GENDER IN HISTORY

Series editors:
Lynn Abrams, Cordelia Beattie, Pam Sharpe and Penny Summerfield

The expansion of research into the history of women and gender since the 1970s has changed the face of history. Using the insights of feminist theory and of historians of women, gender historians have explored the configuration in the past of gender identities and relations between the sexes. They have also investigated the history of sexuality and family relations, and analysed ideas and ideals of masculinity and femininity. Yet gender history has not abandoned the original, inspirational project of women's history: to recover and reveal the lived experience of women in the past and the present.

The series Gender in History provides a forum for these developments. Its historical coverage extends from the medieval to the modern period, and its geographical scope encompasses not only Europe and North America but all corners of the globe. The series aims to investigate the social and cultural constructions of gender in historical sources, as well as the gendering of historical discourse itself. It embraces both detailed case studies of specific regions or periods, and broader treatments of major themes. Gender in History titles are designed to meet the needs of both scholars and students working in this dynamic area of historical research.

Gender and housing in Soviet Russia

Manchester University Press

ALSO AVAILABLE
IN THE SERIES

Myth and materiality in a woman's world: Shetland 1800–2000 Lynn Abrams

History, patriarchy and the challenge of feminism
(with University of Pennsylvania Press) Judith Bennett

Gender and medical knowledge in early modern history Susan Broomhall

'The truest form of patriotism': pacifist feminism in Britain, 1870–1902 Heloise Brown

Artisans of the body in early modern Italy: identities, families and masculinities
Sandra Cavallo

Women of the right spirit: paid organisers of the Women's Social and Political Union (WSPU) 1904–18 Krista Cowman

Masculinities in politics and war: gendering modern history
Stefan Dudink, Karen Hagemann and John Tosh (eds)

Victorians and the Virgin Mary: religion and gender in England 1830–1885
Carol Engelhardt Herringer

Living in sin: cohabiting as husband and wife in nineteenth-century England
Ginger S. Frost

Murder and morality in Victorian Britain: the story of Madeleine Smith
Eleanor Gordon and Gwyneth Nair

The military leadership of Matilda of Canossa, 1046–1115 David J. Hay

The shadow of marriage: singleness in England, 1914–60 Katherine Holden

Women police: gender, welfare and surveillance in the twentieth century Louise Jackson

Noblewomen, aristocracy and power in the twelfth-century Anglo-Norman realm
Susan Johns

The business of everyday life: gender, practice and social politics in England, c. 1600–1900
Beverly Lemire

Women and the shaping of British Methodism: persistent preachers, 1807–1907
Jennifer Lloyd

The independent man: citizenship and gender politics in Georgian England
Matthew McCormack

The feminine public sphere: middle-class women and civic life in Scotland, c. 1870–1914
Megan Smitley

GENDER AND HOUSING IN SOVIET RUSSIA
PRIVATE LIFE IN A PUBLIC SPACE

— Lynne Attwood —

Manchester University Press

Copyright © Lynne Attwood 2010

The right of Lynne Attwood to be identified as the author of this work has been asserted by her in accordance with the Copyright, Designs and Patents Act 1988.

Published by Manchester University Press
Altrincham Street, Manchester M1 7JA, UK
www.manchesteruniversitypress.co.uk

British Library Cataloguing-in-Publication Data is available

ISBN 978 1 5261 2286 5 paperback

First published by Manchester University Press in hardback 2010

This edition first published 2017

The publisher has no responsibility for the persistence or accuracy of URLs for any external or third-party internet websites referred to in this book, and does not guarantee that any content on such websites is, or will remain, accurate or appropriate.

Printed by Lightning Source

Contents

ACKNOWLEDGEMENTS		*page* vi
	Introduction	1
1	New *byt*, new woman, new forms of housing	22
2	The New Economic Policy	40
3	Housing cooperatives	61
4	Communes, hostels and barracks	76
5	The 'second socialist offensive'	87
6	The retreat from new *byt*	107
7	Communal living by default	123
8	The Great Patriotic War and its aftermath	140
9	The Khrushchev era: 'To every family its own apartment'	154
10	The Brezhnev years	180
11	The Gorbachev era: the end of a socialist housing policy	200
12	Personal tales	219
	Conclusion	241
BIBLIOGRAPHY		249
INDEX		259

Acknowledgements

This book would not have been possible without the support of a number of people in Moscow and St Petersburg. I am particularly grateful to Marina Drozdova for her help in procuring material and arranging some of the interviews, for her comments on sections of the book and, most of all, for her friendship and hospitality. It was certainly due to her that my field work in Moscow was enjoyable; it was also due to her, at least in part, that it was possible. I would also like to thank Sasha Breigin, Ol'ga Issoupova and Roza Gef for their assistance. Rachel Platonov kindly read and commented on one of the chapters of the book. I would also like to acknowledge the support of my employer, the University of Manchester, in giving me research leave for one semester. Finally, I would like to thank the AHRC for providing me with a grant to relieve me of my University work for an additional semester, and for its tremendous patience when illness delayed the completion of the project.

Some of the material in Chapter 9, on the Khrushchev period, has appeared in previous publications. These are L. Attwood, 'Housing in the Khrushchev Era', in Melanie Ilic, Susan E. Reid and L. Attwood (eds), *Women in the Khrushchev Era* (Basingstoke: Palgrave, 2004), pp. 177–202; and L. Attwood, 'From the "New Soviet Woman" to the "New Soviet Housewife"', in D. Hipkins and G. Plain (eds), *War Torn Tales: Literature, Film and Gender in the Aftermath of World War II* (Oxford and Bern: Peter Lang, 2007), pp. 143–62. I would like to acknowledge my thanks to these publishers for allowing me to use the material in this book.

Introduction

[T]hey're ordinary people, ... except that the housing shortage has soured them ... (Mikhail Bulgakov, *Master and Margarita*)¹

Housing is clearly one of the most crucial features of daily life. As Marx famously noted, 'life involves before everything else eating, drinking, *a habitation*, clothing and many other things'.² One would expect that the first socialist country in the world, which was explicitly organised in accordance with Marxist principles, would be determined to ensure that these fundamental needs were met. Housing, however, was to prove an intractable problem throughout the country's history.

The Soviet regime inherited an urban housing crisis of enormous proportions from the Tsarist era. While resolving this crisis presented a huge challenge, it also provided an opportunity to reorganise and redistribute housing in accordance with socialist principles. Opinions differed, however, as to what this actually meant. The kind of housing that was considered appropriate in a socialist society was inevitably informed by people's attitudes towards the family, gender relations, and what form *byt*, or 'daily life', should take.

This book will explore these ideas, and the ways in which they were reflected in successive housing programmes, from the time of the Revolution in 1917 to the collapse of Soviet power in 1991. We will see how the original plans for a socialist form of housing were distorted, sometimes almost beyond recognition, by ideological confusion, financial constraints, corruption, ineptness, the banality of daily life – as Mayakovskii famously put it in his suicide note, 'the love boat has crashed against *byt*' – and by tacit obstruction on the part of citizens. We will consider how the peculiarities of Soviet housing could be said to have led to a distinctly Soviet understanding of the home and of 'private life'. Above all, we will look at the interaction between the Soviet housing programme and gender relations. We will consider the extent to which the authorities saw new forms of housing as a route to women's emancipation, and the ways in which different types of housing either challenged or reinforced gender stereotypes.

The study is concerned only with housing in the cities. Cities were seen as the springboard of socialism. Marx and Engels had emphasised their importance, and Lenin described them as 'the centres of the economic, political and spiritual life of the nation ... and the main motor of progress'.³ It was specifically the organisation of urban life and urban housing which was supposed to bring about a transformation in daily life. As David Smith explains, it was meant to 'promote collective sentiments, as well as giving practical material expression to egalitarian ideas'.[4] These included the creation of a new type of relationship between men and women. Cities would provide the facilities to free women from domestic servitude, the opportunities which would enable them to work alongside men in social production, and the lectures and classes which would encourage them to embrace a more collective orientation. The type of housing people lived in, and their understanding of home life, inevitably had a crucial role to play in this process.

Housing and 'home'

What constitutes a home? English-language dictionaries define it as a 'place of refuge', 'the place in which one's domestic affections are centered',[5] 'an environment offering security and happiness'[6] and 'a congenial environment'.[7] A sense of cosiness is conveyed by these definitions, and, as Natal'ya Lebina puts it, of 'spiritual comfort'.[8] Western researchers Tim Dant and D. Seamon add a feeling of self-control[9] and the ability to be, or at least to feel, alone[10] as key elements in the perception of home.

In the liberal democracies of the West the home is generally seen as a private realm. This may have been challenged to some extent by the arrival of 'reality TV', which brings film crews into people's homes and turns their private lives into entertainment for others.[11] For most people, however, the home is still considered to be largely immune from public scrutiny, with the state entitled to intervene in domestic matters only in the event of child neglect or abuse of one family member by another. The notion that the home functions as a protective barrier between its members and the outside world is exemplified by the proverb 'an Englishman's home is his castle', to which we will find some envious references in the material we look at from the late Soviet period.

In countries with private housing markets, people with sufficient money have been able to exercise control not only over how they live inside their homes, but also over what kind of homes they have, and in what location. This has led to the development of districts segregated by class and status. As Moscow sociologist Victoria Semenova has put it, in liberal democracies, where people live is an indication of their position in the social hierarchy, and relocation is strongly linked to social mobility. 'Housing strategies are built around active choice and closely related to social status, mobility and identity', she argues.[12] She fails to mention that this has only ever been the case for the relatively wealthy. Nonetheless, in the Soviet Union virtually the entire population was denied such choice.

Curiously, there is no distinct word for 'home' in Russian. The word *dom* refers both to a home and to a building, whether this be a small house or a multi-storey apartment block. From the Stalin era onwards, reference was made to the 'family hearth', a term redolent of the nineteenth-century middle class and a bizarrely incongruous image, given the conditions in which most people actually lived in the Soviet Union. The bland term 'living space' (*zhilaya ploshshad'*) conveys a rather more accurate understanding of how people lived.

As cities grew at unprecedented and unanticipated speed, the vast majority of urban citizens found themselves living at least for part of their lives with strangers. The so-called 'communal apartment', or *kommunalka*, became the predominant form of Soviet urban housing until the Khrushchev era, and a defining feature of the country itself. This was an apartment which, if it had been built before the Revolution, had then housed a single family, but now had one crammed into every room, with everyone jostling for space in the one kitchen and queuing up to use the one toilet. In some cases the original rooms had been subdivided so that still more people could be accommodated, with the partitions so flimsy they could provide little sense of separate space.[13] Some families did not even have partitions dividing them and their neighbours.

The Bolsheviks believed that social justice could only be achieved through state control and distribution of the housing stock. This would enable them to ensure that all citizens had similar living conditions, and to eradicate the differentiation of city space along class lines, with the bourgeoisie living in elegant districts in the city centre and workers in run-down settlements on the periphery. A small amount of private house building was actually permitted, and was even encouraged in certain periods of Soviet history, when state resources were stretched and private capital provided a welcome supplement to the state housing budget. However, this sat awkwardly with Soviet ideology, which proclaimed private ownership to be a feature of capitalism. The state came to own around 80 per cent of urban housing,[14] and had almost total control over its distribution. This had major implications for the feeling of 'self-control over one's own private space'.[15]

There were no segregated districts in Soviet cities, and people with very different types of work and levels of education were housed in the same streets, and often in the same apartments. Semenova views this mixing up of different social groups as a negative phenomenon which 'numbed or destroyed earlier cultural traditions' and 'gravely hindered the intergenerational transmission of different social class and familial cultures'.[16] What emerged from the wreckage of the old social hierarchy, she concludes, was 'the new everyday culture of barrack socialism'.[17]

Living space was not subjected to the same degree of scrutiny and control as more obviously public places such as the workplace,[18] but this did not mean that it functioned as a private space, at least not for 'ordinary' Soviet citizens. Limited resources account for the fact that state did not exercise greater control. There was no understanding that some areas of a Soviet citizen's life might legitimately lie outside of state attention and intervention.

The blurring of boundaries between public and private space, combined with the overcrowding, meant that the Soviet home had little in common with its counterpart in capitalist countries. The Soviet authorities seem to have made a conscious attempt to develop in citizens a broader sense of home; they encouraged them to look beyond the confines of their own room or portion of a room and see their 'socialist city' in its entirety as their home. In the material we will analyse, we will find that the emphasis is invariably placed on the city's open spaces rather than its cramped interiors. Collective leisure was promoted instead of relaxation at home. Citizens were encouraged to stroll en masse through their city's parks, squares and boulevards, make use of communal recreational facilities, and see their 'living space' as simply somewhere to sleep.

Home extended even beyond the city, to the country as a whole. This patriotic understanding of home was enshrined in the lyrics of a popular song of the 1970s, which proclaimed:

> Our address is not a house or a street,
> Our address is the Soviet Union.[19]

We will find some indication that Soviet citizens did internalise this message, though this does not mean they were indifferent to their housing situation. The struggle to improve their housing functioned as a perennial backdrop to most people's lives throughout the decades of Soviet power. Many wrote letters to government officials and agencies begging for better housing.[20] Some got married to apartments rather than people – that is, they chose marriage partners in accordance with what accommodation they lived in.[21] In the years of Stalin's Terror, 'apartment denunciation' was not uncommon: neighbours in a communal apartment would denounce one another to the authorities in the hope that if they were arrested, their living space might be up for grabs.[22] All goods and services which were in short supply were vulnerable to speculation, and housing was no exception; we will find examples of people engaging in illicit and often illegal practices to get better housing, whatever their attitude to the Soviet authorities and however loyal they were in other respects.

Semenova holds that '[d]ense lodging was thought to be not merely sufficient, but meritorious' by the Soviet authorities, since it allowed them to exert greater control over their citizens' lives.[23] The material drawn on in this study does not support that view, however. I would argue that forcing people into insufficient space was not a policy decision but was the result of a number of unanticipated factors. These include the fact that housing was seen as a public service under socialism, so the state was forced to provide housing of some sort for all of its citizens; that the rate of urbanisation far outstripped expectations; that industry was seen as the overwhelming economic priority, and took the lion's share of resources; and that the income derived from low rents and service charges was insufficient even to maintain existing housing, let alone to fund new construction.

Yet even if the authorities did not consciously promote crowded accommodation, they did manipulate it. Although housing was supposed to be a public service, the housing shortage made it possible for it also to be used as punishment, incentive and reward.[24] In the 1920s, certain categories of people were deprived of the right to any housing on the grounds that they were class enemies: the *byvshie* or 'former people', i.e. members of the bourgeoisie, and the *lyshentsy*, people deprived of voting rights, usually because of their class or professional backgrounds. In the Stalin era, favoured individuals or social groups, such as shock workers and Stakhanovites, would receive better-quality housing as a reward for their contribution to society and their loyalty to the regime. With an increasing amount of housing placed under the control of enterprises and factories, housing also became a means of controlling workers, of luring and then tying them to their jobs. Those who had control over housing distribution derived considerable personal power in relation to others.

The organisation of communal apartments made it possible to monitor the behaviour of tenants much more readily than if they had lived in single-family homes. This was particularly the case with large communal apartments in the Stalin era. One tenant would be given responsibility[25] for ensuring the smooth running of the apartment, which involved drawing up the rota which dictated when each tenant could use the bathroom, determining who would do what chores to maintain cleanliness and hygiene, dividing up the charges for communal services such as the telephone and electricity – and reporting to the police. These 'senior tenants' (*otvetsvennyi kvartiros'emshchiki*) clearly had considerable power over the other tenants, not just on account of their relationship with the authorities, but also because they insisted on the right to observe and interfere in the domestic habits and personal lives of their neighbours.[26]

The Khrushchev era marked a significant turning point in housing policy and provision. The plan was to replace the *kommunalka* with the single family apartment, rehousing every urban family within twelve years. Although this aim was not achieved, the results of Khrushchev's housing programme should not be underestimated. Between 1957 and 1963, an astonishing seventy-five million people moved home, a third of the total Soviet population.[27] Yet the new apartments had many deficiencies. They were poorly built, and the rooms, particularly the kitchen, were uncomfortably small. Moreover, no attention was paid to the fact that a family's needs would change over time. An apartment which suited a husband and wife with two dependent children was not appropriate for a family which, a decade later, included adult children ready to start families of their own. The single family apartment could eventually end up as crowded as a communal one.

The move to the single-family apartment was not meant to result in the authorities having less control over their citizens' 'private' lives. Indeed, in some respects state intervention in the domestic sphere was greater in the Khrushchev era than it had been under Stalin. Attempts were also made to ensure that families did not close their new front doors on the rest of society; to this end, residents were encouraged to turn their new apartment blocks into communities in themselves.

The situation changed dramatically in the last years of Soviet power. Privatisation of housing was hailed as the only way to deal with the continuing housing shortage. The state's role would be pared down to the minimum; it would be obliged to provide housing only for the impoverished and vulnerable. Others would have to buy their own homes or rent them from private landlords. The development of a private rental market was encouraged as a means of ensuring a steady supply of reasonably priced rental properties. Homogeneous districts which housed people with similar educational levels and professions were no longer considered anathema. The emergence of wealthy 'new Russians' with the means to renovate apartments to a high standard led to a yawning gap between those with Western-style housing and those who remained trapped in the Soviet era. So-called 'cottages' also began to appear around city perimeters: large detached mansions, some with crenellated walls and turrets. The new Russian elite had taken on, almost literally, the English notion that the home was a castle.

INTRODUCTION

Public and private space

The relationship between public and private space is clearly an important aspect of this study. To put the situation in historical context, the split between the public and the private resulted largely from the processes of industrialisation and urbanisation. In pre-industrial societies there were no distinct boundaries between the workplace and the home, but in industrialised societies paid work took place in a separate location, and the home assumed a new role as the place where workers would rest and recuperate. The public world came to be seen largely as man's domain, while the home was considered primarily female, a place where the wife would minister to her husband's needs and send him back to work refreshed and revitalised.

Jurgen Habermas has written the most influential work on the development of the public space in Western democracies. He charts the emergence of a distinct public sphere in the late seventeenth century, when feudalism was giving way to capitalism. It consisted of a range of cultural, legal and social institutions which allowed the newly emerging bourgeoisie to meet together, engage in open discussion, and develop opinions on matters that had previously been considered the province of experts and those wielding political power. Literary salons, museums, art galleries, theatres, musical concerts,[28] the rise of the novel, the emergence of newspapers and periodicals, and the proliferation of coffee houses contributed to the creation of a cultural and social space in which public opinion could develop and 'the public' could become a critical authority in its own right.[29] Hence, according to Habermas, this rise of the public sphere was a crucial factor in the development of democracy and egalitarian principles.

Yet this was a very limited form of democracy. This public sphere was an exclusively bourgeois phenomenon, open only to householders, and it was also largely the province of men. The all-important coffee houses, for example, did not even admit women.[30] As Christina Kiaer and Eric Naiman point out, this supposedly open, egalitarian public sphere had a 'dialectical complement': the private sphere, to which women were largely confined. 'On a literal level, the overtly feminised, domestic spaces of private life provided a necessary safe haven from the masculine trials of competitive capitalism.'[31]

Antoine Prost and Gerard Vincent approach the public and private from a rather different perspective. Their focus is on people at the lower end of the social hierarchy, and on the development of the private rather than the public sphere. While Habermas' public space was an exclusively bourgeois phenomenon, so too, they point out, was private space in the same period. Until the twentieth century, 'only the bourgeoisie, those who owned property or lived on private incomes, were fully entitled to a private life'[32] – that is, to a life separate from work and over which people could exercise some degree of choice.[33] Others were defined by their work. While Habermas saw the development of the public sphere as the route to greater democratisation, Prost and Vincent link democratisation with the spread of private life. Industrialisation set the process in motion, but at first the divide between the home and the workplace was far from complete; factories often bought up adjacent land on which to build housing for their workers, and some workers were actually required to live at their places of work. During the course of the twentieth century, however, increasing worker militancy and the development of collective bargaining resulted in labour legislation which acknowledged the right to a life outside of the job for everyone.[34]

The development of private life also required improved housing. In France, the focus of Prost and Vincent's study, there was little chance of any genuine private life until the middle of the twentieth century. Until then, overcrowding meant that privacy and solitude were impossible: 'Each [person] had to wash and dress in the presence of others',[35] and '[p]eople slept several to a room and often several to a bed'.[36] Accordingly, 'individuals enjoyed privacy only in common with others who shared the same living space ... Private space was nothing more than the public space of the household.'[37] This changed when a huge housing programme was launched in the 1950s, which led, twenty years later, to the average French home containing 3.5 rooms and the average French person having 267 feet of living space.

The examples given above relate to Western societies. Let us now look at the situation in Russia, both before and after the Revolution. Pre-revolutionary Russia was a country subject to tight governmental control and censorship, which made the development of both a public and private space problematic. As William Mills Todd III explains, a system of patronage held sway in relation to the arts, with the Imperial family among the chief patrons. They were able 'to interfere capriciously in every aspect of the literary process, imposing a crippling subservience upon writers, ... dictating the themes and forms of imaginative literature'.[38] In the eighteenth and nineteenth centuries, a network of literary circles and salons began to develop alongside patronage, which imposed rather less control over writers and could be said, to some extent, to constitute the beginnings of a public sphere. Literary circles were still rather formal and included speeches, rules and the taking of minutes. Salons were more light-hearted; they were presided over by a host or hostess (usually the latter), and conversation was much more 'free and easy' than in the literary circles.[39] However, Russia was rather different from her West European neighbours. While one of the aims of the literary groups in France was 'to create and shape public opinion', this was not the case with Russia, which, 'with its powerful Tsarist system, ... preferred obedience to talent and intelligence'.[40] In the nineteenth century there was an attempt to reach a wider audience through the publication of literary journals, though these were heavily censored by the authorities. Some of the journals were aimed at a relatively low-brow readership, referred to disparagingly by some intellectuals as 'provincials'. All the same, in a country in which more than 80 per cent of the population was illiterate, even the most popular journals could only reach a small educated elite.[41]

In the Soviet Union, governmental control and censorship became even stronger than it had been under the Tsars. There was no way that the public sphere, as described by Habermas, could exist; its crucial feature was the development of an independent public opinion, and this was anathema to the Soviet authorities, who insisted that there was a unity of interests and opinions between the rulers and the ruled – that is, between the Communist Party and Soviet citizens. In any case, state ownership and control over all aspects of society, including the media and places of public recreation and entertainment, meant that the conditions did not exist for the development of an independent cultural and social space. Communal activity which was strictly under the control of the Party remained at the centre of Soviet ideology.

As for the development of a private sphere, this was thwarted both by practical and political factors. Like the working class in France before the launching of the mass housing programme, Soviet citizens had no possibility of being alone in their homes. Indeed, the overcrowding was even worse in the Soviet Union; until the launching of Khrushchev's housing programme, the 'public space of the household' was peopled not only by family members but by others with whom one had no relationship. Moreover, this was not an exclusively working-class phenomenon in the Soviet Union. In general, white-collar professionals did little better than manual workers. It could be said that the Soviet Union succeeded in its aim to achieve equality in the sphere of housing, but, to quote Semenova, it was 'equality in poverty'.[42]

The housing shortage meant that many activities which we would consider private took place in full view of others. Oleg Kharkhordin refers to an incident which took place in the mid-1920s, in which a man was brought before the court charged with rape. He worked for a trade union, and his job included finding work for young people. He had been using this position to extract sexual favours from young women, one of whom subsequently went to the authorities claiming that he had forced himself on her when she refused his advances. He acknowledged that he had had sex with her, but denied it was rape, and expressed surprise that it had led to such "'excessive talk and suspicion; he considered it his personal affair'". Kharkhordin points out that the man 'had presumably had sexual relations with women before, in workers' dorms in the full sight of his comrades, and it had not produced talk or suspicion'. He was now honestly confused as to 'how a workers' state could punish him for such a trifle.'[43] Kharkhordin relates this tale as part of a discussion on the collective and the role it was supposed to play in enforcing appropriate behaviour. For our purposes, however, its significance lies in its illustration of the extent to which the boundary between public and private had been breached; the ultimate intimate act was performed in what was, in effect, a public space.

According to the writer Walter Benjamin, the Soviets set about simultaneously destroying private and public life, at least in the Habermas sense. After visiting Moscow for two months in 1926–27, he made the famous and oft-quoted comment that the Bolsheviks had 'abolished' private life.[44] As Boym explains, 'for Benjamin, the "collectivisation" of private life and the disappearance of cafes are connected, and both conspire to turn a critically thinking intellectual into an endangered species'.[45] The state's control over private life became still more pronounced with Stalin firmly in power. As Figes asks, 'what did private life mean when the state touched almost every aspect of it through legislation, surveillance and ideological control?'[46]

Vincent and Prost do not include Eastern bloc countries in their study, but Vincent does make a brief reference to life in 'totalitarian regimes' in which 'all barriers between private life and public life seem to be broken down'. All the same, he cautions against assuming that private life did not exist at all. Even in extreme situations, he argues, people find ways to 'preserve their secrets', and to exercise some degree of choice, however small.[47]

This claim is echoed by Steven E. Harris, who refers to studies conducted by the German school of everyday life history, *Alltagsgeschichte*, which indicate that even in Nazi Germany people had choices. These were not reduced to either supporting or opposing the regime; in fact, 'most people existed somewhere between these extremes. One and the same person could shift or "meander" among acts of resistance, passive compliance, and even support for the regime.'[48] Catriona Kelly has made a similar point in relation to the Soviet Union: 'One resists, without necessarily rejecting, by assessing, making tolerable, and, in some cases, even turning to one's advantage the situation one is confronted with.'[49]

Yet there were severe limits to the extent to which resistance was possible in the Soviet Union, especially in the Stalin era. Cynthia Hooper points out that the Soviet regime of the 1930s was actually more intrusive in personal matters than its Nazi counterpart. The latter 'rarely sought to interrogate domestic relations', and '[s]eparations between public and private spheres were accepted, even embraced'.[50] In the Soviet Union, in contrast, 'all "private" relations (meaning all affiliations grounded in personal inclination rather than professional necessity) became a primary subject of investigation and incrimination'.[51] A citizen's loyalty to the Soviet Union, which was itself, from the 1930s, portrayed as a giant family, had to override loyalty to his or her own family. Indeed, loyalty to the family was a cause of considerable alarm on the part of the authorities, which had a tremendous fear of intimacy.[52] The nature of Soviet housing – the overcrowding, combined with the probability that one resident was reporting on the others – meant that the usual relationship between the public and private was in some respects turned on its head. As H. Kent Geiger made clear in his classic study of the Soviet family, some Soviet citizens felt it was possible to achieve a greater sense of 'privacy' in the city streets than they could at 'home'.[53]

A number of commentators have queried the relevance of the notion of private life at all in the Soviet context. Svetlana Boym argues that even before the revolution there was no strong adherence to the private sphere.[54] As Kiaer and Naiman put it, '"private" or personal life was considered by the intelligentsia to be negative, inauthentic, and foreign, something to be overcome. The private individual of the West, acting in his own self-interest, was opposed to the "myth of the Russian soul", a soul joined with the Russian people or *narod*.'[55]

What emerges from this discussion is that the private and public are not polar opposites, and that portraying them as such risks distorting our understanding of daily life in the Soviet Union. As we shall see in this study, intimacy, domesticity and the chance of achieving some sense of solitude are not necessarily confined to a separate private sphere.[56]

Methodology

My primary research method is textual analysis of articles and short stories appearing in a range of Soviet magazines and journals. These magazines were, for the most part, geared at 'ordinary' Russians, by which I mean those who were not part of the *nomenklatura* or the political elite, and had little or no voice in decisions about housing. Two of the publications I focus on appeared throughout the span of this study, from the 1920s to the end of the Soviet era (and, indeed, beyond). These are *Rabotnitsa* (The Woman Worker) and *Ogonek* (Little Flame).

Rabotnitsa was the Soviet Union's principal publication for working-class urban women, the so-called 'female mass'. It was launched in 1914, but folded with the outbreak of the First World War. It was briefly revived between May 1917 and January 1918, but was brought to a halt again due to a paper shortage during the Civil War. It resumed publication in 1923 as a monthly magazine, was appearing twice monthly by the end of the 1920s, and reverted to monthly publication in the post-war era. Its main concerns when it was first launched were to educate women about the aims of the new regime and to draw them into the political community. However, it also contained a considerable amount of material on housing, new *byt* (i.e. the new approach to daily life), and women's relationship to both, and continued to do so throughout the Soviet period.

Ogonek made its first appearance in December 1899 as an illustrated supplement to a stock-market bulletin. It was relaunched by the Bolsheviks in 1923 as a weekly magazine concerned with news, culture and entertainment. It was a middle-brow magazine with a broad appeal, and proclaimed itself to be the most popular publication in the country. In the Gorbachev era it became one of the principal flag-bearers of *glasnost'* (which we will translate as 'openness'), with a circulation in the millions.[57] The housing situation was one of its regular themes, and its popularity meant that its views on the subject would reach a particularly wide audience.

Magazines like *Rabotnitsa* and *Ogonek* were used to disseminate information about official policies and to persuade citizens to go along with them. As such, they can be seen as mouthpieces of the authorities. It could be argued that they set about developing a specific Soviet understanding of home which, it was hoped, would be internalised by their readers.

I have also drawn on publications aimed primarily at people with a professional interest in housing. These have proved particularly useful for periods when housing policy was being worked out or was undergoing major change. For the 1920s I have made considerable use of a monthly journal, *Zhilishchnoe delo* (The Housing Matter), put out by the Leningrad Union of Housing Associations (*Zhilishchnie tovarishchestva*). It made its first appearance in June 1924, with the main aim of providing assistance to housing cooperatives, which were at that time being encouraged by the authorities as a way of dealing with the housing shortage. The journal gave information and advice on a vast range of issues relating to housing, including the legal situation, the measures being taken to tackle the housing shortage, the rules governing rent assessment, how residents should carry out repairs, what credit was available to them for the purpose and how the courts dealt with conflicts between neighbours living in the same apartment or the same room. The relationship between housing and *byt* was an ever-present background theme, as well as the subject of many articles in its own right.

Although the editors of *Zhilishchnoe delo* hoped to reach a broad readership, the journal did not enjoy the popularity of *Rabotnitsa* or *Ogonek*. Indeed, one of its contributors lamented that in some districts the only people who actually read the journal were the managers of apartment blocks.[58] However, it contains a wealth of information on the housing situation in the 1920s, and provides some candid reflections on the new regime's attempts to deal with the problem. It also indicates the variety of approaches both to housing in the post-revolutionary period, and on how people should live their lives in a socialist society. The journal abruptly ceased publication in early 1930, possibly for financial reasons; the paper it was printed on in 1929 was of very poor quality, suggesting that its small readership was not sufficient to keep it going. In the 1930s a Moscow journal aimed at housing workers, *Zhilishchnoe khozyaistvo* (Housing Management), took up virtually where *Zhilishchnoe delo* left off, presiding over the demise of the cooperative movement rather than promoting it.

The Khrushchev era represented a major turning point in the Soviet approach to housing, with a commitment to provide every family with its own apartment. This pledge required a huge building programme and necessitated new and cheaper methods of construction. These were discussed in detail in architectural publications, which I have drawn on as appropriate. I have also made use of the trade union newspaper *Trud* (Labour), since an increasing amount of housing was by now in the hands of enterprises and factories, and the trade unions played a major role in the distribution of the new single family apartments.

It is important to understand what sort of information we can get from these publications. In the 1920s there were some candid discussions on the housing situation, but these were interspersed with less than honest claims about the cause of the problem (it was all down to the policies of the Tsarist regime and the damage inflicted on cities during the First World War), over-optimistic assessments of the rate and extent of improvements, and a rather desperate insistence that housing in the countries of Western Europe was in at least as bad a state as that in Russia.⁵⁹ In the Stalin era, even these types of criticism were rare. The journalistic writings we will look at gave an officially endorsed image of Soviet society which bore little relationship to reality. They provide us not with information about what was actually happening in Soviet society, but about what the regime wanted to pretend was happening. Svetlana Boym's comment on an idealised image of housing in a painting of the late Stalin era, Aleksandr Laktionov's *The New Apartment* (1952), could apply equally to the presentation of housing matters in the print media: this 'is the way the culture wishes to see itself and to be seen'.⁶⁰

In relation to housing, this generally meant putting a socialist gloss on the failure to house people adequately. It turned out that Soviet citizens would have no desire to retreat behind their own front doors, even if they had them. Their main concern was to make their contribution to society through productive work. Housing was not so important to them; and, in any case, sharing personal space encouraged a sense of community.

Ironically, the short stories appearing in the magazines provided more honest commentaries on the housing situation. This was especially the case in the Stalin era. Fiction seems to have offered authors a way of painting a more nuanced picture of Soviet society. In some stories, the overcrowded apartment served as a stage on which the absurdities of daily life could be acted out for dramatic or comic effect. In others, the housing crisis formed the backdrop to a tale which was ostensibly about something else entirely, with telling details on housing hovering in the background of the story. Sometimes serious observations were concealed behind a veil of humour. The lack of privacy, the fear of informers, the noise, the irritation and aggression which stemmed from living in too little space with too many people, were used to elicit what must have been, to readers, rather bitter laughter.

This use of fiction was not a uniquely Soviet phenomenon; as the historian E.H. Carr has noted: 'The use of fiction for the discussion and dissemination of social ideas was … a nineteenth century Russian tradition.'⁶¹ The radical political movements which had emerged in the latter half of that century were constrained by strict censorship, and their members found that they were less likely to attract the censors' attention if they hid their political commentary in fiction rather than broadcasting it in political tracts. Chernyshevsky, whose novel *What Is to Be Done* is a notable example of political fiction, defended his 'lack of talent' as a novelist on the grounds that: 'Truth is a good thing which compensates even for an author's faults.'⁶² It could be argued that the fiction writers in the popular journals analysed in this study were continuing this tradition in the post-revolutionary era.

In the Khrushchev era, relaxation of censorship and the encouragement of anti-Stalinist protestations made it possible to criticise housing provision and conditions, at least as they had been in the Stalin era. Criticisms continued to be voiced after Khrushchev had been deposed, though, as Mary Buckley has noted, 'these were generally pitched as problems that would be solved as society moved towards communism'.[63]

This was to change when Gorbachev came to power in 1985 and launched *glasnost'*. Journalists were now able to cast a much more discerning eye on Soviet society, and many of them went much further than Gorbachev wanted. In the last years of the Soviet Union we will see a huge transformation in writings on housing, as well as on the approach to the housing problem.

In addition to Soviet magazines and journals, I have also drawn on a number of published memoirs, including those of foreigners living in the Soviet Union. The rationale is that these people might be expected to have cast a rather different eye on the housing situation than Soviet citizens, who had no comparison to make with housing in other countries. They might also be expected to have different attitudes towards gender roles.

My other primary source is a series of interviews with people from the former Soviet Union who had a range of housing experiences. My intention was not to contrast the falsities of the 'official' view put forward in the magazines and journals with the 'reality' of people's lives, but to find out how my respondents had experienced the various types of housing they lived in, how they organised their personal and family lives in such cramped conditions, and how they related to the idea of privacy and personal space. In the words of three Western scholars working on oral history projects in the former Soviet Union: 'If we want to understand living through Soviet Russia, we simply cannot do without the testimony of the Russians who lived through it.'[64]

Interviews with Soviet citizens began to come into their own as a research method only from the late Gorbachev era. Until then, it was a risky venture for people in such a repressive society to talk about their lives. To quote Bertaux et al., this was a society 'dominated by a giant system of internal espionage', and people got used to concealing aspects of their pasts; too much knowledge could compromise all involved. Even close relatives were often kept in the dark.[65] Talking to strangers would have been unimaginable, then. This changed when Gorbachev came to power and launched *glasnost'*. While Soviet scholars began to fill in the blank pages of their country's history, 'Russian family members began opening up their own family secrets. The result was a flood of reminiscence.'[66]

Yet this reminiscence was not all anti-Soviet. Bertaux et al. point out that 'many Russians believed they were indeed helping to create a new world', and feel that 'almost all Soviet citizens to some extent internalised ... anti-capitalist and pro-socialist values.'[67] We will find this to be the case even in relation to the housing situation. Some memories of life in communal apartments produced shudders of horror, but a few of my interviewees expressed nostalgia for the idealism which underpinned their creation, and sadness for the loss of a way of life which was, if nothing else, distinctly Soviet.

There are a number of existing books charting the history of Soviet housing. Gregory Andrusz and Alfred DiMaio have written the classic works on the subject; they have proved invaluable in providing the historical background to my own work and I have drawn on them at some length.[68] More recently, work has appeared on specific forms of housing or housing in specific periods of Soviet history; most notably, Katerina Gerasimova and Victoria Semenova have written on the communal apartment, and Susan E. Reid, Victor Buchli and Steven E. Harris on housing in the Khrushchev era. There is also a growing literature on daily life in various periods of Soviet history which has looked at housing conditions as a crucial aspect of daily life; the work of Svetlana Boym, Sheila Fitzpatrick, Stephen Kotkin and Susan E. Reid are particularly noteworthy. There has, however, been no systematic study of the ways in which the Russian home has been differentially experienced by men and women. Nor has there been any work on the ways in which official ideas on housing and family life in Russia were disseminated to the public through the media.

The particular contributions this study will make to the field are to look at the relationship between housing and daily life throughout the entire span of Soviet history, to explore the gender implications of Soviet housing, and to look at the ways in which official ideas on housing and daily life were propagandised through the print media.

Chapter outline

The book consists of twelve chapters. Particular emphasis is placed on the early Soviet period, with the first eight chapters dealing with the first four decades of Soviet power. The reason for this imbalance is that this was the time when ideas about socialist housing were being discussed and developed – and, to a rather lesser extent, put into practice.

Chapter 1 places the study in its historical and cultural context. It outlines the urban housing crisis before the Revolution and explores

INTRODUCTION

the new regime's attempt to deal with this crisis in accordance with its ideas concerning a socialist approach to housing, new *byt* and gender relations. It discusses Soviet ideology on the collectivisation of daily life, the socialisation of housework and the importance of female engagement in social production. It also looks at how these ideas were discussed in the media, and how they were translated into lived experience. Chapter 2 is concerned with the 1920s, the time of the New Economic Policy. It deals with the return to private housing, the establishment of an official norm of living space, and the policies of 'compression' and 'self-compression'. Chapters 3 and 4 look at different forms of communal living: while Chapter 3 discusses housing cooperatives, Chapter 4 looks at house-communes, hostels and barracks. Chapter 5 explores the early Stalin era and the launching of the first Five Year Plan, paying particular attention to the 'socialist cities' which were to be built around new industrial plants; it also discusses the renewed enthusiasm for communal living which accompanied the Plan. This did not last, and Chapter 6 looks at the retreat from 'new *byt*', charting the ideological transition from the promotion of communal living to the revival of the individual family and, in theory, the individual family home.

Yet, even if the individual family home was now the ideal, the authorities were unable – or unwilling – to provide the financial means to make it possible. Accordingly, Chapter 7 looks at the reality beneath the dream, focusing on the so-called 'communal apartment' which became one of the defining features of Stalin's Russia: an apartment housing several families, usually one family to each room, sharing washing and cooking facilities but refusing to live communally, and instead attempting to achieve whatever semblance of privacy was possible in those overcrowded conditions. Chapter 8 deals with the Great Patriotic War and its aftermath, up to the end of the Stalin era.

Chapters 9 to 11 deal with the last four decades of Soviet power. Chapter 9 is concerned with the Khrushchev era and the enormous housing programme which attempted to deliver 'to every family its own apartment'. Chapter 10 looks at the Brezhnev era and the unanticipated problems which the 'single family apartment' had spawned in the course of a generation. Chapter 11 turns to the Gorbachev era, exploring the more honest appraisal of the housing crisis which appeared in the press, the move towards a private housing market, and the end of a socialist housing policy. Finally, Chapter 12 draws on the memories of Soviet citizens themselves, presenting the results of a series of in-depth interviews with people who, between them, lived through the full range of Soviet housing possibilities.

Notes

1. M. Bulgakov, *Master and Margarita*, translated by M. Glenny (London: Fontana, 1983), p. 137.
2. K. Marx, from *The German Ideology Part I*; this translation taken from *The Portable Karl Marx*, edited and translated by E. Kamenka (Harmondsworth: Viking Penguin, 1983), p. 163.
3. G. Andrusz, *Housing and Urban Development in the USSR* (Basingstoke: Macmillan, 1984), p. 4.
4. D. Smith, 'The Socialist City', in G. Andrusz, M. Harloe and I. Szelenyi, *Cities After Socialism: Urban and Regional Change and Conflict in Post-Socialist Cities* (Oxford: Blackwell, 1966), p. 77.
5. *Random House Dictionary* (New York: Random House, 1990), p. 418.
6. www.thefreedictionary.com/home, accessed 6 November 2007.
7. Merriam-Websteronline, accessed 6 November 2007.
8. N.B. Lebina, *Povsednevnaya zhizn' Sovetskogo goroda: normy i anomalii, 1920–1930 gody* (St Petersburg: Zhurnal 'Neva' – izdatel'stvotorgovyi dom 'Letnii sad', 1999), p. 178.
9. T. Dant, *Material Culture in the Social World: Values, Activities, Lifestyles* (Buckingham: Open University Press, 1999), p. 70. He holds that this feeling of self-control is precisely what makes 'the private space distinct from any other space'.
10. Quoted by Dant, Ibid., p. 70.
11. Antoine Prost makes the interesting point that while 'soap operas ... socialise private life and make it out to be a community and give viewers the community they lack in real life in their own streets and houses', reality TV 'turns *real* people's lives into soap opera for other viewers'. A. Prost, 'The Family and the Individual', in A. Prost and G. Vincent (eds), *A History of Private Life*, vol. V, *Riddles of Identity in Modern Times* (Cambridge, Mass. and London: Belknap Press of Harvard University Press, 1991), p. 51.
12. V. Semenova, 'Equality in Poverty: The Symbolic Meaning of *kommunalki* in the 1930s–50s', in D. Bertaux, P. Thompson and A. Rotkirch (eds), *On Living through Soviet Russia* (London and New York: Routledge, 2004), p. 57.
13. One of the people interviewed by Semenova recalled living in an apartment which had, before the Revolution, consisted of six rooms which had housed just one family, but which now had fourteen rooms and fourteen families. The partitions dividing up the original rooms did not even reach the ceilings, 'so we could hear all [the neighbours'] conversations.' Ibid., p. 60.
14. See N.B. Kosareva, A.S. Puzanov and M.V. Tikhomirova, 'Russia: Fast Starter – Housing Sector Reform 1991–1995', in R.J. Struyk (ed.), *Economic Restructuring of the Former Soviet Bloc: The Case of Housing* (Avebury: Urban Institute Press, 1996), p. 255.
15. Ibid.
16. Semenova, 'Equality in Poverty', p. 59.
17. Ibid., pp. 66–7.
18. See B. Holmgren, *Women's Works in Stalin's Time: On Lidiia Chukovskaia and Nadezhda Mandelstam* (Bloomington, Ind.: Indiana University Press, 1993), p. 9.
19. Referred to by T. Virkunen and I. Zhuravskaya, 'Kak postroit' obshchii dom?', *Rabotnitsa* no. 6 (1990), pp. 4–5. The song, 'Moi adres – Sovetskii soiuz', was written by Kharitonov and Tukhmanov, and released by the band Samotsvety in 1971.

INTRODUCTION

20 S. Fitzpatrick, *Tear off the Masks! Identity and Imposture in Twentieth-Century Russia* (Princeton and Oxford: Princeton University Press, 2005), p. 160. See also the discussion of patronage in Fitzpatrick, Ibid., and L. Siegelbaum, ' "Dear Comrade, You Ask What We Need": Socialist Paternalism and Soviet Rural "Notables" in the Mid-1930s', in S. Fitzpatrick (ed.), *Stalinism: New Directions* (London and New York: Routledge, 2000), pp. 210–30.

21 Orlando Figes tells of a woman who paid a young soldier to marry her because he was about to join his unit and would not be needing his small room. She met him only once, to pay him and marry him. See O. Figes, *The Whisperers: Private Life in Stalin's Russia* (London: Allen Lane, 2007), p. 161.

22 From S. Fitzpatrick, *Tear off the Masks!*, p. 228.

23 Semenova, 'Equality in Poverty', p. 56.

24 This point is made by A.J. DiMaio, Jr, *Soviet Urban Housing: Problems and Policies* (New York and London: Praegar, 1974), pp. 2–3.

25 Figes explains that the person holding this position was supposed to be elected by the residents, but that in practice 'it was more common for them to elect themselves, and to be accepted by the residents, either through the force of their personality or else their standing in society'. See Figes, *The Whisperers*, p. 179.

26 Semenova gives the example of a 'senior tenant' called Praskov'ya, who 'thought herself entitled to reprimand anyone for infringement of the rules for order in the life of the flat. So she demanded to be told about who was visiting whom; spotted those whose electricity consumption was above the norm; reprimanded those who missed their turn for washing the floors; and so on.' This 'regulatory power relationship in everyday life', Semenova argues, 'with its implicit acceptance of obedience to the authorities and deprivation of personal freedoms and privacy', replicated the power relationship in society as a whole. 'On the one hand, there was the tight hierarchy of vertical subordination; on the other, the weakness of communal or neighbourly links. Any person identified as a dissident "object of guidance" would directly confront the accredited representative of authority in the person of the "senior tenant", but could count on little support from "the others"'. Semenova, 'Equality in Poverty', p. 62.

27 See K. Zhukov, 'Bol'shoe novosel'e i bol'shie zadachi', *Novyi mir* no. 2 (1963), pp. 230–8; I. Mendzheritskii, 'Zdes' byla derevnya', *Sovetskaya zhenshchina* no. 3 (1963), pp. 9–12.

28 Habermas means by this musical concerts which had no purpose other than entertainment, i.e. which were not used 'to enhance the sanctity and dignity of worship, the glamor of the festivities at court', etc. J. Habermas, *The Structural Transformation of the Public Sphere: An Inquiry into a Category of Bourgeois Society*, translated by T. Burger with the assistance of F. Lawrence (Oxford: Polity Press, 1999), p. 39.

29 Ibid., pp. 40–1.

30 Ibid., p. 33.

31 C. Kiaer and E. Naiman (eds), *Everyday Life in Early Soviet Russia: Taking the Revolution Inside* (Bloomington Ind., Indiana University Press, 2006), p. 9.

32 Prost and Vincent, *A History of Private Life*, p. 22.

33 G. Vincent, 'A History of Secrets?', in Prost and Vincent, *A History of Private Life*, p. 148.

34 Ibid., pp. 20–2.

35 Ibid., p. 62.

36 Ibid., p. 63.

37 Ibid., p. 62.
38 W. Mills Todd III, *Fiction and Society in the Age of Pushkin: Ideologies, Institutions and Narratives* (Cambridge, Mass.: Harvard University Press, 1986), p. 51.
39 Ibid., p. 58.
40 Ibid., p. 61.
41 Ibid., p. 97.
42 This is the title of Semenova's article in Bertaux, Thompson and Rotkirch, *On Living through Soviet Russia*, pp. 54–67.
43 O. Kharkhordin, *The Collective and the Individual in Russia* (Berkeley and London: University of California Press, 1999), pp. 128–9.
44 S. Boym, *Common Places: Mythologies of Everyday Life in Russia* (Cambridge, Mass.: Harvard University Press, 1994), p. 73. See also E. Bershtein, '"The Withering of Private Life": Walter Benjamin in Moscow', in Kiaer and Naiman, *Everyday Life in Early Soviet Russia*, p. 217.
45 Boym, *Common Places*, p. 309, fn. 111.
46 Figes, *The Whisperers*, p. xxx.
47 Vincent, 'A History of Secrets?', p. 147.
48 S.E. Harris, 'In Search of "Ordinary" Russia: Everyday Life in the NEP, the Thaw, and the Communal Apartment', *Kritika: Explorations in Russian and Eurasian History* 6.3 (2005), pp. 591–2.
49 C. Kelly, 'Ordinary Life in Extraordiinary Times: Chronicles of the Quotidian in Russia and the Soviet Union', *Kritika: Explorations in Russian and Eurasian History* 3:4 (2002), p. 639.
50 C. Hooper, 'Terror of Intimacy: Family Politics in the 1930s Soviet Union', in Kiaer and Naiman, *Everyday Life in Early Soviet Russia*, p. 65.
51 Ibid., p. 62.
52 Ibid., p. 71.
53 See H. Kent Geiger, *The Family in Soviet Russia* (Cambridge, Mass.: Harvard University Press, 1968), p. 212.
54 Boym, *Common Places*, pp. 31, 73, 84.
55 Kiaer and Naiman, *Everyday Life in Early Soviet Russia*, p. 8.
56 I am grateful to fellow participants, particularly Sheila Fitzpatrick, at the symposium 'The Prospect of Privacy: Rethinking Twentieth Century Modernism', held at the Victoria and Albert Museum, London, 3–4 June 2005, for these insights concerning the public versus the private.
57 S. Lovell, '*Ogonek*: the Crisis of a Genre', in *Europe-Asia Studies* 48:6 (1996), pp. 989–1006.
58 P. Zakharov, 'Dorogu domokhozyaike', *Zhilishchnoe delo* no. 1 (1926), p. 31.
59 See, for example, 'Zhilishchnyi krizis v Moskve', author not named, *Ogonek* no. 1 (1923), pages not numbered; M. Broide, 'Stroyushchayasya Moskva', *Ogonek* no. 15 (1923), p. 14; and Doma kommuna v Moskve', author not named, *Ogonek* no. 7 (1923), p. 16.
60 Boym, *Common Places*, p. 7.
61 E.H. Carr, from the Introduction to N. Chernyshevsky, *What Is to Be Done: Tales about New People* (London: Virago, 1982), p. xvi.
62 Chernyshevsky, *What Is to Be Done*, p. 12.
63 M. Buckley, *Redefining Russian Society and Polity* (Boulder, Colo., and Oxford: Westview Press, 1993), p. 115.

64 From the Introduction of Bertaux, Thompson and Rotkirch, *On Living Through Soviet Russia*, p. 11.
65 Ibid., p. 7.
66 Ibid., p. 1.
67 Ibid., p. 4.
68 On housing, I found the following works particularly helpful (see the bibliography for details): the classic studies on housing by G. Andrusz and A.J. DiMaio; K. Gerasimova's work on the communal apartment in the Stalin era, enlivened with interviews with people who have lived in them; I. Utekhin's monograph on the communal apartment, though this focuses on the post-Soviet era; S. Reid and V. Buchli's studies on the home in the Khrushchev era. On daily life in the Soviet Union, see in particular, the work of S. Boym, S. Fitzpatrick, B. Alpern Engel, W.Z. Goldman, S. Kotkin, and R. Stites; also the edited collections by C. Kiaer and E. Naiman, and by D. Bertaux, P. Thompson and A. Rotkirch.

I

New byt, new woman, new forms of housing

Before we start exploring the Soviet approach to housing, we need to understand the state housing was in when the Bolsheviks came to power, and hence what they had to deal with before they could start putting their own ideas into practice. Accordingly, we will start this chapter with an outline of the housing situation in Russian cities before the Revolution. We will then look at the revolutionary government's attempts to develop a distinctly socialist housing policy in the chaotic conditions of the Civil War and War Communism, paying particular attention to their views on new *byt* and gender relations.

The background: urban housing before the Revolution

Although Russian industrial development had lagged behind that of northern Europe, it had been growing in the latter half of the nineteenth century, and this had inevitably led to increased urbanisation. In 1811 only 6.6 per cent of the population lived in towns and cities, but this had risen to 18 per cent by 1914.[1] Population growth was particularly acute in the capital, St Petersburg, where it trebled in the forty years before the First World War, reaching two million by 1914.[2]

Housing construction did not keep pace with the increase in the population. On average there were six people living in each room in St Petersburg, twice as many as in any other European capital,[3] paying some of the highest rents in Europe. In the decade before the war there was a burst of housing construction in Moscow and St Petersburg, but the new apartments were not designed for ordinary workers, and were beyond the financial reach of most of the urban population.[4]

Some factories had their own hostels or barracks for workers, housing forty or so per room in long lines of bunk beds. These had been hastily built with little regard for safety regulations, and the overcrowding, the use of hazardous building materials and the lack of ventilation resulted in a high death rate.⁵ Yet they were not the worst type of accommodation. The housing shortage enabled private landlords to make a very profitable business out of other people's desperation. A common form of accommodation was called a 'bunk and closet'; this was one small section of a room which was divided entirely into such sections, each rented out to a different individual or couple. Many people lived in a corner of another family's room. It was also not uncommon for a worker to rent a bed for just a few hours per day, with the result that the same bed was used by two or more people working different shifts. According to Andrusz, by the early 1900s, 400,000 people in St Petersburg, or 35 per cent of the city's inhabitants, lived in 'bunk and closets', basements or attics, while a further 155,000 lived in a corner of a room.⁶

Some people got together to create residential communes, which, as Stites explains, developed out of the artel movement, which predated industrialisation. An artel consisted of 'a small band of like-minded people of the lower classes ... who hired themselves out for temporary work and then shared the proceeds equally'.⁷ With increased industrialisation and urbanisation, the artel tradition moved to the cities, and began to include communal housing. 'The so-called *artelnaya kvartira* or cooperative-communal apartment ... sprang from need, the housing shortage, and a clinging sense of community. Groups of workers would hire a communal apartment, share the rent, buy food and dine together, and even attend leisure events in groups ... [H]undreds of thousands of workers lived in this way in the generation or so before the revolution.'⁸

Communes of various types were common amongst students. Some constituted little more than a pooling of money to pay for food and rent, while others were based on ideological principles and 'became incubators of revolution'.⁹ Lebina also talks of young people setting up phalansteries inspired by the French socialist Charles Fourier.¹⁰ Yet, for the most part, communal living in the pre-revolutionary era was a response to the housing shortage, not to ideological conviction.

In the last years of the Tsarist regime the government started to take a more active role in housing, introducing a series of decrees which attempted to improve the situation for workers. In 1915, controls were imposed on the rent increases which landlords could demand. These were extended in 1916, when a Tenants' Protection Act gave landlords the right to raise rents only in accordance with an increase in expenditure on maintaining the property.¹¹ All the same, by the time of the Revolution urban workers were still paying extortionate rents for dismal accommodation.

The situation was rather different for those on the other side of the class divide. In the capital, St Petersburg, there were thousands of *barskie kvartiry*: luxurious mansion apartments, each inhabited by a single family, and containing dining rooms, reception rooms, libraries, even billiard halls.[12]

Inequality existed not only between the classes, but also between the genders. Barbara Alpern Engel has written extensively on women's experience of urban life in Russia in the years before the Revolution and how it differed from that of men, and it is worth looking in some depth at her discussion.[13] Women constituted one in three factory workers by 1914, she explains, and found themselves in a rather vulnerable situation. Men were likely to have wives and children back home in the countryside, so were not available for marriage; yet they could not get home very often, and were not averse to some light relief in between home visits. In contrast, most urban women were single or widowed. They earned less than men, which placed them in a worse position in terms of housing. It was virtually impossible for them to rent rooms of their own, and the danger they were placed in by the indiscriminate mixing of men and women in shared accommodation is indicated by the high incidence of illegitimate births in the cities. Their best options were to try to get accommodation with a group of women (some urban artels consisted only of women) or to rent a corner of a room inhabited by a couple.

Domestic work was the major source of employment for urban women and, while the pay was worse than in a factory, at least the job came with accommodation. However, overcrowding was such that the young woman might have to sleep behind a screen in the corridor, in the kitchen, or even by her employer's bed.[14] It was very likely that other people unconnected with her employer would be living in the same apartment: 'In the crowded and expensive housing of Russia's major cities, a middle-class couple who hired a maid-of-all-work might live in only one or two rooms of an apartment with many rooms. Next door might dwell another couple, or a group of students, who hired a servant too. ... This meant that a single apartment might have as many as three or four servants working for different employers.'[15] The young woman was potentially at risk not only from her own employer, but from all of the men in the apartment.

For a married woman with children, the home might be a less dangerous place, but it was still oppressive. Men had an escape route: they could flee the 'overcrowded apartments, wailing infants, and dulling routine'[16] and socialise with their workmates in a bar or tavern. This was not an option for their wives. Even if they worked outside the home, women were unlikely to meet up with their co-workers in their free time, for the obvious reason that the double burden of paid work and domestic work did not leave them with any free time. In any case, they had nowhere to meet. Women who frequented bars and taverns were taken to be prostitutes, which was obviously a disincentive to those who were not; and their homes were almost certainly too cramped to allow for entertaining.

Alcohol was a ubiquitous feature of male socialising, and had an inevitable impact on a family's well-being. On payday, it was common for housewives to gather at the factory gates in the hope of extracting at least part of the contents of their husbands' wage packets before it was all exchanged for alcohol at the nearby tavern. Men were drawn as much by 'the masculine society' of the tavern as by the drink, Engel tells us. If a wife attempted to save money by persuading her husband to drink at home, she rarely succeeded in keeping him there for more than a couple of evenings.[17]

The home, in contrast, was primarily a female space. Women formed their social networks within and around the home, mainly with neighbours and relatives. Neighbourly relations were traditionally strong, with '[t]he poor practic[ing] a customary kind of philanthropy, sharing the little they had with those who had even less'.[18] These relations were harder to sustain in the city than in the countryside, however. The urban poor tended to move frequently in an attempt to improve their housing situation, which hindered the development of stable networks of neighbours and 'left families more isolated and vulnerable and probably more dependent on the wages of the husband'.[19] We might also suppose that the densely populated city housing led to tensions which were not conducive to the development of neighbourly friendships. For women, then, the city must have been a rather lonely place.

New *byt* and the new woman

Following the October Revolution, the new regime set out to radically alter relations between the genders, so that men and women would live and work together as equal partners in the new society. However, they were far from certain as to how to bring this about. As a number of commentators have noted, the concept of socialism was initially rather vague, and there was 'a great deal of speculation, experimentation and negotiation' in the early post-revolutionary years.[20] Indeed, as Svetlana Boym puts it, the country was 'a creative laboratory of various conflicting utopian projects'.[21]

As noted in the Introduction, one of the most crucial features of the Bolshevik plan in the revolutionary years was the creation of a completely new type of daily life, or *novyi byt*, which would be lived by a completely new type of person. New forms of housing were required which would both reflect these changes and help to bring them about. Solving the housing problem was not just an economic issue, then, but an ideological one.[22] Above all, housing had to be organised in such a way that it would encourage a collective orientation in its residents, a willingness to put the social good above their own personal interests.

The new person would emerge from the industrial proletariat, the 'victorious class'. Yet workers had a long way to go before they would be transformed into new people. Commentators pointed to a mixed bag of negative characteristics which collectively constituted the old way of life, or *staryi byt*. These included being uncultured and uncouth, having philistine or petty-bourgeois habits, keeping oneself and one's living space in a dirty and unhygienic state, lacking social awareness, engaging in alcohol abuse, committing acts of violence and hooliganism, and adhering to unequal gender roles, including the physical abuse of women by men The new way of life, *novyi byt*, would overturn these negative traits and replace them with a range of positive attributes, such as cultured behaviour, a collective orientation, rational and healthy leisure activities, a commitment to cleanliness and hygiene and an understanding of basic housekeeping principles.

Education and the encouragement of a more cultured outlook would play a significant role in the creation of new *byt*. Much of this would take place through the 'Red Corner', an area set aside in the workplace or the apartment block in which lectures and classes would be held on a variety of topics relating to the new way of life, and appropriate newspapers and journals would be available.

Women were the principal targets of propaganda on new *byt*. In an era which lacked any labour-saving domestic devices and in which shopping for basic foodstuffs involved standing in queues for hours every day, housework was extremely labour-intensive. Even those women who did not work outside the home claimed that '[w]ashing, looking after the children, making the dinner – these take up the whole day, and there is absolutely no time left for [anything else].'[23] It was obviously worse for those who went out to work. As one woman complained in *Rabotnitsa*; 'We, women who are mothers and workers, do not have even a minute of free time. Having come home from work, we do not even know what to start with; the meal needs cooking, the cleaning needs to be done, there is always something to sew or mend for the family, the children are crying, and so on.'[24] Clearly women had the most to gain from the transition to new *byt*, which, according to the propaganda, would reduce the burden of domestic work by turning it into a social institution. As the principal homemakers, they also played the major role in ensuring that the home was kept clean and hygienic, and in maintaining the health of their families.

For men, the transition to new *byt* involved becoming more socially and politically aware, developing a more responsible attitude towards work and leisure, reducing their alcohol consumption, being less handy with their fists, and coming to see their wives as partners rather than servants.

As this outline suggests, new *byt* was an awkward combination of a utopian vision of the new society and a set of rather mundane domestic goals. This was bound to result in disappointment, at least among the more radical revolutionaries. Svetlana Boym holds that the plans for new *byt* reflected a deeply held Russian desire to transcend 'the ordinary, transient and everyday'.[25] Russian intellectuals of the nineteenth century had been preoccupied with the opposition 'between *byt* (everyday existence) and *bytie* (spiritual being)'.[26] This concern was taken up by the intellectuals of the Revolution and incorporated into their understanding of new *byt*. What they wanted was a total transformation of society, a 'complete restructuring of both time and space'.[27] Yet the trifles of everyday life refused to go away. This failure to transcend banality was a tragedy to the more sensitive revolutionaries. It has been cited as the main reason for the suicide of the Revolution's unofficial poet laureate, Vladimir Mayakovskii, in April 1930: his suicide note, written in the form of a poem, included the enigmatic lines:

> the love boat
> has crashed against *byt*.[28]

The combination of idealistic and practical considerations was particularly acute when it came to housing. The destruction wrought by the First World War and Civil War had taken its toll on the already inadequate housing stock. The practical issue was an absolute priority: people had to be housed, immediately, in whatever way possible. The ideological concern was manifested in an attempt to do away with housing privilege (and, indeed, to do away with the former privileged classes), distribute housing in an egalitarian way, and develop the type of housing which would be conducive to creating a new socialist way of life and transforming gender relations.

Communal housing would deal to some extent with both the practical and ideological concerns. It constituted the most economical use of space, and it would help develop in residents a collectivised approach to life; this would then form the foundation of the new socialist person. There were differences of opinion on the extent to which life should be lived communally, but shared kitchens, dining rooms and laundries were seen as fairly fundamental. These would not only foster collectivism, but would also liberate women from doing the domestic chores for their own families. This, in turn, would free them for work in social production, which was one of the cornerstones of female emancipation and an essential step in the transformation of gender relations. Appropriate housing was seen, then, as a key element in the creation of gender equality.

There was broad agreement amongst the Bolsheviks, at least in principle, that the pre-revolutionary family had constituted an instrument of oppression for women. It had forced them to devote their time and energy to the mind-numbing drudgery of housework, and had reduced them to a state of such financial dependence that they were unable to leave their husbands even if they were subjected to appalling brutality. Decrees aimed at creating equality between the sexes were among the first introduced by the new regime. They gave women the same legal rights as men, entitled them to divorce on demand, made it possible for them to claim child support from the fathers of their children whether or not they were married, and much else.[29]

However, there was confusion and disagreement amongst the new rulers about the fate of the family under socialism. Would it 'wither away' and be replaced by the commune, or could it survive in a new form? Would men and women settle down into long-lasting unions, or would women's financial independence, and hence their ability to move on when they chose, result in more fluid and short-lived relationships? Who would care for the children these relationships produced? Would they live with one or both parents, or would they be housed in separate quarters?

Lenin and his wife, Nadezhda Krupskaya, were on the conservative end of the spectrum. Both rejected the 'bourgeois marriage', with 'its license for the husband and bondage for the wife',[30] and supported women's right to leave abusive husbands. However, they did not envisage the end of marriage, but, rather, its transformation into a new and improved form, a partnership of equals. As Krupskaya put it: 'Devoid of its bourgeois traits – the domination of the man and the suppression of the woman under the burdens of domestic work – the conjugal family, a long-term union dedicated to the building of a shared life, the birth and upbringing of children, is the only form [of the family] which we need.'[31] In 1919, two years after the Revolution, Lenin insisted that Soviet Russia had done more than any other country to ensure the *legal* equality of its female citizens, but acknowledged that there had been insufficient change in daily life. Housework had still not been turned into a fully socialised industry, and the woman remained a 'domestic slave':

> *petty housework* crushes, strangles, stultifies and degrades her, chains her to the kitchen and to the nursery, and she wastes her energy on barbarously unproductive, petty, nerve-wracking, stultifying and crushing drudgery. The real emancipation of women, real communism, will begin only where and when an all-out struggle begins ... against this petty housekeeping, or rather where and when its wholesale transformation into a large-scale social economy begins.[32]

The first steps had been taken with the creation of some public dining facilities, crèches and kindergartens, Lenin continued. As these developed, relations between husband and wife would become more harmonious and egalitarian.

For many communists in Soviet Russia, the family would not survive in any form; it would simply have no role to play under socialism. The transition to a nationalised economy would remove its productive function; socialised child care would remove its role in upbringing; and the sexual needs of its adult members would be released from its confines and dealt with, as Aleksandra Kollontai famously put it, 'like the satisfaction of hunger or thirst'.[33] I. Brandenburgskii, spokesman of the People's Commissariat of Justice, was confident that '[t]he family ... will disappear, and will be replaced by the state organisation of social upbringing and social security'.[34] Sociologist Semen Vol'fson was equally uncompromising: 'socialism carries within itself the death of the family'.[35] V. Dyushen, a pedagogue, insisted that the family was not only unnecessary but harmful since it only concerned itself with 'people connected by blood ties', supporting and helping them at the expense of other members of society.[36] Kollontai, the Bolsheviks' principal theorist on gender relations, insisted that the family would be replaced by the collective, which would accommodate a wide range of intimate relationships: 'the more numerous these inner threads drawing people together, the firmer the sense of solidarity and the simpler the realisation of the working-class ideal of comradeship and unity'.[37]

Whatever their position on the family, the Bolsheviks were in agreement that the rearing of children should be socialised. Having children was a social duty rather than a matter of personal choice; and since children represented the country's future, it followed that their material care and upbringing should be taken over by society. State child care institutions would also ensure that children developed an appropriate socialist orientation. There was disagreement, however, as to whether they would be cared for in these institutions only during the day, and return to their parents in the evenings, or whether they would live apart from their parents at all times. Krupskaya reassured mothers that there were no plans to forcibly remove their children from them: 'When we talk about the social upbringing of children, what this means ... is that the worry about the support of the children will be taken from the parents and that the state will guarantee not only the means to keep the child alive, but will also concern itself with providing it with everything necessary for full and comprehensive development.'[38] However, Zlata Lilina believed that the upbringing of children was too important to be left to parents at all: 'children, like soft wax, are very malleable and they should be molded into good communists ... we must rescue children from the harmful influence of family life ...We must nationalise them.' It was the revolutionaries' task, she continued, 'to oblige the mother to give her child to the Soviet state.'[39]

Dyushen, who was herself involved in a Moscow child care centre, stressed the benefits of communal upbringing to children themselves. She acknowledged the argument that small children need their mother's love and caresses, but insisted that mothers did much more harm than good because, consciously or unconsciously, they inculcated their own traits and characteristics in their children rather than allowing them to develop their own. Socialised child care would, she argued, with a touch of contradiction, give children the freedom to develop their own personalities, and inculcate in them the qualities appropriate to communism. In her vision of the future, children would live from the age of 3 to 17 in separate children's settlements, each containing between 800 and 1,000 children. The settlement would consist of a series of houses, with forty to fifty children, of different ages and sexes, living in each house. These groups would be further divided into smaller collectives in accordance with age. Each house would be governed by a house council made up of children, pedagogues and support staff. Ultimately, all children would be brought up in such settlements, but while families continued to exist, it was important that children of the collectives had contact with them so that they could see for themselves how awful family life could be.[40]

Kollontai's views on child rearing seem somewhat inconsistent. In a pamphlet aimed at working-class women, she wrote that: 'The working woman and mother need not take fright; communist society is not getting ready to snatch children from their parents, to tear the infant from its mother's breast or violently split up the family.'[41] Children would only spend 'the greater part of the day' in state child care institutions, and would return to their families in the evening.[42] However, in her other writings she anticipates the death of the family and its replacement by the commune, which suggests that this more moderate picture was only intended to placate anxious mothers. Elsewhere she paints a rather limited role for mothers, with their only duty in relation to their children being to breastfeed them in order to give them a healthy start in life. In fact, she argued that to insist on a special attachment to one's own children was un-socialist; in due course the Soviet woman would 'rise to a point where she no longer differentiates between yours and mine; she must remember that there are now only our children, those of the Communist state, the common possession of all the workers'.[43]

The 'housing question' in the time of War Communism

Before many of these ideas could be put into practice, the country had to get through what J.N. Westwood describes as 'the confusion, chaos, and anarchy of post-revolutionary Russia'.[44] During the so-called War Communism period, when the country was in the throes of Civil War, '[f]requently, the policies of the Bolsheviks bore little resemblance to their earlier intentions; it was a case of riding on the tide or perishing.'[45]

These were truly appalling times. The American anarchist Emma Goldman visited Petrograd in 1920, and found it 'almost in ruins, as if a hurricane had swept over it. The houses looked like broken old tombs upon neglected and forgotten cemetaries. The streets were dirty and deserted; all life had gone from them ... The people walked around like living corpses'.[46] There was little food, and no fuel for heating; accordingly, many starved or froze to death. Children were abandoned by parents incapable of caring for them, and roamed the streets in gangs, surviving – if they did survive – from begging, theft and prostitution. There was, as Wendy Goldman puts it, a 'complete cessation of anything approaching normal life.'[47]

However important an issue housing was in ideological terms, the Bolsheviks' attempt to solve the housing crisis against this background was bound to be driven largely by desperation. All the same, Friedrich Engels' suggestions as to how to go about it provided their starting point. Basing his observations on Manchester, the capital of England's textile industry (and home to the Engels family's own cotton mill), Engels had argued that 'there is already a sufficient quantity of houses in the big cities to remedy immediately all real "housing *shortage*", provided they are used judiciously. This can naturally only occur through the expropriation of the present owners and by quartering in their houses homeless workers or workers overcrowded in their present homes.'[48]

In accordance with this approach, the October Revolution was immediately followed by a housing revolution.⁴⁹ In towns with a population of more than 10,000, all housing which exceeded a certain value, which was set by the local authorities, would be taken from its owners and nationalised, along with all residential accommodation which had been empty for three months or more. It would then be distributed to workers. This was described as 'the first step in the battle against the housing crisis'.⁵⁰

In 1919 the Commissariat of Health (*Narkomzdrav*) decided on a 'sanitary norm' of living space per person – that is, the minimum amount of space needed to maintain a reasonable state of health. At first it was set at 8.25 square metres per person, but this was raised to 9 square metres in 1926. This remained the official norm throughout Soviet history, though until the end of the Stalin era few people actually received anything like this much space.

At first the crisis in urban housing was partly offset by the depopulation of the cities, resulting both from the high death rate, and from people fleeing to the countryside in search of food. According to Goldman, by 1921 Moscow had lost half of its population, and Petrograd two-thirds.⁵¹ All the same, there was still little possibility of an urban worker and his family having self-contained single-family accommodation, and even less of anyone having a room of his or her own. Indeed, the fact that housing was allocated not by room but in accordance with a 'sanitary norm' of 'living space' was a tacit acknowledgement that rooms were supposed to accommodate more than one person.

If the so-called 'victorious class' found life difficult in the early years of the Revolution, the 'formers' – members of the 'former exploiting classes' – had their lives completely turned upside down. If they had ever hired labour for profit, lived off 'unearned income' (the interest on private capital, for example, or the rent derived from their property), engaged in private trade, worked in the Tsarist police force, prison system or security forces, served as officers in the White Army, or been religious professionals, they were liable for disenfranchisement, which meant that they would not be allowed to vote or serve in local government bodies or soviets.⁵² Most of them were also evicted from their homes – as Richard Stites puts it, 'shoved onto the streets unceremoniously with or without their possessions'.⁵³ This was most often the fate of members of the aristocracy. Princess Ekaterina Meshcherskaya, who was thirteen when the Revolution broke out, relates in her memoirs how she and her mother at first threw themselves on the mercy of friends and acquaintances when they were kicked out of their apartment, but when these people became nervous of associating with such 'enemies', they had no alternative but to sleep in railway stations. Eventually her mother managed to get a job as a canteen cook, which came with meagre accommodation. As a former aristocrat, menial work was all she was allowed, despite the fact that there was a great need for educated people.[54]

In some cases, large confiscated houses were used not to accommodate workers but to house military detachments or administrative departments. This was what happened to the Volkonskii family's Petrograd town house, which became the headquarters of an army brigade. When Princess Volkonskaya visited her old home, she found that '[e]verything in the house had been broken, spoilt or stolen; the books in the library used for cigarette paper, the furniture mostly burnt as fuel, the pictures cut and slashed. (Piercing the eyes of family portraits with bayonets had always been a favorite pastime of the Red warriors.)'[55]

Some 'formers' were allowed to continue living in one or two rooms of their homes, while the other rooms were assigned to workers. This process, termed 'compression' (*uplotnenie*), was an astonishing exercise in social engineering. As Stites notes, it 'brought together in almost daily association two kinds of people who had theretofore been as from two different planets.'[56] For the former owners, the experience was not a happy one. Lebina talks of the new residents bringing 'to the former bedrooms, studies, nurseries and living rooms of the "bourgeoisie" the habits and morals of city slums. They used the possessions of their former owners without ceremony – after all, the settlement involved also the confiscation of possessions. The interior decoration of the apartment also suffered – the decoration of the ceilings and walls was destroyed by a range of conveniences, the ancient parquet was wrecked by lack of care.'[57] As class enemies, the former owners were also likely to have their movements monitored and reported to the authorities, both by their neighbours and by the *dvornik* or janitor of the apartment house.

As for the empty apartments, it would seem that little attempt was made by the authorities to determine whether an apartment was genuinely unoccupied. Lebina gives the example of a General A.S. Potopov, whose Petrograd apartment was unoccupied for several months in 1918 only because he had been sent abroad on official business. When he returned he found strangers living in it, making use of his personal possessions.[58]

While smaller properties were supposedly exempt from 'municipalisation', the seizure of buildings was left largely to the discretion of local soviets, which had rather vague criteria as to which properties they were entitled to take over. Lenin had pronounced that a wealthy apartment was one 'in which the number of rooms is equal to or exceeds the number of persons normally living there', which would include some fairly modest homes. Some of the more zealous officials decided that virtually everything was up for grabs, even small wooden houses.[59] The situation also varied enormously from city to city. In Moscow and Petrograd more than three-quarters of all residential properties were requisitioned. In smaller towns it was generally only around a quarter.

The *dacha*, the country house to which the bourgeois family had traditionally decamped during the summer months, was also vulnerable to seizure. This was especially the case if it was close to one of the capitals and could be used as year-round accommodation for workers for whom no accommodation could be found in the city itself. Stephen Lovell explains in his study of the *dacha* that, as a second home to a family who also had a large city apartment, it was viewed as a particularly reprehensible form of private property and aroused heightened passions on the part of both the authorities and the people. Accordingly it was not only liable to seizure, but to vandalism and outright destruction. Many owners abandoned their *dachas* rather than see them occupied, robbed or ransacked.[60]

By the time of the Eighth Communist Party Congress, held in March 1919, the process of municipalisation was said to be complete. The Party programme proclaimed that all housing which had belonged to capitalists was now under the control of city soviets, and that there had been a large-scale resettlement of workers into houses formerly owned by the bourgeoisie.[61]

The periodical publications put out by the new regime talked in positive terms of the benefits resettlement had brought to workers. They had been moved from outlying districts and 'given comfortable, light and spacious apartments in the most comfortable homes' in the city centre.[62] Yet many workers were not happy with the arrangements. According to Lebina, resettlement was carried out primarily for propagandistic reasons: taking over the apartments of the aristocracy and the bourgeoisie was a symbol of the effectiveness of the new regime. The comfort and well-being of the workers was actually not that well served by the move. One problem was that the factories were located in the outskirts. Workers had to spend money they could ill afford commuting by tram – if they could get onto a tram, which was not that easy, since the public transport system could not cope with the new demands being placed on it. Otherwise they wasted hours walking to and from work.[63]

There were also problems with the apartments themselves. Firstly, there was the cost of heating the enormous rooms, especially with the complicated heating systems designed for wealthy occupants who were more concerned with aesthetics than economy. In addition, apartments intended for single-family occupation did not always lend themselves to multiple occupancy. Some of the new residents found themselves living in 'walk-through' rooms, through which all of the other people in the apartment had to pass to reach their own accommodation. The housing shortage also meant that kitchens and bathrooms were often turned into living space, which made the maintenance of basic hygiene difficult for the other residents.[64] Food was another problem. In the workers' settlements in the outskirts, people had the possibility of growing their own vegetables and keeping some livestock for milk or meat, but this was clearly impossible in the central districts.[65] According to one contemporary observer, some workers also 'felt uncomfortable in the luxurious apartments, and the previous owners gave them dirty looks'.[66] While there were dissenting voices,[67] more candid commentators would later acknowledge that the policy of rehousing workers in the city centre had been a failure.[68]

The leaders of the new regime accommodated themselves in the Kremlin, or in the grand hotels of pre-revolutionary Russia. These were now renamed 'Houses of Soviets'. Moscow's Metropol Hotel, for example, became the official residence of Foreign Office personnel. Although they did experience shortages, the residents of these hotels enjoyed lives of incomparable privilege for those desperate times. Most crucially, they did not have to forage for themselves, but received regular meals.[69] Accordingly, these were a much-sought-after form of accommodation. Hopeful prospective tenants would emphasise in their applications that being protected from 'petty domestic chores' would enable them to devote more of their energy to service to the state.[70] These 'elite communist phalansteries', as Lebina calls them, were occupied by the new elite until the beginning of 1923, when the single-family self-contained apartment became more popular and was considered a sign of having made it in the new society.[71]

Payment of rent was virtually abolished under War Communism. Rampant inflation had made money worthless; this, combined with the fact that the state had almost total control over the economy, resulted in an almost money-free society.[72] A decree of January 1921 formalised the situation, declaring that workers were not required to pay either for their accommodation or communal services such as gas and electricity. However, this did not last long. With the Civil War now at an end, the New Economic Policy (NEP) was launched in 1921, reviving private industry and putting many of the more radical socialist decrees on hold. In April 1922 rents and payments for services were reinstated. Workers were charged much less than people in other social groups, regardless of the standard of accommodation.

There is little discussion in the literature on the ways in which the housing situation was experienced differentially by men and women in the years following the Revolution. We can make some informed assumptions, however. As we noted earlier, the working-class home in the pre-revolutionary era was a largely female environment. Men escaped its confines to socialise with workmates in bars and taverns; for them, the home was primarily a place to sleep and be fed. For women it was also a workplace and a social environment. However, frequent moves hindered the development of stable neighbourly relations in the cities, and since these were more important to women they must have experienced a greater sense of isolation. This situation would have been worse in the years following the Revolution. With the resettlement of workers into city centre apartments, the women had to share their domestic space with those bourgeois neighbours who, as Stites put it, were creatures from a different planet and, furthermore, resented the intrusion of the newcomers. The overcrowding would hardly have been conducive to the development of friendships; as we shall see in the next chapter, the magazines of the 1920s make frequent references to fights breaking out amongst women jostling for space in shared kitchens. We would expect, then, that women suffered most from the resettlement programme, and from the urban chaos of War Communism in general.

In the workers' settlements on the outskirts of the city, life was not much easier for women. A *Rabotnitsa* article describes the daily routine in one settlement, attached to a china factory. Most families kept a few animals – a cow, a pig, a goat, some chickens – and it was the woman's job to tend to them, in addition to doing the housework and holding down a full-time job in the factory. Accordingly:

> women workers usually get up at 5.00 a.m., clean out and feed the livestock, prepare breakfast, and at 8.00 a.m., already tired, go to the factory, where they work until six in the evening with a break between twelve and two for lunch. In this break they have to tend to the family again: make their lunch, feed the livestock again, wash the little children, and again run to the factory, often just eating a scrap of bread themselves on the way. In the evening there is more work: getting the livestock ready for the night, feeding the husband and children their dinner, and then the washing, sewing, and darning still has to be done.[73]

While women struggled under this phenomenal workload, the author pointed out, they would hardly have the time to take part in the building of a new way of life.

Notes

1. G. Andrusz, *Housing and Urban Development in the USSR* (Basingstoke: Macmillan 1984), p. 7.
2. Ibid.
3. Ibid.
4. W.C. Brumfield, 'Building for Comfort and Profit', in W.C. Brumfield and B.A. Ruble (eds), *Russian Housing in the Modern Age: Design and Social History* (Cambridge: Cambridge University Press, 1993), p. 76.
5. See Andrusz, *Housing and Urban Development*, p. 9.
6. Ibid., p. 10.
7. R. Stites, *Revolutionary Dreams: Utopian Vision and Experimental Life in the Russian Revolution* (Oxford and New York: Oxford University Press, 1989), p. 207.
8. Ibid
9. Ibid.
10. N.B. Lebina, *Povsednevnaya zhizn' Sovetskogo goroda: normy i anomalii. 1920–1930 gody* (St Petersburg: Zhurnal 'Neva' – izdatel'stvotorgovyi dom 'Letnii Sad' 1999), p. 159.
11. Andrusz, *Housing and Urban Development*, pp. 12–13.
12. See the descriptions of these apartments in *Zhilishchnoe delo*. For example, Ya Golubenskii, 'Barskie kvartiry i st. 1-ya. grazhd. kodeksa', *Zhilishchnoe delo* no. 7 (1926), pp. 17–19; L.V., 'Eshche o bol'shikh komnatakh', *Zhilishchnoe delo* no. 14–15 (1927), p. 37; Buksui, 'Leningradskii zhilishchnik', *Zhilishchnoe delo* no. 18 (1927), p. 11.
13. B. Alpern Engel, *Between the Fields and the City: Women, Work and Family in Russia, 1861–1914* (Cambridge: Cambridge University Press, 1994), especially pp. 126–32, 141–5, 151.
14. Ibid., p. 141.
15. Ibid., pp. 144–5.
16. Ibid., p. 232.
17. Ibid., pp. 233–4.
18. Ibid., p. 231.
19. Ibid., p. 232.
20. V. Buchli, *An Archaeology of Socialism* (Oxford and New York: Berg, 1999), p. 24. See also S. Fitzpatrick, *Everyday Stalinism* (Oxford and New York: Oxford University Press, 1999), p. 111.
21. S. Boym, *Common Places: Mythologies of Everyday Life in Russia* (Cambridge, Mass.: Harvard University Press, 1994), p. 126.
22. O. Bessanova, 'The Reform of the Soviet Housing Model in Search of a Concept', in B. Turner, J. Hegedus and I. Tosics, *The Reform of Housing in Eastern Europe and the Soviet Union* (London and New York: Routledge, 1992), p. 276.
23. B-va, 'Delegatki, na liniyu ognya', *Zhilishchnoe delo* no. 21 (1927), pp. 17–18.
24. 'Golos rabotnitsy', author not named, *Rabotnitsa* no. 5 (1923), pp. 15–16.
25. Boym, *Common Places*, p. 31.
26. Ibid., p. 29.
27. Ibid., p. 33.
28. In Russian, Mayakovskii's lines read as follows: 'Любовная лодка / Разбилась о быт'. Svetlana Boym seems to be suggesting that Mayakovskii killed himself for this reason – i.e. because the 'love boat' had crashed against the banality of daily life. See Boym,

Common Places, p. 29. One of my interviewees, Vladimir Nikolaevich, was also of this opinion; he repeated these lines from Mayakovskii's poem several times during our interview. However, Soviet commentators generally rejected the idea. See A. Koloskov, 'Tragediya poeta', *Ogonek* no. 23 (1968), pp. 26–31. Koloskov insists that the suicide had nothing to do with disillusionment with the Soviet system, and that 'the enemies of communism to this day use his death to make slanderous attacks on him and the Soviet Union'.

29 For a more detailed discussion, see L. Attwood, *Creating the New Soviet Woman: Women's Magazines as Engineers of Female Identity, 1922-1953* (Basingstoke and London: Palgrave, 1999), pp. 44–5.
30 C. Zetkin, 'My Recollections of Lenin', Appendix to *Lenin on the Emancipation of Women* (Moscow: Progress Publishers, 1965), p. 105.
31 N.K. Krupskaya, 'Brachnoe i semeinoe pravo', quoted in Mikhail Olesin, *Pervaya v mire: biograficheskii ocherk ob A.M. Kollontai* (Moscow: Izdatel'stvo, 1990), p. 21.
32 V.I. Lenin, *Selected Works* (Moscow: Progress Publishers, 1977), p. 488. Originally published in pamphlet form in June 1919. Original emphasis.
33 A. Kollontai, 'Tezisy o kommunisticheskoi morali v oblasti brachnykh otnoshenii', *Kommunistka* no. 12–13 (1921), pp. 28–34.
34 Quoted by V.I. Isaev, *Kommuna ili kommunalka? – izmeneniya byta rabochykh sibiri v gody industrializatsii* (Novosibirsk: Nauka: Sibirskaya izdatel'skaya firma RAN, 1996), pp. 25–6.
35 Ibid., p. 35.
36 V. Dyushen, 'Problemy zhenskogo kommunisticheskogo dvizheniya: Problemy sotsial'nogo vospitaniya', *Kommunistka* no. 12–13 (1921), pp. 25–8.
37 A. Kollontai, *Selected Writings*, translated, and with commentary, by A. Holt (London: Allison and Busby, 1977), pp. 287–8.
38 N. Krupskaya, 'Zhenshchina i vospitanie detei', from *Deti – nashe budushchee* (Moscow: Proveshchenie, 1984), p. 41.
39 Quoted in O. Figes, *A People's Tragedy: The Russian Revolution 1891-1924* (London: Jonathan Cape, 1996), p. 630.
40 V. Dyushen, 'Problemy zhenskogo kommunisticheskogo dvizheniya', pp. 25–8.
41 A. Kollontai, *Sem'ya i Kommunisticheskoe Gosudarstvo* (Kiev: Ukrainskoe tsentral'noe agenstvo, 1919), p. 17.
42 Ibid., p. 14.
43 A. Kollontai, *Revolyutsiya byt* (Moscow: Gosudarstvenno izdatel'stvo, 1923), p. 151.
44 J.N. Westwood, *Endurance and Endeavour: Russian History 1812-1971* (London: Oxford University Press, 1973), p. 271.
45 Ibid., p. 271.
46 Quoted by Figes, *A People's Tragedy*, p. 771.
47 W.Z. Goldman, *Women, the State and Revolution* (Cambridge: Cambridge University Press, 1993), p. 61. See pp. 59–100 for a detailed description of *besprizornost'* (child abandonment/homelessness), and the state's attempts to deal with it.
48 Quoted by Lenin, *Selected Works*, p. 302.
49 See Y. Larin, 'Zhilishchnaya revolutsiya v SSSR', *Zhilishchnoe delo* no. 7 (1927), pp. 1–3.
50 'Zhilishchnyi krizis v Moskve', author not named, *Ogonek* no. 1 (1923), pages not numbered.
51 Goldman, *Women, the state and Revolution*, p. 61.

52 G. Alexopoulos, *Stalin's Outcasts: Aliens, Citizens and the Soviet State, 1926-1936* (Ithaca, NY: Cornell University Press, 2003), pp. 15-16.
53 Stites, *Revolutionary Dreams*, p. 128.
54 E. Meshcherskaya, *Comrade Princess: Memoirs of an Aristocrat in Modern Russia* (London and New York: Doubleday, 1990), pp. 9-21.
55 S. Volkonskaia, 'The Way of Bitterness', in S. Fitzpatrick and Y. Slezkine, *In the Shadow of Revolution: Life Stories of Russian Women* (Princeton, NJ: Princeton University Press, 2000), pp. 145-6.
56 Stites, *Revolutionary Dreams*, p. 129.
57 Lebina, *Povsednevnaya zhizn' Sovetskogo goroda*, p. 182.
58 Ibid., p. 180.
59 Andrusz, *Housing and Urban Development*, p. 29.
60 S. Lovell, *Summerfolk 1710-2000: A History of the Dacha* (Ithaca and London: Cornell University Press, 2003), p. 122.
61 Andrusz, *Housing and Urban Development*, p. 29.
62 'Doma-kommuna v Moskve', author not named, *Ogonek* no. 7 (1923), p. 16; See also Y. Larin, 'Zhilishchnaya revolutsiya v SSSR', pp. 1-3.
63 A. Zazerskii, 'Kakie doma stroit' dlya rabochego zhilishcha?', *Zhilishchnoe delo* no. 6/7 (1924), p. 16.
64 Lebina, *Povsednevnaya zhizn' Sovetskogo goroda*, p. 182.
65 A. Zazerskii, 'Kakie doma stroit' dlya rabochego zhilishcha?', p. 16. See also 'Svet', 'Rabochim nado pomoch' svoim zhenshchinam', *Rabotnitsa* no. 13 (1925), p. 17.
66 Quoted in Lebina, *Povsednevnaya zhizn' Sovetskogo goroda*, p. 182.
67 Larin, for example, still insisted it was a great success. See Y. Larin, 'Zhilishchnaya revolutsiya v SSSR', pp. 1-3.
68 A. Zazerskii, 'Kakie doma stroit' dlya rabochego zhilishcha?', p. 16.
69 Stites, *Revolutionary Dreams*, p. 142.
70 Lebina, *Povsednevnaya zhizn' Sovetskogo goroda*, p. 161.
71 Ibid., pp. 163-4.
72 See Westwood, *Endurance and Endeavour*, pp. 273-4.
73 'Svet', 'Rabochim nado pomoch' svoim zhenshchinam', *Rabotnitsa* no. 13 (1925), p. 17.

2

The New Economic Policy

The New Economic Policy, or NEP, was introduced by Lenin in 1921. It was initially intended as a short-term measure to deal with the acute crisis in food production. Under War Communism, grain which was considered surplus to the peasants' own needs – and this was open to interpretation – had been requisitioned by the authorities and used to feed the urban workers and the army. The furious peasants had rebelled; if the food they produced would be taken from them, they would simply produce less. A severe drought in 1920 and 1921 turned the food shortage into a famine, which claimed around five million lives. Urban workers fled the cities in the vain hope of finding something to eat in the countryside. The *besprizorniki*, the abandoned and orphaned children whose numbers had swelled into the millions,[1] were forced onto trains and sent to makeshift children's homes in provinces which supposedly still had food. As conditions worsened, cannibalism became almost commonplace.

The NEP replaced requisitioning with a tax, which peasants would pay on the surplus grain they produced. They could sell the rest at local fairs and markets. For this to be an effective incentive there had to be something worth buying with the money they made, and so small private businesses were allowed in order to encourage the production of manufactured goods. What began, as Goldman puts it, as a 'simple measure to increase grain production'[2] led to a complete transformation of the Soviet economy, which constituted in many respects a return to capitalism.

A new class divide came into being. On the one side stood a new breed of entrepreneurs, the so-called Nepmen, who flaunted their wealth in the privately owned cafes and restaurants which had opened to serve them. On the other was the working class, many of whom were not working since the NEP had brought about mass unemployment.

This resulted from a move to strict cost accounting, the closure of many unprofitable enterprises, and the return of some four million demobilised soldiers to the workforce.³ Women were hit particularly hard, partly as a result of protective legislation introduced by the Bolsheviks; this was aimed at shielding them from hazardous work conditions and excessive workloads, but made them less attractive employees in what was now a competitive job market. Even in the state-owned industries, women were the first to be laid off on the often erroneous grounds that they would be supported by husbands. The combination of moneyed Nepmen and unemployed women resulted in prostitution, which had disappeared during War Communism, returning to the city streets.

Housing under NEP: ownership, tenancy, rents and repairs

The 'housing revolution' of War Communism came to an end with NEP. Municipalisation was brought to a halt, and there was even a partial re-privatisation; smaller apartments which were not considered useful to the local soviets were returned to private ownership, and sometimes even to their previous owners. As Andrusz notes, this new legislation 'had an aura of "back to normalcy" about it: the revolution was over, the expropriators had been expropriated and now evictions should cease, or at least be carried out properly.' A decree introduced in April 1922 made it necessary to prove that people had a 'predatory relationship to the accommodation' before they could be evicted; this would be indicated by their refusal to pay rent, or by their vandalising the property. Another decree, introduced a month later, legalised the individual's right 'to own and dispose of property that had not been muncipalised'.⁴

One reason for this demunicipalisation was that the authorities did not want the financial and administrative burden of repairing and maintaining residential property, much of which was in a very dilapidated state. Owners and tenants were now held responsible for the maintenance of the buildings they lived in, contributing their own money and labour in accordance with the amount of space they occupied.⁵ As noted in the last chapter, rents and payments for services were also reinstated in April 1922. However, the way in which these were determined rather challenges the idea of a return to 'normalcy'. The sums which different tenants had to pay were established by means of an extraordinarily complex set of criteria which included class status, income, whether or not there were dependants, the age and condition of the property, the amount of space they had, and so on. For workers rents were low, amounting to only around 14 per cent of their budget.⁶ For members of other social groups, however – 'formers', 'non-working elements', private traders, those in 'the free professions' – they could be astronomical.

The complexity of the system seems to have confounded owners, tenants and the authorities alike. *Zhilishchnoe delo* published regular reports on cases brought before the housing section (*zhilishchnaya kamera*) of the People's Courts, many of which concerned disputes over rent. To give one example, a woman called Sergeeva appeared before the court in 1925 threatened with eviction for non-payment of rent. She had been an office worker in a hospital, but had been made redundant several months earlier and was now eking out a living selling apples. The chair of the housing association which had authority over her room saw her as a private trader, and was charging her seven rubles; she considered herself to be a worker, and insisted she should only have to pay two. The court decided in her favour and reduced both the rent she had to pay and the back rent she owed; it also accused the chair of the housing association of trying to evict her in order to free up her room for one of his friends.[7]

Confused readers bombarded the journal with queries about the regulations. How, one asked, would the rent be determined in the case of a son and mother who lived together, when he worked on the railways and she was a pensioner? If the house management had no evidence that he was supporting his mother, he was told, the rent would be determined in accordance with his salary since he had the higher income. Did a cohabiting mother and son constitute a family, another wanted to know, since this would entitle them to an extra seven square metres on top of the norm for two single adults? This would only be the case, he was informed, if one of them was dependent on the other. If a mother and son lived in two rooms, asked a third, and one of these was a walk-through room, should they not receive a rebate on the floor space of this room? They should not, was the reply, since they were close relatives, and so were considered less likely to disturb each other than two strangers. If a husband lived separately from his wife and his children but gave them a monthly allowance of thirty to thirty-five rubles, how would his rent be determined? The reply was that the allowance he gave them, as well as the overall material position of the wife, would be taken into consideration.[8] How much space was a housemaid entitled to? It turned out that she should have the same amount as any other member of the family.[9]

If tenants had more than the established norm of living space they had to pay extra rent for it, and at a higher rate, whether or not they actually wanted the extra space. This was particularly galling for residents of Petrograd – or Leningrad, as it was renamed after Lenin's death in 1923 – who had been settled in cavernous rooms in the luxurious apartments of the former bourgeoisie. As a contributor to *Zhilishchnoe delo* pointed out: 'Willingly or otherwise, someone has to live in huge, high-ceilinged, cold and often inadequately furnished "ballrooms", "reception rooms", "billiard rooms", etc.; they have to pay higher rent for space they do not need, and at the same time they get through a great quantity of fuel.' It was not always possible to divide these rooms into smaller units. 'Suppose that [the room] has three or four windows; one door into the entrance hall, the other into the next room; two partition walls, and one main wall with one flue, located in the corner furthest from any of the windows. If you divide it into two rooms, one will be a walk-through room, and it will only be possible to enter the other by way of the next room; the "remote" room will have the stove, and the walk-through room will be left with no form of heating.' The family occupying this huge room 'should not have to pay half or two thirds of their salaries for surplus space they do not want, nor take in "corner residents" which would infringe both the sanitary norms and their own domestic tranquillity. Big rooms which are occupied by a single family, and which cannot be divided in such a way that both rooms have even the most primitive conveniences, should be exceptions to the understanding of surplus space.'[10] As the decade wore on, more and more of these apartments were divided up, whether or not they lent themselves to the division. One article in *Zhilishchnoe delo* discussed a relatively successful conversion of twenty-eight aristocratic apartments into sixty-two smaller ones, each consisting of two or three rooms; all of them had their own bathrooms, and some natural light. However, the writer admitted that this was an exception and that 'the conversion of large apartments into small ones rarely turns out successfully'.[11]

In the immediate wake of the Revolution, tenants' committees had been given the authority to collect rent from tenants in their apartment house, to evict those who refused to pay, and to ensure that order was maintained in areas of common use, i.e. the corridor, kitchen, bathroom and toilet. However, it had been difficult to perform these duties properly in the chaos of the Civil War, when the tenants of an apartment were frequently changing.[12] The situation had been particularly difficult in Petrograd, where the apartments of the bourgeoisie were now inhabited by a vast number of tenants, each of whom, as *Zhilishchnoe delo* acknowledged, felt responsible 'only for the room or whatever accommodation he occupies himself'.[13] The need to find some way of ensuring that communal areas were kept in a reasonable state, and that rents were paid, resulted in the creation of a new institution, the 'apartment manager', who in many cases was the former owner of the apartment. The apartment manager's activities were overseen by a House Committee, led by a house manager, who had ultimate responsibility for all of the apartments in the house.

Judging from the articles in *Zhilishchnoe delo*, the majority of apartment managers were women. This may, at least in part, have been due to the fact that they were less likely than their husbands to be employed outside of the home; maintaining the apartment, and ensuring their own privileged place in it, had become their job. It might also result from the fact that the domestic environment was seen as a largely female responsibility.

Apartment managers were viewed by the authorities as a necessary evil. The articles in *Zhilishchnoe delo* refer to them as class enemies, 'formers', members of the 'free professions', self-employed traders and crafts people (*kusari*). They had apparently made sure that they were armed with 'firm knowledge of [their] rights'[14] and exploited the housing crisis for their own ends. They retained the best rooms for themselves and ensured that most of the other good rooms were taken by wealthy Nepmen, who would pay them extra. Workers were forced to live in the worst rooms and corners, including former storerooms, corridors and communal kitchens.[15] Apartment managers often imposed rules which made life wretched for the other residents: 'Carping on about every trifle, not unlocking the apartment in the evenings [to let the other residents in], and even forbidding the use of the toilet – this is a very frequent occurrence.'[16] They also sometimes refused to allow tenants to move a close relative, such as a parent, spouse or sibling, into their living space, and without the apartment manager's permission, the new tenant could not be registered. This meant that 'the tenant has to either arrange for his wife, or whoever, to live in a different apartment, or pay the landlady more for the "inconvenience".'[17]

Some apartment managers were said to exert a control over their tenants which was malicious and hypocritical. *Zhilishchnoe delo* reported that in one apartment

> a three year old boy is enjoying himself, running along the corridor playing with his nanny or just being noisy (like a three year old resident of an apartment can be noisy). The landlady comes in and orders him to be quiet because her other half is resting: this happens, of course, in the daytime. Two days later, the 'virtuous landlord and landlady' organise a party which goes on until the morning, with singing and shouting. The boy is not able to sleep, but there is no way to complain because they are the landlord and landlady and they do what they want – the flat is in their names.[18]

If it was not possible for the house (i.e. building) manager to curb an apartment manager's excesses, and if she refused to make full and appropriate use of the living space under her control, the apartment could be communalised.¹⁹ The 'communal apartment' would acquire a rather different meaning in the Stalin era, but during the NEP it was one which was run by a tenants' committee rather than an apartment manager: 'A cooperative takes the place of the owner; this is better for the tenants, since the apartment is no longer managed by an individual who acts in his or her own interests.'²⁰ In Moscow, *Zhilishchnoe delo* reported, communal responsibility for apartments had become the norm.

An unscrupulous apartment manager could also be evicted. A woman called Chudor lived in one room in the flat she had once owned, the other three rooms of which were rented out. She was brought before the court by the Housing Committee for failing to pass on the tenants' rents. In her defence she explained that she lived in one room with her two daughters, one of whom was a cripple; that she was separated from her husband, who was unemployed and gave her insufficient child support to keep the family; and that she had problems collecting rent from the other tenants in the apartment. However, the plaintiff produced a damning character reference which claimed that she derived a good income from selling milk, that she had many valuable items of furniture stored in one of the apartment's rooms, and that she was well able to pay the rent from her own finances. The court ordered her to pay the back rent, and gave her notice of eviction.²¹

The courts had less control over people whose apartments had been returned to them under the demunicipalisation programme and who now rented out rooms as private landlords or landladies. This was referred to as 'wild housing' (*dikie doma*), since it was not under the supervision of any of the official state organs.²² It formed a crucial part of housing provision during the NEP – according to Katerina Gerasimova, more than half of the Leningrad population was engaged in a private housing arrangement by 1926.²³ However, it was hardly consistent with socialist principles. Furthermore, many private landlords exploited the laws which were intended to encourage the private housing market to make a tidy income for themselves. If they provided tenants with furniture they were legally entitled to charge an additional sum of their choosing, but some became so greedy that the authorities had to 'place a limit on the orgy through a special order concerning the price for which a furnished room can be rented out',²⁴ and to tax the income from the rental of furnished rooms at a premium rate.²⁵ One commentator in *Zhilishchnoe delo* was so incensed by profiteering on the part of private landlords that he demanded a return to requisitioning: 'Given the housing crisis, the freedom to rent out rooms, with or without furniture, is evil.'²⁶

Zhilishchnoe delo came across a particularly bad case in 1927. A Leningrad landlord, Gorshkov, rented out his entire apartment to so-called 'corner tenants'. He had nine tenants in one room, which measured eighteen square metres, the sanitary norm for two people. A husband and wife paid an astronomical six rubles per month to live in one corner, while the other three corners were occupied by a family of six: a trader called Trikhin, his wife, their three small children and their nanny. There were three more rooms in the apartment, which were packed with seasonal workers, who were only let in to sleep. Gorshkov did not live in the apartment himself, in contravention of the rules, but just paid occasional visits, leaving Trikhin in charge. The scam came to light when the apartment had a visit from a sanitary inspector. In view of the seriousness of the case the apartment was requisitioned, and Trikhin and his family were given a month's notice to leave.[27]

'Compression', 'self-compression' and apartment overcrowding

The housing crisis had been bad enough in the War Communism years, but it actually deteriorated during the NEP. As we noted earlier, pressure on urban housing had been partly offset during the Civil War by a reduction in the urban population. The regeneration of industry under NEP resulted in people returning to the cities. This was a relatively slow process; Lebina holds that in the early 1920s it was still possible to find a single-family apartment in Leningrad.[28] However, between 1920 and 1926 the urban population grew from 20.9 million to 26.3 million,[29] and this had an inevitable impact on demand for housing. Standardised construction was also promoted to reduce construction costs, with a company called 'Standardbuild' (*Standartstroi*) set up to produce prefabricated houses.[30] An attempt was also made to supplement state expenditure on housing construction with private capital. House construction cooperatives were introduced; individuals or groups of people were allowed to build their own housing on spare plots of land; and Nepmen were offered tax breaks and other perks if they invested in housing. Most proved reluctant to do so, however. They did not trust the government, and with good reason, since those who did venture into housing were treated like urban *kulaks* – wealthy peasants who were now pronounced enemies of the Revolution – once Stalin was in power.[31]

Since none of these efforts was sufficient to meet the increasing demand, further 'compression' was required on the part of the population. While the official 'sanitary norm' of living space was still nine square metres, the amount of space the average urban resident actually lived in went from 6.4 square metres in 1923 to 5.8 by 1926. There was considerable variation between people from different social classes; ironically, manual workers, the 'victorious class', found themselves at the bottom of the pile, with an average of 4.8 square metres, compared to the seven square metres of the white collar employee.[32]

A curious new concept was introduced in August 1927, 'self-compression' (*samo-uplotnenie*). People who still had 'surplus' space – anything in excess of the sanitary norm, even if it was just a few extra metres of floor space in their only room – might find themselves invited to exercise their 'right' to offer it to another person of their choice. They had three weeks to do so before a lodger was imposed on them. Housing committees would assess the living conditions of the residents in the buildings for which they were responsible, identify likely candidates for self-compression, and report their findings to the local soviet and militia. This leads Lebina to argue that 'self-compression' was not just a way of easing the housing crisis, but also of monitoring citizens' daily lives and exerting control over them. The involvement of the NKVD (*Narodnyi Kommissariat Vnutrennikh Del*, or People's Commissariat for Internal Affairs) in housing distribution certainly does suggest that there was an element of control in the process. This was the organisation responsible for political repression under Stalin. It was the forerunner of the KGB, the *Komitet Gosudarstvennoi Bezopasnosti*, or Committee for State Security. The first people to fall victim to self-compression were those the regime most disapproved of, such as 'formers' and private traders.[33] However, they were probably the only people, apart from Party and government officials, who had any surplus space at this time. Some resolved the matter as best they could by finding an amenable lodger from their own circle of acquaintances; for example, the adult son or daughter of a 'good family'.[34]

As the housing situation continued to deteriorate, people found ways of 'abusing the right to self-compression'[35] by renting out, on their own initiative, a corner of their room to desperate people whose legal rights they then refused to acknowledge. This led to accusations that it was no longer only apartment managers and owners who were exploiting the housing crisis for personal gain, but ordinary tenants. Victims who attempted to seek redress through the courts were not always successful because the legal profession was itself confused about the situation. Five years after the introduction of self-compression, publications were still appearing to attempt to explain the concept and its legal consequences. One pamphlet explained to readers that self-compression did not mean that someone moved into the living space of an existing tenant, but only into genuine surplus space, over which the new tenant would acquire legal rights. For example, if Ivanov occupied a room of sixteen square metres (that is, almost twice the sanitary norm), and invited Petrov to move in, Petrov would become a permanent resident, would acquire an independent right to half of the room, would be responsible for paying his own rent and could not be evicted by Ivanov.[36] In reality, the chance of anyone actually having that much space was extremely remote.

Disputes between neighbours

Overcrowding inevitably led to tensions between neighbours, some of which were serious enough for the authorities to intervene. These were dealt with by two bodies: the housing section of the People's Court, and the Conflict Commission of the *Otkomkhoz* (the Department of Housing Matters).[37] In many cases, complaints were lodged against neighbours solely in order to get them evicted and free up their living space. Others, however, indicate more genuine animosities. The regular reports in *Zhilishchnoe delo* on cases dealt with by the People's Court give an inkling of the extent of the misery which could result from overcrowding and from living with people with very different domestic habits. They also provide curious insights into the authorities' attitudes towards both gender and the concept of 'private' domestic space.

Many of the disputes took place between women. This is not surprising, since female unemployment was particularly high in the 1920s and so women spent much of their time at home. They also had to deal more than men with other tenants in 'places of common use', such as the kitchen. In one case, two elderly female neighbours, Potemkina and Galina, were attempting to get each other evicted through the court. They were always arguing, sometimes to the point of physical violence, with each claiming that the other was the aggressor. The court decided they were each as bad as the other, and warned them that if they did not change their ways they would both be evicted.[38] In another case, Praskov'ya Solovskaya wanted the court to evict her tenant, Nadezhda Troyan, on the grounds that she had a quarrelsome disposition, was always picking fights and stayed out late at night (probably a covert reference to prostitution). The court decided that the quarrels were all of a petty nature, that this was corroborated by witness statements and that, in any case, Solovskaya was equally quarrelsome.[39] Two other female neighbours, Stoyarova and Bystrushkina, shared a room, from which Stoyarova wanted Bystrushkina evicted. She explained that Bystrushkina was dirty, refused to pay her share of the heating costs, and was visited by such 'shady' (*podozritel'nye*) people that Stoyarova feared for her own safety. The court decided that

Stoyarova had not provided convincing evidence for her claims and refused to evict her neighbour.[40] From these examples, it would seem that the courts could be rather dismissive of disputes between women: the protagonists were portrayed as foolish, their conflicts frivolous and their 'evidence' unconvincing.

While there were discrepancies in the decisions taken by the courts, it is also interesting to note that some quarrels between neighbours were judged to be 'private matters' in which the court should not intervene. Savel'ev, for example, wanted the court to evict his neighbours, the Vasil'evs, on the grounds that Vasil'ev had a difficult disposition which made him impossible to live with, the couple were always having loud fights with each other, and the wife traded in *samogon* (home-brewed vodka), which resulted in unsavoury people coming to the apartment. The court could find no evidence of the *samogon* trading, decided that the discord was of a 'personal nature' and refused the eviction.[41] In another case, all of the other residents of a multi-occupancy apartment sought the eviction of Novikov and his wife because they had poor sanitary standards, did not pay their rent and had moved in without the permission of the house manager. More surprisingly, since this case involved tangible factors like non-payment of rent and illegal occupation of living space, the court again decided that the conflict was of a 'petty and purely family nature' and refused the eviction.[42]

That some disputes were dismissed as personal matters which did not fall under the court's jurisdiction suggests that there was still an understanding of home as a 'private' realm which was immune from state intervention – at least, when it suited the authorities to see it this way. Yet these were conflicts between people who had not chosen to live together, and who had been strangers when they found themselves sharing a domestic space. One could argue, then, that they actually constituted 'the public' in relation to each other. The court's refusal to get involved can be seen as an abdication of responsibility rather than a respect for privacy. In Western societies, neighbours sometimes come to blows over the state of a garden fence, but at least they are able to close their front doors on each other. In 1920s Russia, some of these battles were over fundamental matters of daily life, between people who were forced to go on living in the same room.

Not all of the cases involved disputes between strangers. In one case, brothers Mikhail and Semen Batrasov shared a four-room apartment with their wives and children. Mikhail tried to get Semen's family evicted on the grounds that his own family, which numbered seven people, had too little space, that Semen was continually swearing in front of Mikhail's daughter and that the discord between the families had become so intense that living together was intolerable. Semen agreed with the latter sentiment, but gave the court a rather different explanation of the cause of the antagonism. Despite being married, Mikhail had started a relationship with another woman, had made her pregnant and had then refused to support the child, and Semen's wife had appeared in court as a witness for the woman. Mikhail had not forgiven her or his brother for the betrayal. The court decided against the eviction, however, leaving the warring brothers to continue living in the same apartment.[43]

Drunkenness and violence on the part of men featured prominently in disputes. In some cases, a wife tried to use the court to rid herself of a drunken husband. For example, 'S' sought the eviction of her unemployed husband, Kozlyakov, since he 'he systematically taunts me, scolds me in the most foul and uncensored language, pushes me about unmercifully and repeatedly, has torn up my clothes, has broken and burned domestic utensils. I have a son and all of this has been having an effect on the child'. The court took her side and gave her husband two weeks' notice.[44]

In another case, a woman called Pudova had been given a room, which she shared with her partner, Medvedev, in the children's home where she worked as a dishwasher. He was frequently drunk and disruptive, burst into the rooms of other residents and behaved towards them 'in an outrageous and violent manner'. The neighbours wanted to get rid of both Pudova and Medvedev, but the court only agreed to the eviction of Medvedev.[45]

Violence against women

There was one advantage to living in such crowded conditions. The close proximity of neighbours might provide women and children with some protection against violent partners or parents. *Rabotnitsa* encouraged its readers to keep an eye on their neighbours and to report them to the authorities if they suspected them of violent or abusive behaviour. While some of the cases reported in *Zhilishchnoe delo* were dismissed as a 'private matter', *Rabotnitsa* insisted that the family should in no way be seen as private; it must be transparent and answerable to society. Accordingly, the magazine reported with approval the comment made by a judge when applauding the action of vigilant neighbours: 'the *byt* of the family must be placed under the control of the collective and of society.'[46]

This neighbourly vigilance was clearly facilitated by the housing shortage. As *Rabotnitsa*'s reports make clear, it was virtually impossible to do anything in private; every act was observed by others. It is interesting to note that in the court cases referred to in the magazine, it is invariably female neighbours who have brought the action; there is rarely any specific mention of men getting involved.

In one case, a widower, Myshechkin, remarried mainly to get a new mother for his two young children. However, his new wife did not take to the children, starved them and frequently beat them. When the neighbours attempted to intervene she insisted that the children were none of their business. The neighbours took the case to court, the stepmother was sentenced to a year's imprisonment, and the children were turned over to the care of their grandmother.[47]

Most of the cases concerned women being abused by violent husbands. In one case, six neighbours gave evidence against a man who repeatedly beat his young wife, egged on by his vindictive mother who lived in the same room. The neighbours often heard the young woman screaming, and saw her covered in bruises; on one occasion, they saw the mother-in-law smear her face with human excrement. After this the chair of the house management committee let her stay in his room for a while. This is a rare mention of male involvement in the protection of an abused wife, and it is surprising that a single man would take a young married woman into his room. There is no explanation as to why one of her female neighbours did not do so. There is one obvious possibility, but it would surely be a brave man who would risk antagonising such a monster of a husband by seemingly stealing his wife. Perhaps he simply had more space, or his official position was felt to offer more protection. All the same, she went back to her husband, and the beatings resumed. After one particularly noisy attack, a neighbour forced her way into the family's room and found the husband sitting on the bed smoking a cigarette, while his wife lay semi-conscious on the floor; this finally prompted the neighbours to bring the matter before the court.[48]

In another case, a young woman who was often beaten by her drunken husband had on several occasions 'saved herself [by running to] her neighbours (*ona spasalas' u sosedei*)'. The violence continued to escalate, however, until one day she tried to escape by climbing through the window of their second-floor room onto a ledge. She fell, and 'the neighbours came running over and carried the senseless Zarezina into the flat.' She was taken to hospital, where she died the next day. The court held her husband responsible for her death, and sentenced him to five years in prison.[49]

Rabotnitsa also reported a case of neighbours intervening when a man beat his pregnant wife in an attempt to bring about a miscarriage. A neighbour took him to court, explaining that she had witnessed him 'standing with one foot on the floor and kneading his wife's stomach with the other as she lay on the bed. In this way he drove out the foetus.'⁵⁰ One can only assume that everything that happened in this bed did so in view of the neighbours.

If the housing shortage offered women some protection from violent husbands, it also forced them to stay in relationships that had effectively ended. In a case reported in *Rabotnitsa*, a young woman was killed by her drunken ex-husband when she refused to have sex with him. They had long been separated, but, the magazine pointed out, 'The housing crisis forced them to live in one apartment.'⁵¹

Men as obstacles on the path to new *byt*

While women were said to have the most to gain from new *byt*, men were portrayed as one of the major obstacles to bringing it about. One of the problems was their failure to comprehend that women were equals in the new society; they saw them as household servants, and were reluctant to let them go to meetings, join clubs, or do anything which might make them less inclined to devote themselves to their families. In one case referred to in *Rabotnitsa*, 'when the housewives decided to open a Red Corner and meet together there twice a week, their husbands began to yell: "Why do these women get together so often? We have to wait without supper and we get worn out by the children!"'⁵²

Another problem was their propensity for violence. A *Rabotnitsa rabkorka* (worker-correspondent)⁵³ suggested that working-class men had become accustomed over the centuries to taking out their frustrations and failures on their families, and seemed unable to grasp the fact that this was no longer condoned.⁵⁴

Alcohol was inevitably a factor in this violence. Drinking was the main form of male recreation, and on public holidays many men spent the entire day in an alcoholic haze: 'the courtyards resound with noise, there are fights, a pregnant woman is beaten by her husband.'⁵⁵ Alcohol not only destroyed families, but also made it hard for women to engage in activities which would help them to embrace new *byt*. As a reader complained in a letter to *Rabotnitsa*, 'if a woman wants to go to a meeting, she has to leave the children with their father, and he is drunk every day and beats the children for nothing. A lecture will hardly sink in when you know that your children might be suffering a beating from their drunken father.'⁵⁶

A number of suggestions were put forward as to how to wean men off the bottle. Lectures on the problems which stemmed from alcohol abuse, notices on wall newspapers naming and shaming the culprits, a ban on alcohol in cooperative houses, consultations with doctors about possible cures, 'might prevent more than one case of wife-beating, and they might force many drinkers, as well as those who just "like a drop", to think about the possible consequences of alcohol'.[57] However, for some participants in the discussion the only long-term way of dealing with alcoholism was to introduce a total ban on alcohol consumption. Moscow had 25,000 alcoholics, one claimed in *Zhilishchnoe delo*, and all of them had begun with just 'a couple of beers' or 'a glass of wine'.[58] They inevitably passed on their addiction to the next generation, either by setting a bad example to their children or even by actively encouraging them to drink. Sobriety had to be an element in new *byt*: it was 'the first and most basic condition of the protection of health in our daily life', and an essential feature of the new culture.[59]

Communal living would help bring an end to many of these problems, it was claimed. It would provide socialised domestic facilities to free women from housework, and educational programmes to save men from their ignorance. We will see in subsequent chapters if these expectations were borne out.

The housing crisis as portrayed in the magazines' fiction

The appalling overcrowding, and the enforced cohabitation of large numbers of strangers who had nothing in common, gave the magazines' short-story writers a plethora of material. Unlike the non-fiction accounts of the housing crisis, these stories often applied a large dose of resigned or ironic humour to the subject.

One story in *Ogonek* is worth citing at length, since it conveys so well the flavour of involuntary communal living. The story simply describes a day in the life of a multi-occupancy apartment housing fifteen different individuals or families. These included Margarita Karlovna, thirty years old and a self-employed artist and pianist; Shura, 'a small and bad-tempered girl' of twenty-seven, who worked in a school; Anastas Trofimovich, a manual worker, and his wife, Mariya Tilkhonovna, an electrical engineer; a Nepmen family, the aptly named Miserskiis; a poet, Vadim Motorov; and a cleaner, Dunya. There were also two cats and a fox terrier; these unfortunate creatures, who belonged to Margarita Karlovna, served as a butt for the other residents' frustrations. The corridor had once been wide and spacious, but was now full of the surplus possessions of the residents:

> the walls are crammed up to the ceiling with trunks, commodes, wardrobes, boxes. All that remains is a narrow black tunnel leading from the entrance hall to the lavatory. You must walk along it skilfully and cautiously. If you walk too briskly, you will bash your head on a

sharp corner of some piece of furniture, or, as often happens to new people, you will be struck in the face by the underwear which [a] female resident has hung up to dry in the corridor.

The corridor functioned as a playroom for the apartments' children, and a bedroom for the poet, who had partitioned off a corner by means of a rug suspended between a wall and a cupboard. 'There, in the darkness, is a fold-up bed, a stool, and a suitcase: this is all of the poet's furniture.' The corridor also housed the communal telephone, on which the Nepman's daughter held interminable conversations. When a queue of people formed around her and stared at her with menace, she snapped at them that they would not have a phone at all if her father had not paid for it.

If the front doorbell rang, strict rules governed who was to answer it. For example, if it rang three times, the visitor was for Shura; if it rang five times, it was for Margarita. If it rang the wrong number of times, this would inevitably prompt an argument. When one of Shura's visitors rang five times and summoned Margarita to the door by mistake, Shura was admonished to 'teach your guests to ring the bell correctly. It is clearly written out in the entrance!' The visitor pointed out that it was dark on the landing outside the apartment and impossible to read the notice, but his explanation was ignored.

The ringing of the doorbell, and the arguments which often followed, were just two elements in a perpetual cacophony. On this particular evening the apartment throbbed with the sounds of the poet reciting stanzas, a pupil of Margarita's singing the scales, and the Nepmen's daughter and some guests dancing the foxtrot. The story was illustrated by photographs which, the caption joked, showed 'several bright moments in the daily life of a Moscow apartment': these included a group of women arguing in a communal kitchen, and a steaming row of pots bubbling on Primus stoves.[60]

Overcrowding resulted not only from the number of people living together, but also from the volume of their possessions. In another *Ogonek* story, a 'vast, luxurious apartment' and its contents had been requisitioned and reassigned to workers. This included some grand furniture – 'a splendid olive green silk ottoman', for example, and 'an inlaid card table and a tall silk armchair' – over which the residents constantly bickered. One of them, Nastas'ya, who had been the former owner's maid, had managed to amass a particularly fine haul, which included 'a commode ..., several armchairs, some other odds and ends' and, most importantly, a red wooden bed, which was the envy of her neighours. Unfortunately she lived in the kitchen, which was so full of her new possessions that it 'was not easily able to perform its normal functions'. The neighbours complained bitterly about this, even though they did not actually need to use the kitchen because they preferred to cook on Primus stoves in their own rooms. They quarrelled, all the same, 'out of irritability and greed, and especially over the bed that Nastas'ya had managed to get for herself'.[61]

Zhilishchnoe delo, a rather earnest journal which was much more concerned with information than entertainment, still chose to share an occasional joke with its readers by means of what it referred to as a '*feuilleton*'. One of these concerned the desperate attempts on the part of a recent arrival in Leningrad to get himself a room. Each of the rooms he found came with a 'condition' which he could not agree to: he would be obliged to lie, or participate in a scam, to get more space or money for his prospective landlady. He eventually resolved his housing problem by taking up with a woman who had her own accommodation. 'Well, within three months we were "registered", that means we were married. Now I live like a gentleman. I have a room.' The housing crisis had turned this principled young man into a gigolo.[62]

Apartment managers provided much opportunity for ironic or bitter humour. Another *Zhilishchnoe delo* story told of apartment managers who picked on particular residents and tried to make their lives so miserable that they would have to move out. In one case, the apartment manager took against her neighbours, a young couple, because they had had a child, and this was a 'direct breach of [their] agreement'. Accordingly she left piles of dirty crockery in the kitchen, removed their belongings, fed their food to her cat, and forbade them to have their light on after midnight. In another case, an apartment manager wanted to install one of his friends in a room currently occupied by a young woman, and when she refused to leave of her own volition he began entering her room in the middle of the night and trying to physically pull her out of bed.[63] These stories make the point that enjoying a sense of control over one's living space – which, as we saw in the introduction, was one of the criteria denoting 'home' – was impossible for the majority of people in 1920s Russia.

The ways in which the housing shortage impacted on relationships between men and women was a particularly popular subject for fiction writers. One *Rabotnitsa* story was concerned with the difficulty of leaving an abusive relationship when there was nowhere else to go. Ol'ga and Andrei had just had their first child, but Andrei's pride evaporated when Ol'ga confessed that the child was not his but the result of a brief affair she had had when he was away on a business trip. Unable to accept the situation, Andrei took to drink, started a relationship with another woman and began to beat Ol'ga. She asked her parents to take in her and the baby, but they only had one room in a communal apartment and insisted they were 'cramped enough here as it is, you can see for yourself'. Ol'ga had no choice but to go on living with Andrei. She tried to act as his housekeeper rather than his wife, preparing his meals, washing his clothes and sleeping on the floor, but Andrei continued to beat her. Ol'ga then made the mistake of confiding to a neighbour – indeed, their room-mate – that Andrei was not the child's father, and soon all of the neighbours knew. Andrei beat Ol'ga so badly for her indiscretion that she suffered a nervous breakdown and attempted to kill the child. The case came to court and the room-mate acted as Andrei's main character witness, with the result that he was not charged. Ol'ga, on the other hand, received a prison sentence.[64] That Ol'ga and Andrei did not even have a room to themselves but shared it with another woman was revealed in the story in passing, presumably because it was so common a situation as to be unremarkable. We are given no indication as to how the room-mate coped with living in one room with a warring couple and a fractious baby.

The housing shortage made it difficult both to start and end relationships. This was the point of a story in *Ogonek* by Ivy Litvinov, the English wife of the Russian diplomat Maksim Litvinov. The protagonist was a young woman called Kate, a Muscovite by birth who had been living in England for the past ten years but had recently returned to her native city. Endowed with a spirit of adventure, she had been lured back to Moscow by reports in the British press of the 'familiarity and immorality of Bolshevik Russia', which she found both shocking and exciting. Yet how was one to engage in this immoral behaviour when there was so little chance of finding any private space? She slept in the dining room of her sister's apartment, and 'every night she had to wait until her sister's husband chose to vacate the dining room, or until guests dispersed, before she could make up a bed on the hard sofa and lie down to sleep in the smoky room'. When she found a boyfriend, he turned out to be in an even worse position, explaining to her that:

> 'Very often when I arrive home I find one of my comrades already sleeping in my bed.'
> 'Where do you sleep, then?'
> 'I must make do with half of the bed', he answered.

Eventually he persuaded his room-mate to go out for the evening so that he and Kate could consummate their relationship. When it was time to leave, she found a young woman waiting outside the room to take her place. This, it turned out, was her boyfriend's ex-wife, the 'comrade' with whom he shared his bed. 'Is it my fault if she has nowhere to live?', he asked the horrified Kate. 'We've been separated for two years already, but I can't throw her onto the street.' The story ended with Kate 'search[ing] in a Russian–English dictionary for the meaning of the word "separated"' (*razoshlis'*), which in Russia had assumed an ironic new twist.[65]

When there was such a shortage of living space that people had no control over where they lived, women might find themselves subjected to sexual abuse from men they were not even involved with. In a *Rabotnitsa* story, a young female factory worker shared a room 'six paces long and four wide' with a married couple and a single man. Waking up on a typical morning,

> [she] pulls the blanket down ... And then pulls it quickly to herself again. The metal-worker Lekseich is beginning to stir. Agh, the moment has slipped by. They were all sleeping, she could have got dressed. Damn. Now she will have to wait until Lekseich goes out to the hallway to the washstand.

Lekseich spat on the floor to irritate her, and when she rose to the bait, he taunted her: 'Find yourself a room of your own. Perhaps one with a terrace with carved fretwork?' She asked him to leave the room so she could get dressed, but he responded:

> 'Just get dressed here, darling. I'll watch you.' There was venom in Lekseich's voice. 'Who do you think you are? You're a working lass, but you're ashamed to show your legs?'

By the end of the story the married man had joined in the game.[66]

The child's perspective on communal living also made an appearance in the magazines' fiction. In a story in *Ogonek* by Vera Inber, who would later become famous for her diaries and poems about Leningrad during the siege, the protagonists were an eight-year-old girl called Mura and her five-year-old brother, Tosik. They spent much of their time entertaining themselves, since their widowed mother was out at work all day and had a 'private arrangement' in the evenings, typing up a writer's manuscripts.

> The apartment had a long corridor, with rooms along both sides. In each room there were people who were completely different. But even though they were different, they were all the same in one respect: they did not like children who disturbed them. One day Mura and Tosik made a train out of stools in the corridor, and set off [on a journey]. An armchair was the engine. They set off nicely, quickly, merrily, with train crashes and [other] adventures. But then comrade Gil'kina emerged from room no. 6 with a cigarette and a teapot, fell over the engine in the poor light, and broke her pince-nez.

This was not the first accident the children had caused, and their mother received a stern caution from the head of the house management committee.

> Now Mura and Tosik go into the corridor quietly, on foot rather than by train, and talk in whispers. And when they are coming up to room no. 1, they go completely silent. In room no. 1 lives an 'Answerable Communist' [*otvetstvennyi kommunist*], the most important person in the whole apartment. If he asks you something, you have to answer the absolute truth; this is why he is 'answerable'. The 'answerable communist', having put on a leather coat, and with a pipe poking out of his beard, would usually run along the corridor and go out. But sometimes he was at home the whole day, and then it was quiet in the apartment and even his cook did not throw other people's saucepans off the stove and did not throw firewood around.

One day, convinced he was out, Mura and Tosik tried to peer through his keyhole, but their combined weights caused the door to fall open and they found that he was in after all, sucking on his pipe and writing at his desk. As they tumbled into the room they sent the washstand flying, breaking a glass and a jug and drenching the 'answerable communist'. Furious, he interrogated the children about their lives and circumstances. Mura told him everything, including the fact that their mother had a 'private arrangement' with a writer, 'because the communist was answerable and needed to know everything'. By the time the other residents had returned from work the children and the communist had become friends and were making paper aeroplanes together. Yet when they opened his door to leave, they found their terrified mother pressed against it, trying to hear their conversation.[67] Presumably she was scared that the 'answerable communist' would be writing reports on his neighbours' activities, including her 'private arrangement' with the writer. While from a child's perspective the multi-occupancy apartment was a place of adventures and strange characters, for adults it was a rather more oppressive environment.

Notes

1. According to Wendy Goldman, there were an estimated 7.5 million *besprizorniki* by 1922. See W.Z. Goldman, *Women, the State and Revolution* (Cambridge: Cambridge University Press, 1993), p. 59.
2. Ibid., p. 71.
3. Ibid., p. 110.
4. G. Andrusz, *Housing and Urban Development in the USSR* (Basingstoke: Macmillan, 1990), p. 30.

5 Ibid., p. 16.
6 N.B. Lebina, *Povsednevnaya zhizn' Sovetskogo goroda: normy i anomalii. 1920–1930 gody* (St Petersburg: zhurnal 'Neva', publishing house 'Letnii sad', 1999), p. 188.
7 'V zhilishchnoi kamere', *Zhilishchnoe delo* no. 10 (1925), pp. 23–4. See also, in the same report, the case involving a man called Tarasov, who considered himself a worker and thought he should only pay twenty kopecks, whereas the house management was demanding fifty kopecks. Again, the court decided in Tasasov's favour.
8 'Pochtovyi yashchik', *Zhilishchnoe delo* no. 9 (1927), p. 45.
9 'Pochtovyi yashchik', *Zhilishchnoe delo* no. 12 (1927), p. 14.
10 L.V., 'Esche o bol'shikh komnatakh', *Zhilishchnoe delo* no. 14–15 (1926), p. 37.
11 Buksui, 'Leningradskii zhilishchnik', *Zhilishchnoe delo* no. 18 (1927), p. 11.
12 Pulik, 'Pora obuzdat' kvaritokhozyaev', *Zhilishchnoe delo* no. 7 (1926), p. 19.
13 Mikh. Ugol'nikov, 'K kapitalizmu ili k sotsialismy', *Zhilishchnoe delo* no. 7 (1926), pp. 22–4.
14 Pulik, 'Pora obuzdat' kvaritokhozyaev', p. 19.
15 G. Mednikov, 'Nuzhny li kvartirokhasyaeva?', *Zhilishchnoe delo* no. 5 (1924), pp. 45–6.
16 'Kvartirokhozyaeva i kvartirnye zhil'tsy': subheading 'Eshche po zhilishchnomy voprosy', by an unnamed member of a ZhAKT, *Zhilishchnoe delo* no. 19–20 1926, p. 2.
17 Ibid.
18 Ibid.
19 Ibid.
20 Ya. Golubenskii, 'Barskie kvartiry i st. 1–ya grazhd. kodeksa', under rubric 'Kvartirokhozyaeva i komnatnye zhil'tsy', *Zhilishchnoe delo* no. 7 (1926), pp. 17–19.
21 'V zhilishchnoi kamere', *Zhilishchnoe delo*, no. 6–7 (1924), p. 29.
22 'Kak likvidirovat' "dikie doma"', author not named, *Zhilishchnoe delo* no. 5 (1928), p. 43.
23 Cited by Lebina, *Povsednevnaya zhizn'*, p. 184.
24 Ya. Golubenskii, 'Barskie kvartiry i st. 1–ya grazhd. kodeksa', pp. 17–19.
25 'Bor'ba so spekulyatsiei komnatami', *Zhilishchnoe delo* no. 20–21 (1925), pp. 45–6.
26 Aru, 'Kvartirokhozyaeva i komnatnye zhili'tsy', *Zhilishchnoe delo* no. 11 (1926), p. 35.
27 *Zhilishchnoe delo*, no. 23 (1927), p. 43.
28 Lebina, *Povsednevnaya zhizn' Sovetskogo goroda*, p. 184.
29 Andrusz, *Housing and Urban Development*, p. 16.
30 See *Ogonek* no. 47 (1924), author not named, pages not numbered; advertisements for *Standartstroi* on inside back cover of *Ogonek* no. 3 (1925) and back cover of no. 6 (1925); and K. Polinin, 'Rabochii poselek v Ivanovo-Voznesenske', *Ogonek* no. 1 (1926), p. 15.
31 Andrusz, *Housing and Urban Development*, p. 44.
32 Ibid., p. 17.
33 Lebina, *Povsednevnaya zhizn' Sovetskogo goroda*, p. 189.
34 Ibid., p. 192.
35 Kochkin, 'Ob otmene instituta kvartirokhozyaev', *Zhilishchnoe delo* no. 7 (1929), p. 3.
36 N.M. Nemtsov (ed.), *Zhilishchnye dela* (Moscow: Sovetskoe zakonodatel'stvo, 1932), pp. 8–9.
37 See Mikh. Vyborgskii, 'Kak uprostit' razbor zhilishchnykh konfliktov', *Zhilishchnoe delo* no. 13 (1925), pp. 13–14.

38 'V zhilishchnoi kamere', *Zhilishchnoe delo* no. 8–9 (1925), pp. 27–8.
39 'V zhilishchnoi kamere', *Zhilishchnoe delo* no. 3 (1925), pp. 45–6.
40 'V zhilishchnoi kamere', *Zhilishchnoe delo* no. 1 (1925), pp. 23–4.
41 'V zhilishchnoi kamere', *Zhilishchnoe delo* no. 6 (1925), p. 26.
42 'V zhilishchnoi kamere', *Zhilishchnoe delo* no. 3 (1925), pp. 45–6.
43 'V zhilishchnoi kamere', *Zhilishchnoe delo* no. 6–7 (1924), p. 29.
44 'V sude', *Zhilishchnoe delo* no. 23 (1927), p. 43.
45 'V zhilishchnoi kamere', *Zhilishchnoe delo* no. 3 (1925), pp. 45–6.
46 M. Dmitrieva, 'Byt sem'i – pod kontrol' obshchestvennosti', under rubric Sud i byt, *Rabotnitsa* no. 9 (1930), p. 19.
47 A.E., 'Khotela "v lyudi" proisvesti', under rubric Sud i byt, *Rabotntisa* no. 12 (1926), p. 24.
48 M. Dmitrieva, 'Byt sem'i – pod kontrol' obshchestvennosti', p. 19.
49 'D', 'Sud i byt', *Rabotnitsa* no. 3 (1929), p. 3.
50 E. Rozenblyum, 'Geroi kulachnoi raspravy' ('a Hero of "Fist Law"'), one of a series of short pieces under the heading 'Po bytovym ukhabam', *Rabotnitsa* no. 29 (1930), p. 18.
51 V. Mel'nikov, 'Sud i byt: trebuet strozhaishego nakazaniya', *Rabotnitsa* no. 13 (1929), p. no. 3.
52 N. Kaptaltseva, 'Byt rabotnits po ikh pis'mam', *Rabotnitsa* no. 1 (1926), pp. 15–17. For other examples, see L. Attwood, *Creating the New Soviet Woman: Women's Magazines as Engineers of Female Identity, 1922–53* (London: Palgrave, 1999), especially pp. 52–65.
53 A *rabkorka*, or female worker-correspondent, was usually a factory worker given a certain amount of time off so that she could pen her observations of life around her.
54 N. Kaptaltseva, 'Byt rabotnits po ikh pis'mam', pp. 15–17.
55 Ibid.. See also Bor. Chudin, 'V bor'be s khuliganstvom', *Zhilishchnoe delo* no. 19 (1928), pp. 20–1.
56 N. Kaptaltseva, 'Byt rabotnits po ikh pis'mam', pp. 15–17.
57 M. Zimina, 'Bor'ba s alkogolizmom i ZhAKT'y: ZhAKT'y i p'yany byt', *Zhilishchnoe delo* no. 15 (1928), p. 15.
58 Ibid., p. 15.
59 I.M., 'Deti-p'yanitsy', *Rabotnitsa* no. 1 (1929), p. 18.
60 N. Pogodin, 'V Moskovskoi kvartire tesnovato...', *Ogonek* no. (1927), pp. 8–10.
61 S. Vashentsev, 'Baba, moyushchaya poly', *Ogonek* no. 30 (1929), pages not numbered.
62 I. Nelin, 'Zhilishchnaya svad'ba', *Zhilishchnoe delo* no. 5 (1926), p. 39.
63 A. O-v, 'Pochemy ne napisan fel'eton', *Zhilishchnoe delo* no. 6 (1928), pages not numbered.
64 Sverchikov, 'Staroe derzhit...', serialised in *Rabotnitsa* no. 5 (1927), pp. 9–12 ; no. 6 (1927), pp. 9–12; no. 7 (1927), pp. 9–11; and no. 8 (1927), pp. 9–11.
65 A.[I.] Litvinova. 'Ona ne ponyala', *Ogonek* no. 3 (1926), pp. 4–5.
66 Z. Chagan, 'Zhilishchnyi krizis', *Rabotnitsa* no. 3 (1926), p. 8.
67 V. Inber, 'Trudnaya Zhizn' Mury', *Ogonek* no. 9 (1925), pp. 3–4.

3

Housing cooperatives

The revival of the private housing market in the NEP period was seen by the Bolsheviks as a necessary but temporary evil. Not only did it encourage speculation and exploitation, but it was inconsistent with the socialist principle of collectivism. It would be eradicated once the housing crisis had been brought under control. Though the private family home still had its supporters, the predominant view was that in a communist society people should live communally. Here, ideology dovetailed neatly with economics. Proponents of communal housing stressed that it was both the most ideologically correct, and the most cost-effective, form of housing. Housing cooperatives were hailed as a first step on the path to communal living.

The cooperative movement

Housing cooperatives were a logical extension of the broader cooperative movement which had been heavily promoted during the War Communism period. These had concerned themselves with a range of domestic needs. They had procured foodstuffs for their members; they had helped them sell their own produce, such as home-grown vegetables; and they had set up sewing and knitting artels through which members could produce and sell clothes. They had also played a part in the organisation of social services such as crèches, kindergartens, dining rooms and laundries.[1] All of these activities were traditionally part of the woman's domain, and commentators were quick to point out that cooperatives were particularly useful to women. Aleksandra Artyukhina, one of the most prominent women in the political elite, pointed out that cooperatives enabled the woman worker to 'reconstruct her own daily life, [and also to] actively participate in the building of socialism'.[2] All the same, cooperatives were seen as a temporary phenomenon which had an important role to play in the so-called 'transitional period' but would serve no purpose once socialism had been achieved.[3]

Housing cooperatives were an exception. They were seen as a crucial long-term weapon in the battle against the housing crisis, since they would add the personal reserves and wages of the population as a whole to the state housing fund. They were not a purely post-revolutionary phenomenon; some had been set up in the major cities in the years before the revolution to build relatively low-cost, not-for-profit apartment blocks. However, these were still too expensive for ordinary workers, and did little to alleviate the housing shortage.[4] The housing cooperatives of the post-revolutionary era were to serve a different constituency.

A decree introduced on 8 August 1921 provided for the transfer of municipalised housing to residents' collectives in order to relieve the soviets of some of the burden of repairing and maintaining the housing they had requisitioned. Three years later, on 19 August 1924, the situation was formalised, and a set of rights and duties was established for housing cooperatives. There were to be two distinct types: those which leased municipalised property, and those which built new housing or brought back into use buildings which had suffered major damage during the war years.

The accommodation-leasing cooperatives were known by the acronym ZhAKT, which stood for *Zhilishchno-arendnoe kooperativnoe tovarishchestvo* (Accommodation-Leasing Cooperative Association). These were now considered the most efficient way of managing municipalised accommodation, and an increasing amount of property was transferred to them. By 1931 they had control of 70 per cent of the entire housing stock.[5]

The principal form of house-building cooperative was the Workers' Housing Construction Cooperative Association, or RZhSKT (*Rabochoe Zhilishchno-stroitel'noe kooperativnoe tovarishchestvo*). Shareholders would provide a down payment, and then pay additional sums as work on the housing progressed. A RZhSKT was entitled to credit from the state bank at a low interest rate; this would vary in accordance with the average salary of its members, but would not exceed three per cent. The RZhSKT could also apply for free building materials. Membership was restricted to those who worked in the state sector, the Party or the cooperative movement. Initially there was another type of house-building cooperative open to other groups of citizens; this was the General Housing Construction Cooperative, or OZhSKT (*Obshchegrazhdanskaya zhilishchno-stroitel'noe kooperativnoe tovarishchestvo*). As non-workers the shareholders of a OZhSKT did not qualify for any state benefits and had to rely entirely on their own capital. Probably for this reason they failed to take off, and after building a small number of houses they disappeared.

Only people who had election rights could join a ZhAKT or RZhSKT. In theory this excluded 'formers', as well as religious professionals and anyone with a criminal record. However, the rules were inconsistently applied, and not all formers had been disenfranchised. When a member of a housing cooperative died, his or her accommodation could be passed on to other family members, but again only if they had election rights.[6] It was possible to rent space in a housing cooperative without being a member, but these residents did not have the right to use any domestic facilities provided by the ZhAKT, such as canteens, laundries and children's facilities – though these, as we shall see, were usually rudimentary, if they existed at all.

The majority of shareholders were men. According to figures published in *Zhilishchnoe delo* in 1927, women constituted 52 per cent of the residents of ZhAKT housing, but only 38 per cent of shareholders. In construction cooperatives the figure was far worse: only 5 per cent of shareholders were women.[7] For the most part, those who were not shareholders in their own right were counted as dependants of their shareholder husbands, and were entitled to use the cooperative's domestic facilities. However, if the marriage were to break down, they were clearly in a vulnerable position.

Housing cooperatives and new *byt*

The housing cooperatives did not concern themselves only with increasing and maintaining the housing stock. They were also supposed to ensure, as one contemporary observer put it, that 'the cooperative principle is carried into the utilisation of housing'.[8] This meant that they had a duty to encourage their residents to embrace new *byt*, and ensure that they had the knowledge and skills to do so. This was to be done through education, and through the establishment of communal facilities such as shared kitchens, dining rooms and laundries.

The 'Red Corner' was the first step in the process of socialist education. At its most basic, it was simply a physical space – a room, or part of a corridor – which was set aside for residents to gather together, read newspapers and, it was hoped, discuss political and social issues with one another. When resources permitted, the Red Corner put on classes, clubs, circles, lectures and excursions. These were aimed at eradicating illiteracy, teaching residents about the new society they lived in, encouraging their support for the new regime, and ensuring that they engaged in 'intelligent' recreational pursuits, such as chess, amateur drama and handicrafts.

Many of the lectures and classes were aimed at female residents, since they had primary responsibility for all domestic matters, and had the most to gain from the transition to new *byt*. Hence classes on the merits of collective housekeeping and the need for effective child care and upbringing were aimed at them.[9] The suggestion was also made that Red Corners put on classes for women to help them improve their domestic skills. This contradicted the notion that women should be freed from domestic work, but the rationale was that, until communal services such as dining rooms and laundries were more widespread, women would have to go on doing the housework themselves. It was in their interests, then, to learn how to do it more efficiently. Advocates insisted that these classes would appeal not only to the full-time housewife but also to the woman worker, because 'after her work at the factory she returns to the housework and cooking. Home for her constitutes more work, in addition to the time she has already spent at her [paid job].'[10]

The communal kitchen was generally seen as the most crucial feature of socialist *byt*. However, women generally proved resistant to communal cooking and dining. When *Rabotnitsa*'s editors asked readers to tell them what things they considered most important in everyday life, they were disappointed to find that communal dining was hardly mentioned, 'although this is a very important matter in the daily life of the woman worker'.[11] Many of the ZhAKT houses were unable to organise communal kitchens, since they had taken over existing buildings which did not always have a large enough space; but even when they did, women generally persisted in cooking separately for their own families on their own Primus stoves, turning the kitchen into a battleground as they competed for elbow room.

Publications such as *Rabotnitsa* and *Zhilishchnoe delo* attempted to persuade them of the error of their ways. *Rabotnitsa* painted a rosy picture of the future: 'Coming home from work, we will go to the dining room, have dinner, and be free from all superfluous worries so that we will be able to put our time to the greatest use for ourselves and the state.'[12] It called on no less an authority than Krupskaya to convince women of the merits of communal food preparation. She began by deriding the complicated cooking arrangements in a pre-revolutionary factory hostel:

> There is a common kitchen, but every family has its own pot in which it keeps its own cabbage and potatoes. This is given to the factory cook to put on the stove, and the family has to pay two rubles a month for this … If they do not pay, the pot is put on one side and nothing gets cooked

for them ... A big factory, a mass of workers, and every family has its own pot. Does this not seem an absurdity? ... And if we all agree that the method of preparing food in the Thornton factory is absurd, and that instead of everyone having individual pots there should have been one common cauldron, then it should be equally clear that we need to bring an end as quickly as possible to cooking food in 'one's own pot' in one's own apartment.[13]

V. Izmailov, writing in *Zhilishchnoe delo*, pointed out that the communal kitchen offered great savings in terms of time, fuel and food. 'Work in the kitchen on collective food preparation requires ten times less effort, and economises enormously on fuel; and the communal preparation of foodstuffs makes them significantly cheaper, by around 20 per cent.'[14] He acknowledged that some women had a strong attachment to their own kitchens, but insisted that their number was far fewer than generally thought, and reported a conversation he had had with a woman worker who had just received an apartment with an individual kitchen in a RZhSKT house: ' "How do you like your new kitchen?", I asked, and I received an answer in the form of a question: "How would a dog like the fence it was tied to?"'[15]

Another *Zhilishchnoe delo* commentator, Boris Pundol'tsev, visited a number of cooperative houses, and was aghast to find that one which had initially set up a communal kitchen had later dismantled it. He insisted that most women did not want to cook in their own rooms, and be forced to 'live and sleep in soot and oppressive heat'. Nor, contrary to popular belief, were fights inevitable in communal kitchens; they were more likely to break out in the corridors, when drunken male residents returned from the tavern. Pundol'tsev pointed to the experience of another cooperative house which had communal kitchens on each floor, and the female residents were very happy with them and 'love to argue against those who are opposed to them'.[16]

Communal laundries were seen as another crucial step on the road to new *byt*. Indeed, one *Rabotnitsa* commentator went so far as to suggest that they constituted 'the kernel of the new life'.[17] For *Rabotnitsa*, their importance rested primarily on the fact that they would save women an enormous amount of time. *Zhilishchnoe delo*, however, was more concerned about the link between laundry, the condition of a property, and its residents' health. As M.V. Broun explained, if washing and drying laundry took place in the rooms in which people lived, damp was inevitable, and this destroyed buildings and provided a breeding ground for diseases, especially tuberculosis, the great killer of the day. Housing cooperatives were, accordingly, urged to address the issue of damp as a matter of urgency. Female residents should be targeted. As one commentator explained, the cooperative should carry out 'educational work, especially amongst housewives, on the question of how to ventilate housing and about the importance of using the *fortochka* [the small casement window intended for ventilation]'.[18] Secondly, they should work on providing decent communal laundries, or at the very least a separate room in which women could do their own washing. Thirdly, they had to persuade women to use these facilities, since at present they were reluctant to do so – though this was probably because few existing laundries met 'even the most minimal sanitary-hygienic demands',[19] and women needed 'iron health to risk washing in them'.[20]

The third crucial feature of new *byt* was communal child care. This was important for a number of reasons. Firstly, it would ensure that children had appropriate socialist upbringing. Secondly, it would free women from one of their most time consuming domestic tasks; as one commentator put it, it would 'liberate housewives from slavery to their children'.[21] Thirdly, it would make it easier for them to go out to work, and to do so with a clear conscience in the knowledge that their children were being cared for. Cooperatives were, accordingly, called on to set aside special rooms for children and to employ qualified childminders to care for them. This was a particularly tall order, however. In reality, few cooperatives provided any child care facilities at all, and children took care of themselves. This often meant roaming the streets unsupervised and learning tricks such as picking pockets from the gangs of homeless children, the *besprizorniki*.

House construction cooperatives: new housing, new *byt*

House-construction cooperatives should have provided the ideal opportunity to create the infrastructure for new *byt*. Since they were constructing buildings from scratch, they could incorporate laundries, communal kitchens, child care facilities and clubs into the designs. Many, however, did not include these features. In some cases this was because they were built on such a tight budget that they could afford few facilities of any kind. In many cases, however, the shareholders were not convinced of the benefits of communal living. Indeed, despite the theoretical commitment to communal living, there was actually considerable confusion, even amongst writers specialising in housing issues, about the type of housing which was appropriate in the new society.

In the guidance it offered to construction cooperatives, *Zhilishchnoe delo* suggested a range of possible types of housing. Some commentators proposed that different types of accommodation were appropriate for different people, in accordance either with family status or choice.²² A. Zazerskii offered a particularly detailed account of the kinds of accommodation he thought construction cooperatives should be building. Surprisingly, he felt that '[t]he ideal living space is, of course, a private residence; that is, a house intended for one family, with its own entrance to the street, its own patch of land with a little courtyard, and a vegetable garden, where the family can carry out its own business, like in the countryside.' However, if large numbers of people were housed in this way there would be excessive urban sprawl, making it hard to move about the city by public transport. It would also be too expensive to install modern conveniences such as running water, gas, electricity, central heating and telephone in each individual house. More appropriate forms of housing for the city were multi-apartment housing blocks, in which each family had its own apartment, and hostels of the 'hotel' type, in which 'a family or an individual has a sleeping room for its own use, and, in some cases, a room for study', while the remaining space was communal: kitchen and dining area, bathrooms, library, reading room, utilities room, and perhaps a sports hall and workshop. The best solution would be to build all three types of housing, and let people choose the accommodation which best suited them at that particular time in their lives. People who had just come to the city from the countryside and had not yet developed a collective orientation could have the kind of home which would enable them to continue their rural practices; those who were more accustomed to urban life would appreciate the facilities and the social contact they would find in a multi-apartment house; and those who already had a collectivised approach and did not wish to do their own housework would prefer to live in a hostel, where their individual domestic duties would be confined to their own small bedrooms and everything else would come 'in organised social forms'. Shareholders in a construction cooperative should be able to dictate what type of housing was built in accordance with their own needs and preferences.²³

Others had a less flexible approach, and insisted that cooperatives should only build communal houses with shared facilities. V. Izmailov gave a precise outline of a standard cooperative house. The first (ground) floor would house the communal kitchen and dining room, special children's rooms, a leisure room for adult residents to read, play chess, listen to the radio and engage in sports, and a quiet room for study. The next three floors would consist of family apartments, each with two or three rooms. Above these would be individual rooms for single people. Guests would not be able to receive visitors in their own rooms, but this,

Izmailov insisted, was an outmoded custom; it had already vanished in the West, he claimed encouragingly (and fallaciously). Instead people would receive guests in the communal rooms, which the latter would find more interesting and cheerful. Bathrooms and toilets would be located in the basement. (These seem, in Izmailov's vision, to be the only such facilities in the house. How this would work for people living on the upper floors of the building is not explained.) In addition to its social benefits, such a house would also be economical. If, for example, a cooperative built a house containing a hundred apartments which each had its own ten-metre kitchen, 'this would require a floor space of 1,000 square metres ... If we use half of this 1,000 metres for a communal kitchen, dining room and other accommodations of a communal type, we save 500 metres for living space.' They would also need fewer ovens, flues and storage boxes.[24] Izmailov did acknowledge this kind of living situation would only work if the residents 'have more or less the same budget, a similar way of life, habits and tastes, and, finally, an inclination for communal life, an understanding that they will take on themselves responsibility for the building of a new *byt*.' We should bear this in mind when we come to look at the 'communal apartments' of the Stalin era, in which people who had no common tastes or habits, and usually no inclination for communal life, were thrown together.

In fact, few of the houses produced by construction cooperatives in the 1920s had anything more than rudimentary communal facilities. The Red Corner was the most likely nod in the direction of new *byt*, but this could be very basic. *Zhilishchnoe delo* regularly sent its journalists to investigate new cooperative housing, and their reports suggest that most residents were indifferent or even hostile to communal living, and lived their lives in the most private, family-based ways that conditions permitted. V. Adol'fov reported on one new house which consisted entirely of individual apartments with their own facilities. While he expressed concern about the complete absence of any communal facilities, he acknowledged that the female residents were 'thrilled with their new homes, and shower special praise on the way they fit the domestic needs of the working housewife.'[25]

In a different article, Adol'fov reported on a three-room apartment with a total living space of 11 square arshin, or 7.81 metres (an 'arshin' was equal to 71 centimetres), in which two rooms were occupied by a family of eight people and the third by a family of five. One of the women expressed disappointment at how little space they had; her family's one room had to serve as both dining room and bedroom, she complained, and 'children grow up, everyone has to sleep together, and that's not appropriate'. However, she admitted that their previous room had been even smaller, and unpleasantly damp because there had been no separate washing or drying room.[26]

Despite the fact that this new housing was built at least partly with money provided by its future residents, it would seem that they did not know what they would actually get for their money until the housing was completed. Many were disappointed. *Zhilishchnoe delo* acknowledged that some cooperatives were oversubscribed; that is, they had more members than they could comfortably accommodate. One such cooperative had built a house consisting of four- and five-room apartments, each of which had to house between four and six families. Each apartment had a small kitchen which contained only one stove, which meant that the women had to cook on Primuses. There was a communal laundry, but it could hold only six people at time. There was no drying room, which meant that sheets had to be dried in the rooms in which the families lived, and this had already resulted in damp in a brand-new building. There were also only four bathrooms for the entire building, which had a total population of five hundred people. The report did contain one positive observation: most of the residents were trying to adopt a responsible approach to their living space and, even though the rooms were overpopulated, they were generally clean and tidy. There were exceptions, however. Some families had pet dogs, and allowed them to soil the staircases and other common areas. Children were little better; if there were several children living in a room, and they were left to their own devices while their parents were at work, 'the floors are black with dirt, the wallpaper is dirty and in some cases already torn'.[27]

Limited resources often meant that a cooperative was unable, as *Zhilishchnoe delo* occasionally admitted, 'to accommodate the demands of new *byt* in its housing construction'. In one case, all it had been able to do at was lay water pipes where floor space permitted, so that at some time in the future it would be able to install bathrooms.[28] Yet not all cooperatives were forced into a 'battle with kopecks'.[29] One, hailed by the journal as a model of new *byt*, had a well-equipped communal kitchen on each floor, a food storage room with separate containers for each female resident, and four bathrooms. There was a children's room, and a large general hall where residents could gather in the evenings. There was an excellent laundry and drying room which ensured that the rooms were not damp. The residents had the means to hire a pedagogue to work with their children, and to pay someone to clean the common areas and polish the parquet floors twice a week.[30] If one had the money, then, new *byt* could be bought.

Communal facilities did not always result in communal activities. One new house consisted of 280 apartments linked by communal corridors, each of which contained a communal kitchen with two stoves. 'The wives' were said to be particularly pleased with the pantry, which had individual lockable cupboards where each of them could store their family's food; there was also a laundry under construction in the courtyard which would have separate cubicles in which women could do their own washing.[31] Housework remained a largely individual matter, then, even if it was carried out in communal rooms. The lockable food cupboards and separate laundry cubicles do not indicate an enthusiasm for communal living; on the contrary, they hint at mutual suspicion.

In provincial factory towns the housing crisis had reached such proportions that cooperatives had to build not just individual apartment houses, but entire settlements. Again, this provided construction cooperatives with an opportunity to build in accordance with socialist principles. However, they seemed no more inclined to exploit this opportunity when building new settlements than they were when building individual houses. *Rabotnitsa* sent emissaries to report on the settlements, and they were vexed to find that they differed little from pre-revolutionary workers' settlements. For the most part they consisted of small houses, each divided into two apartments, each of which had its own cooking facilities. There was also usually a fenced-off courtyard per family, sometimes with outbuildings, in which they could keep their own chickens and other livestock. Most of the residents had previously lived in overcrowded barracks, and *Rabotnitsa* conceded that this new accommodation was far better; it had also led to a great improvement in attitudes and behaviour, including a reduction in alcohol abuse. All the same, the absence of facilities for communal housekeeping was a huge flaw, and hindered the development of women's equality. *Rabotnitsa* insisted that cooperatives had a duty to provide the conditions for new *byt*: 'the "conveniences" of old *byt* should not grope their way by stealth into the new houses.'[32]

One of the most attractive settlements, in a pine forest on the edge of Glukovsk, came in for particular criticism. *Rabotnitsa*'s reporter acknowledged that the apartments were pleasant and well-equipped, that the location was beautiful, and that the residents were delighted with their new homes. However, the cooperative had shown 'a complete lack of thought about the question of a new life for the workers. Everything was worked out to facilitate separate, petty housework.' As well as being a terrible waste of money, these private facilities encouraged what Lenin had denounced as 'nerve-inducing, stupefying' domestic labour. Ironically, the factory was taking steps to establish new *byt* by setting up a number of communal facilities – a large canteen, a crèche and a kindergarten – just fifteen minutes' walk from the new settlement. Yet the housing cooperative was 'going backwards, encourag[ing] the return of women to kitchen slavery'. The reporter urged women to become more aware of the perils of self-contained accommodation, and insist on the creation of social institutions which would liberate them.[33] In short, even if they were happy with their new self-contained apartments, they should not have them. If they did not have separate facilities they would have no choice but to use communal ones, and this would set them on the road to new *byt*.

The management of cooperative accommodation

According to figures published in *Zhilishchnoe delo* in 1927, women constituted only around 4.2 per cent of the members of management committees.[34] This was cause for concern, since women had the most to gain from the domestic facilities which promoted new *byt*, and were thought to be more likely to push for them.[35] If they got involved in plans being drawn up by housing construction cooperatives, they could insist at the outset that communal kitchens, laundries and special children's rooms be included.[36]

One reason for women's lack of involvement was that they lacked confidence in their organisational abilities. Working-class women, especially full-time housewives who had little experience of dealing with people beyond their own family circle, were said to be 'timid and ashamed to show themselves in front of people'.[37] This lack of confidence was reinforced by the attitudes of men, even those who claimed to champion their cause, since they did not trust them with any important tasks. Two female contributors to *Zhilishchnoe delo* pointed out that women who tried to get involved in the work of the cooperatives were generally assigned jobs which carried no real responsibility, such as 'cultural-domestic work'. They were never put in charge of money, even though they were usually responsible for balancing their own family budgets and so were likely to have more experience of handling money than men.[38]

Another reason for women's lack of involvement was that they had no free time. This was a vicious circle. If women got involved in housing management, this would enable them to insist on domestic institutions which would ease their domestic workload. However, until their domestic work load was eased, they had no time to get involved in housing management. Before they could do anything else, they had to be freed from the '[t]he kitchen, pots and saucepans [which still hold them] in a tenacious grip'.³⁹ How could this be achieved? It was occasionally pointed out, almost invariably by a woman writer, that it would help if men took on a share of the domestic workload,⁴⁰ yet in these times this was a vain hope.

Another cause for concern was that 'class enemies' had found ways of abusing the housing situation. As housing cooperatives took over an increasing amount of municipalised housing, they were forced to relax the rules on who was entitled to membership. This meant that 'class enemies' were able to join cooperatives, and then contrive to take control of management committees and use them for their own ends, ensuring that they and their friends got preferential treatment in the distribution of apartments and the schedules for repair work.⁴¹ *Zhilishchnoe delo* called for a purge of all 'formers' and Nepmen from management committees, and a ban on anyone lacking solid worker credentials from standing for office.⁴²

The cooperatives' failings in relation to new *byt*

If resolving the housing crisis was proving more problematic than had been envisaged, so was the transition to new *byt*. *Rabotnitsa* acknowledged in 1927 that this had turned out to be 'the most complicated thing, the most stubbornly resistant to revolutionary destruction and reconstruction.'⁴³

While women were the main beneficiaries of new *byt*, it turned out that they were not always enthusiastic converts. One female trait which particularly bothered *Rabotnitsa* was a propensity to gossip and to 'sit around the doorways of their houses observing every action of their neighbours'.⁴⁴ There was clearly a fine line to be drawn here. As we saw in the last chapter, taking an interest in the behaviour of neighbours was applauded if it resulted in witnessing and reporting violent behaviour. Otherwise it was seen as uncultured, an aspect of old *byt* which had no place in the new society.

A reluctance to embrace hygiene and cleanliness was one of the major problems. Throughout the 1920s, the journals' commentators lamented the fact that people seemed willing to live in filth, and could not be persuaded to take any responsibility for areas of common use. N. Sanzhar', writing in *Rabotnitsa*, suggested that this was a hangover from the pre-revolutionary past, when workers were used to making do with whatever shelter they could find. It would take a great effort to get them to overcome their passivity and improve their living space. He visited one housing cooperative which consisted of several small buildings grouped around a dirty, stinking courtyard. Goats roamed freely, sickly children played around a foul-smelling shed and rubbish festered in a heap outside a window. The rooms were damp and the air appalling, since the windows were never opened.

Women were held largely responsible for resolving the problem. Sanzhar' reproached the woman whose room overlooked the rubbish dump for not telling people to stop throwing their rubbish there. She told him, with a resigned shrug, that they were used to doing so, and would not want to stop. He asked the other women why they did not open their windows, and was told that the frames were held in place by nails and putty and that if these were removed the glass would fall out. In despair, Sanzhar' decided that those in charge of housing management would have to operate on the principle that 'our citizens [need] rules, discipline and drills, like small children.'[45]

Rabotnitsa also held women largely responsible for any improvements in cleanliness and hygiene. It explained to readers that 'domestic comfort cannot create itself, but arises only through the skill of the housewife, who loves order and works tirelessly to ensure the cleanliness of her living space.'[46] Despite its insistence on the need for socialised housework, it gave its readers reams of advice on how to do their own housekeeping.[47] This suggests that notwithstanding its protestations to the contrary, *Rabotnitsa* actually had little faith that the socialisation of housework would come about in the forseeable future. Even if it did, women were expected to carry on doing the work, albeit as a collective, or as employees in state domestic institutions. In this respect, new *byt* did not look so dissimilar to the old.

Notes

1 See, for example, D. Dosekin, 'Kooperatsiya – drug rabotnitsy i krest'yanki', *Rabotnitsa* no. 1 (1923), p. 31; and 'Golos rabotnitsy', author not named, *Rabotnitsa* no. 5 (1923), pp. 15–16.
2 A. Artyukhina, *Ocherednye zadachi partii v rabote sredi zhenshchin* (Moscow: Gosudarstvennoe izdatel'stvo, 1927), p. 56.
3 See G. Andrusz, *Housing and Urban Development in the USSR* (Basingstoke: Macmillan 1990), p. 38.
4 W.C. Brumfield, 'Building for Comfort and Profit', in W.C. Brumfield and B.A. Ruble (eds), *Russian Housing in the Modern Age: Design and Social History* (Cambridge: Cambridge University Press, 1993), p. 77.
5 *Bol'shaya Sovetskaya Entsiklopediya* (Moscow: Izdatel'stvo 'Sovetskaya Entsiklopediya', 1932), p. 467.
6 See I. Irisov, 'Dekret o zhilishchnoi kooperatsii', *Rabotnitsa* no. 1 (1925), p. 32; Andrusz, *Housing and Urban Development*, pp. 39–41.
7 B-va, 'Delegatki, na liniyu ognya!', *Zhilishchnoe delo* no. 21 (1927), pp. 17–18.

8   N.L. Meshcheryakov, *Zhilishchnaya kooperatsiya v kapitalisticheskom i sovetskom stroe* (Moscow and Leningrad: Knigosoyuz, 1926), p. 18.
9   See, for example, V. R., Torzhestvo kratala no 149', *Zhilishchnoe delo* no. 9 (1927), p. 25; Prof I. Dmitrikov, 'Rabota odnogo krasnogo ugolka', *Zhilishchnoe*, author not named, *delo* no. 18 (1926), pp. 13–15; M. Shitkina, 'Trudyashchiesya zhenshchiny i perevybory v ZhAKT'akh', *Zhilishchnoe delo* no 4 (1927), pp. 6–8; A. Kozhevnikov, 'Bez kustarnichestva', *Zhilishchnoe delo* no. 10 (1927), p. 18; M. Petrov, 'Domokhozyaika vmeste s organizovannoi rabotnitsei stroim novyi byt', *Zhilishchnoe delo* no 11 (1927), pp. 17–19; 'Krasnyi ugolok v byvshei tserkvi', author not named, *Zhilishchnoe delo* no. 11 (1927), p. 20.
10 M. Petrov, 'Domokhozyaika vmeste s organizovannoi rabotnitsei stroim novyi byt', pp. 17–19.
11 'Chto nam pishut o byte', *Rabotnitsa* no. 23 (1926), pp. 15–16.
12 'Golos rabotnitsy', pp. 15–16.
13 N. Krupskaya, 'Rabotnitsa i delo obshchestvennogo pitaniya', *Rabotnitsa* no. 3 (1925), p. 11.
14 V. Izmailov, 'Problema doma', *Zhilishchnoe delo* no. 22 (1928), pp. 8–10.
15 Ibid., pp. 8–10.
16 B. Pundol'tsev, 'Novyi dom – novaya zhizn', *Zhilishchnoe delo* no. 5 (1928), pp. 33–5.
17 M. Yunprof, 'U yartsevskikh tekstil'shchits (Smolenskaya gub.)', *Rabotnitsa* no. 12 (1925), pp. 10–12.
18 M.V. Broun, 'Za zdorovoe zhilishche', *Zhilishchnoe delo* no. 3 (1928), pp. 30–1.
19 R.A. Garen, 'Stroit' novye i uluchshat' starye prachechnye', *Zhilishchnoe delo* no. 4 (1928), pp. 7–8.
20 I. Zaitsev, 'Za kul'turnuyu revolyutsiyu v bytu', *Zhilishchnoe delo* no. 6 (1928), pp. 1–2.
21 B. Pundol'tsev, 'Novyi dom – novaya zhizn', pp. 33–5.
22 See, for example, V. Fedorov, 'Dlya odinokikh – komnaty, dlya semeinykh – kvartiry', *Zhilishchnoe delo* no. 4 (1925), p. 18.
23 A. Zazerskii, 'Kakie doma stroit'', *Zhilishchnoe delo* no. 6–7 (1924), pp. 15–18.
24 V. Izmailov, 'Problema doma', pp. 8–10.
25 V. Adol'fov, 'Po novym rabochim domam', *Zhilishchnoe delo* no. 23–4 (1925), pp. 17–18.
26 V.A., 'Pervye novosely', *Zhilishchnoe delo* no 18 (1927), pp. 7–8.
27 'V novykh domakh', author not named, *Zhilishchnoe delo* no. 1 (1928), pp. 34–5.
28 M. Ya., 'Voina za kopeiku', *Zhilishchnoe delo* no. 19 (1927), pp. 7–8.
29 Ibid.
30 Ibid.
31 'Obraztsovaya stroika', author not named, *Zhilishchnoe delo* no. 19 (1927), p. 19.
32 A. Tamarova, 'Gde vy khotite zhit'?', *Rabotnitsa* no. 8 (1930), pp. 19–20. See also M. Yunprof, 'U yartsevskikh tekstil'shchits (Smolenskaya gub.)', pp. 10–12.
33 'Rit', 'O starom v novom', *Rabotnitsa* no. 3 (1925), pp. 13–14.
34 M. Shitkina, 'Trudyashchiesya zhenshchiny i perevybory v ZhAKT'akh', pp. 6–8.
35 Ibid., pp. 6–8; see also 'Kh.' 'Kak my sorganizovali detskii ochag', *Zhilishchnoe delo* no. 15 (1927), pp. 29–30; and A. Koshevnikov, 'Bez kustarnichestva', *Zhilishchnoe delo* no. 10 (1927), p. 18.
36 S. Radueva, 'Rabotnitsa i zhilishchnoe stroitel'stvo', *Rabotnitsa* no. 3 (1926), pp. 9–10.
37 M., 'Domokhozyaika vmeste s organizovannoi rabotnitsei stroim novyi byt', *Zhilishchnoe delo* no. 11 (1927), pp. 17–19.

38 See M. Shitkina, 'Trudyashchiesya zhenshchiny i perevybory v ZhAKT'akh', p. 7; and B-va, 'Delegatki, na liniyu ognya!', pp. 17–18.
39 A. Kozhevnikov, 'Bez kustarnichestva', p. 18.
40 For example, see 'Svet', 'Rabochim nado pomoch' svoim zhenshchinam', *Rabotnitsa* no. 13 (1925), p. 17.
41 See M. Shitkina, 'Trudyashchiesya zhenshchiny i perevybory v ZhAKT'akh', pp. 6–8, and 'Rabota proletarskikh domoupravlenii: Vse dlya proletarskikh zhil'tsov', author not named, *Zhilishchnoe delo* no. 5 (1924), p. 41.
42 'Kak rosli zhilishchnye tovarishchestva', author not named, *Zhilishchnoe delo* no. 6 (1925), pp. 42–3.
43 N.V., 'Volkhovstroi v kukhne', *Rabotnitsa* no. 19 (1927), pp. 12–13.
44 'Domokhozyaikam nuzhen klub', by an unnamed housewife reader, *Rabotnitsa* no. 2 (1925), p. 26.
45 N. Sanzhar', 'V domakh dlya rabochikh', *Rabotnitsa* no. 7 (1923), pp. 25–6.
46 'Poryadok uborki zhilishcha', author not named, *Rabotnitsa* no. 5 (1926) p. 20.
47 Ibid., p. 20.

4

Communes, hostels and barracks

Housing cooperatives could function as a first step in communal living, but they did not necessarily require their members to live communally. This was not the case with communes, hostels and barracks. Whether or not they wanted to live communally, their residents had little choice in the matter. In this chapter we will explore the various forms of communal housing which existed in Soviet cities in the 1920s, looking both at how they were portrayed in the literature and, as far as we can determine, how they were actually experienced.

Communes

The house commune, or *dom-kommuna*, would be the ultimate in communal living, and according to its supporters it would one day be the only form of housing in the Soviet Union. In the years immediately following the Revolution, the term was used rather loosely, however, and some of the buildings which were registered as house communes had little, if any, communal facilities. Housing blocks which were municipalised and then given to factories and enterprises to be used as housing for their workers were often referred to as house communes; although they were encouraged to provide communal facilities such as kitchens, crèches and laundries, they had such minimal resources that in reality they had no way of doing so, and 'all domestic work was undertaken individually by residents'.[1] Many of the workers' housing blocks in pre-revolutionary Russia had a kitchen shared by several apartments, and these were also now registered as house communes, whether or not the residents cooked communally.[2] If all the former residents of a requisitioned house were evicted and the house was put under the management of its new worker tenants, this was also referred to as a house commune.[3]

The fully communal house commune was acknowledged to be

a thing of the future. Inspired by the Phalansteries set up by French socialist Charles Fourier in the nineteenth century, avant-garde architects produced plans for large buildings or clusters of buildings accommodating hundreds or even thousands of people and including a full range of communal facilities and services. A competition organised by the Moscow Soviet (*Mossovet*) in 1926 to find the best architectural design for a house commune, one of many competitions aimed at redesigning the urban environment in accordance with socialist principles, called on architects to replace the oppressive 'family hearth' with a range of domestic facilities which should including a dining room, kitchen, crèche, kindergarten, laundry, club, library and reading room.[4] Yet despite these practical criteria, few of the designs could actually have been built, since they required a level of technology not yet in existence. Against the background of the new regime's passion for technology and machines, these architects saw their designs as 'abstract explorations' which might eventually be adapted for practical purposes.[5] As Bliznakov explains, they were concerned as much with 'evok[ing] desired feelings and emotions, promot[ing] action, and chang[ing] human behaviour' as with actually housing people.[6] Yet even if their plans could not be translated into bricks and mortar, they looked sensational on paper, and made great propaganda: 'Attractive drawings of new towns and houses were displayed on store windows and in workers' clubs as emblems of an attainable socialist future and symbols of the approaching joyous life.'[7]

According to Svetlana Boym, the commune was intentionally antagonistic to the family; it was supposed to 'radically reconstruct the individualist bourgeois quarters, ... subverting the structure of the bourgeois family and instituting the relationships of proletarian comradeship.'[8] The communal kitchen was a non-negotiable feature of these designs: 'The individual kitchen was the symbolic space of the nuclear family and the cause of women's enslavement by the daily grind', and, as such, had no place in a commune.[9]

Communal child care was another important aspect of life in the commune, though Boym goes too far in her claim that 'children were to be shared.'[10] There were different opinions on how they should be housed and brought up: some wanted them to live separately from adults, on their own floor of the commune or even in a different building, while others thought they should return to their parents in the evening after spending the day in a child care institution. Yet there was a common misconception that joining a commune involved giving up one's children, and this is said to have turned many women against the idea.[11]

All the same, women were meant to have the most to gain from living in a commune. Released from domestic work and child care, it would be easier for them to enter the paid workforce. This would give them financial independence, develop their skills and encourage their self-confidence. The house commune would also foster more egalitarian relations between men and women. Accordingly, in 1919 the VIII Party Congress promoted the house commune as a crucial element in the liberation of women.[12]

There was a huge gap between this idealised image of the house commune and what actually emerged in the 1920s. These were usually small-scale, voluntary associations set up by groups of students or young workers, using whatever accommodation they could find. In some cases they managed to take over an entire requisitioned house or apartment and turn it into a commune. Others had to share accommodation with other people who were not members of the commune. For example, a group of people living in a hostel for students or workers might decide to form a commune and take over a dormitory room, or part of a dormitory room, for this purpose. Sometimes a few of the residents in a multi-occupancy apartment would form a 'mini-commune' in one or more of the rooms. Lebina describes one micro-commune in Rostov which consisted of four people who lived in the bathroom of their apartment: 'One slept on the windowsill, two on the floor; the best place, which they took turns to occupy, was the bath.'[13]

There are no reliable figures on how many communes there were in the 1920s. In 1921, *Ogonek* claimed there were 556 of them in Moscow, housing around 90,000 people.[14] The 1931 edition of the *Great Soviet Encyclopedia* gives the figure of 450 for the same city in the same year,[15] while Richard Stites holds that there were 865.[16] The confusion stems largely from the fact that the term was used so loosely. Furthermore, since most of the communes were informal structures with a rather fluid membership, it was not always possible to keep track of them.

The members of a commune were more likely than residents in a housing cooperative to have chosen to live communally, and to have chosen the people they lived with. This was not always the case, however. The Komsomol had control of some communes, and when a place became free it might simply be assigned to a member in need of accommodation, regardless of the wishes of the other residents. As one member of a Komsomol commune in Moscow explained in her memoirs:

> Our commune was not a voluntary organization in the sense that a group of congenial people decided to live together. Applications for membership were submitted to the district Komsomol committee with a recommendation from the applicant's place of work ... The applicant had to have a good work record and had to be active in Komsomol

affairs. For young people from out of town who had no place to live, a communal residence was preferable to a cot in a factory dormitory, where they would often share a room with ten or fifteen others in a wooden barrack with no basic conveniences.[17]

Even when the members of a commune had control over who moved in, the extent of the housing shortage complicates the notion of choice. The majority of urban people were living in shared accommodation anyway, and joining a commune was seen by some as a way of making the best of the situation.[18] As one contemporary observer noted: 'Sheer lack of accommodation drives some people into collective life.'[19]

All the same, there were communes with a strong sense of ideological commitment. Some required members to put all of their wages into a communal fund, and to share all possessions. One, set up by students at Moscow State University, insisted that 'overcoats, shoes, and even underclothes were at the disposal equally of all the communards. Should it come out that one of the communards preferred to wear his own overcoat and his own underclothes, it would be characterised as a backslide into darkest capitalism; as prejudice originating in a petit-bourgeois ideology.'[20] Others were less dogmatic. They took only a portion of their members' incomes, either a percentage or a set amount which would be the same for all members regardless of how much they earned,[21] and they also allowed their members to keep a few personal possessions, such as certain items of clothing. Yet some commentators insist that these were collectives rather than communes, operating on different principles.[22]

A commitment to women's equality was supposedly a universal feature. Household tasks were supposed to be shared between all members, regardless of gender. In reality, this principle was often compromised. It was not unknown for a commune to employ a woman to do at least part of the housework, and the tasks which members carried out themselves were often differentiated by gender. Women generally turned out to do most of the housework.

The German writer Klaus Mehnert has provided us with a detailed description of one Moscow commune in which he often stayed during the 1920s. It was started in 1925 by ten students, who managed to procure a three-room apartment. The five women slept in one room, the five men in another, while the third room, referred to as 'the club', was used as a living room. Rules of conduct were set out in the commune's Constitution, and daily life was managed by a series of committees. These included: the finance committee, which was in charge of the budget and ensured that essential provisions were in stock; the academic and political committee, which procured appropriate books and newspapers and maintained relations between the commune and the Komomsol; the clothing committee, which dealt with laundry and the maintenance of the clothing stock; and the hygiene committee, which, in Mehnert's words, 'looks after the communards' health and provides them with soap and tooth-powder'.[23] All income went into a communal fund, managed by the finance committee. At the end of every month a general meeting would be held to decide on the budget for the following month and to determine how any surplus money should be spent. A box containing small change was left on a table in the common room; members could help themselves, but had to leave a note detailing how much they had taken and for what purpose.[24] Members were allowed to keep a few things for their personal use, such as some items of clothing, but could not actually own anything.

The original intention was for household tasks to be divided between the members, but when the apartment became worryingly dirty they decided to employ a housekeeper. There was some concern about the ethical implications of this move, but they decided it was not much different to taking their clothes to a laundry or having a shirt made by a seamstress. The communards continued to do some of the housework themselves, and had a long discussion as to whether men were capable of ironing; although the women were worried that their clothes might be ruined, they decided that men had to do their share in the interests of equality. Fetching and chopping firewood were deemed exclusively male tasks, however, because the men were stronger; in exchange, the women did the darning. The institutionalisation of home life, with its plethora of committees and its incessant meetings, did not suit everyone. There was a considerable turnover of members, with one young man explaining that he had 'had enough of collectivism. There's a collective at college, there's a collective at home. I want to be alone.'[25]

This commune was not one of the most rigid, however. Some tried to exert complete control over their members' lives, scrutinising their behaviour for any signs of 'subver[sion] of Communist ethics'.[26] One, founded by 'NOTists' – members of the Scientific Organisation of Labour (*Nauchnaya Organizatsiya Truda*) – was heavily influenced by Taylorism, the American movement aimed at increasing production efficiency, which held that every task could be carried out in a precisely calculated time. Accordingly, the NOTists attempted to account for every minute of their members' time by means of a detailed schedule posted in the living room. As Stites notes, in effect this meant that members not only sacrificed their private space, but also any semblance of private time.[27]

Communes which attempted to exert too tight a control over their members' behaviour experienced a particularly high turnover, however.

As Mehnert explains, people would either leave of their own accord or be expelled for infringing the commune's rules.[28]

Sexual relations posed a particular problem. This was partly because it was thought that a special intimacy between two members of the commune would threaten its cohesion. However, the main problem was lack of space. There was nowhere for a couple to be alone; as Mehnert notes, 'every room was full of people.'[29] Some communes decided that the easiest solution was to prohibit sexual relations between members.[30] This clearly would not work, however, if, as some hoped, communes would one day be the only form of housing.

In the commune Mehnert stayed in, sexual relations and marriage were initially banned, but the prohibition did not last for long. All the same, the shortage of space meant that husbands and wives continued to sleep in separate bedrooms. Presumably they still managed to have sexual relations, because there were deliberations as to whether to permit children in the commune. It was decided that marriage 'must remain without consequences', since they had neither the money nor the space for children, and their presence would make it impossible to work at home. Curiously, abortion was also prohibited, though it had been legalised in Soviet Russia in 1920.[31] Given that contraception was virtually non-existent, one can only assume that 'consequences' were inevitable, and that when a woman became pregnant she had to leave. Eventually the commune acquired a larger apartment and decided to allow children, but they had 'to be regarded as the commune's children and brought up at the general cost'.[32]

The journals we have focused on – *Zhilishchnoe delo*, *Ogonek* and *Rabotnitsa* – were supporters of the commune, but only in its large-scale, custom-built version, since only these could provide the services and facilities which would liberate women from domestic slavery, encourage the collective principles which would lead to the creation of the new Soviet person, and be cost-efficient. 'We must only build gigantic house-communes!', declared one contributor to *Zhilishchnoe delo*; 'Only these will lead us down the road to new *byt*!'[33] One 'model commune' described in the journal had been set up on Leningrad's Prospekt Ogorodnikova, 'a huge house with 720 rooms'. It had been given credit by the Communal Bank to carry out repairs and modifications, and had set up communal kitchens, a wash house and toilets. It also had plans to open a club and dining room.[34] Yet, if this was the ideal, it did not bode well for gender equality. In the photographs which accompanied the article, the only people at work in the communal kitchen were women.[35]

A 1924 *Ogonek* article was explicitly concerned with the gender implications of house communes. The author, D. Mallori, reported on a new house commune in Odessa, which had been set up by the female members of the Union of Textile Workers. Male residents were permitted, but women formed the majority: there were sixty-five of them, compared with thirty-five men. There were also twenty-five children. The main aim of the commune, its founder declared, was 'to free the woman worker from the yoke of housework', and hence to set her on the path to cultural and educational development: 'The woman worker could hardly go to the club after work if she came home hungry and tired and had to continue to work for the next five to six hours "like a convict", washing the floors, washing the sheets and scrubbing the potatoes.' In this commune, most of the housework was done for her:

> When she comes home from work, the woman worker finds at home clean sheets, a tasty meal, a warm room, a bath ... From morning to night the communal dining room is at the service of the house's residents. One can either take [meals] to one's apartment, or eat in the dining room. Hot water is available all day. In the evening the dining room is a merry place. For thirteen chervonny rubles [a *chervonetz* was a ten-ruble note] a member of the commune has a full table ... The communal laundry, communal kitchen, and a splendid club ... make the house commune a comfortable residence for women workers.[36]

The communal services also ensured that the residential rooms were 'free of any signs of "housework" – smoking stoves, sheets hanging up to dry, and so on'. The author concluded that the house commune was 'the only path to a fundamental transformation of *byt*', and to emphasise this point the Odessa commune had been given the name 'New *byt*'. The article did not explain who provided the domestic services, but they seem to have been paid for at the point of use, which suggests that the residents hired staff rather than sharing the work between them. A photograph of this communal kitchen showed, unusually, a man preparing food, which is another indication that the work was not done for free.

In general, despite its insistence that the house commune was the path to women's liberation, *Rabotnitsa* still portrayed the communal kitchen as a female domain. One contributor explained that since women would gain the most from it, it was up to them to set it up and run it: 'Women workers must take this matter on themselves. By organising public kitchens in house communes, women workers will be making a move towards freeing themselves from the domestic kitchen.'[37]

Hostels and barracks

In reality, few attempts at communal living during the NEP period bore any resemblance to the ideal. Hostels and barracks were the most widespread form of communal housing, and they were hardly a model of communal life.

There was some hope for hostels. Their Russian name, *obshchezhitie*, can be translated as 'communal living', and some commentators did suggest that they could function as a first step towards new *byt*. They generally housed a particular cohort of people, such as students, young workers, or recent arrivals from the countryside, and were seen as a way of introducing them to communal ways. However, their inadequacies were frequently acknowledged. *Ogonek* painted a dismal picture of the communal kitchen in one hostel for women and children; too small to meet the needs even of its own residents, it also had to accommodate many of the women's husbands, who lived elsewhere but turned up at regular intervals expecting to be fed by their wives. Overcrowding led to aggressive behaviour, and exacerbated poor standards of hygiene: 'The women who are preparing food in the crowded and smoky kitchen, which has huge stoves and endless rows of cupboards, with four to five women per cupboard, are constantly yelling at each other and jostling each other for space. In the evenings the kitchen is full of people, including drunken men. The kitchen is only quiet at night, but then it is full of empty bottles, jars, scraps of food, etc.'[38] *Zhilishchnoe delo* also made it clear that the sanitary conditions in hostels could be appalling, and urged Komsomol members to get involved in efforts to improve them.[39]

Barracks were even worse. For the most part they were pre-revolutionary buildings which had belonged to factory owners and had been requisitioned by the new regime along with the factories. They were particularly common in provincial industrial towns. In Ivanovo-Voznesensk, frequently described as the 'Russian Manchester', there was a constant stream of prospective new residents hoping to find work, and the existing housing could not cope. The average amount of living space had dropped to four and a half arshin per person (approximately 3.9 square metres) by 1925.[40] In Dulevsk, where there was a large porcelain factory, the only accommodation available for workers was a large stone barracks and a few rotten wooden structures which had been damaged by fire. Some people had less than three square arshin of living space (2.13 metres) – 'the size of a grave', *Ogonek* observed. Men, women and children slept together in the same room, sharing their diseases as well as their living space.[41] In Yartevsk, some 8,500 people lived in factory barracks;

three or so families, each consisting of five or more people, were crammed into each small room. 'The women workers say: "This is not life, but penal servitude (*katorga*)", *Rabotnitsa* reported.[42]

'Swearing, drunkenness, petty and major quarrels', fuelled by *samogon*, were ubiquitous features of barracks life.[43] Male violence against wives and children was common.[44] Conditions were unsanitary: 'there were black, soot-covered ceilings, crumbling plaster, cobwebs in the corners, dirty staircases and floors, on which untended children were constantly sitting.'[45] Children were usually left to their own devices during the day while their parents were at work, and in the evenings were exposed to alcohol abuse, gambling and 'hooliganism'.[46] As a result, they became aggressive themselves from the youngest of ages.[47]

Barracks were universally acknowledged to be a temporary phenomenon, which would be replaced as soon as possible with new forms of housing. As we shall see in the next chapter, however, they would become the predominant form of housing in the early Stalin era.

Notes

1 *Bol'shaya Sovetskaya Entsiklopediya* (Moscow: Izdatel'stvo 'Sovetskaya Entsiklopediya', 1931 edition), p. 78.
2 See M. Bliznakov, 'Soviet Housing During the Experimental Years, 1918–1933', in W.C. Brumfield and B.A. Ruble (eds), *Russian Housing in the Modern Age: Design and Social History* (Cambridge: Cambridge University Press, 1993), p. 96.
3 See N. Meshcheryakov, 'Chto delaet sovetskaya vlast' dlya uluchsheniya zhilishch rabochikh', *Kommunistka* no. 8–9 (1921), pp. 30–2; and 'Doma-kommuna v Moskve', author not named, *Ogonek* no. 7 (1923), p. 16.
4 G.A. Gradov, *Gorod i byt* (Moscow: izdatel'stvo literatury po stroitel'stvu, 1968), p. 44.
5 C. Lodder, 'Searching for Utopia', in C. Wilk (ed.), *Modernism 1914–1939: Designing a New World* (London: V&A Publications, 2006), p. 36.
6 Bliznakov, 'Soviet Housing During the Experimental Years', p. 971.
7 Ibid., p. 101.
8 S. Boym, *Common Places: Mythologies of Everyday life in Russia* (Cambridge, Mass.: Harvard University Press, 1994), p. 127.
9 Ibid., p. 128.
10 Ibid., p. 127.
11 K. Mehnert, *Youth in Soviet Russia*, translated by M. Davidson (London: George Allen and Unwin, 1933), p. 221.
12 G. Andrusz, *Housing and Urban Development in the USSR* (Basingstoke: Macmillan 1990), p. 114.
13 N.B. Lebina, *Povsednevnaya zhizn' Sovetskogo goroda: normy I anomalii. 1920–1930 gody* (St Petersburg: Zhurnal 'Neva' – izdatel'stvotorgovyi dom 'Letnii Sad', 1999), p. 166. This example was taken from the memoirs of V.F. Panova, *O moei zhizni, knigakh i chitatelyakh* (Leningrad 1980), p. 88.

14 'Doma-kommuna v Moskve', *Ogonek* no. 7 (1923), p. 16.
15 *Bol'shaya Sovetskaya Entsiklopediya*, p. 78.
16 R. Stites, *Revolutionary Dreams: Utopian Vision and Experimental Life in the Russian Revolution* (Oxford and New York: Oxford University Press, 1989), p. 213.
17 M.M. Leder, *My Life in Stalinist Russia: An American Woman Looks Back* (Bloomington, Ind.: Indiana University Press, 2001), p. 41.
18 See A.M. Kairov, 'Kratkaya istoriya odnogo doma', *Zhilishchnoe delo* no. 22 (1927), pp. 27–8, for a description of one house taken over by a group of workers.
19 Mehnert, *Youth in Soviet Russia*, p. 184.
20 Ibid., pp. 182–3.
21 Klaus Mehnert, a frequent visitor to Russia in the 1920s, differentiated between the communes and collectives, and held that in communes all earnings went into a communal fund, and in collectives only part of it. Other commentators make no such distinction, however. See Mehnert, *Youth in Soviet Russia*, p. 182; also V.I. Isaev, *Kommuna ili kommunalka?* (Nauka: siberskaya izdatel'skaya firma RAN, Novosibirsk, 1996), pp. 25–6; and Stites, *Revolutionary Dreams*, pp. 213–19.
22 See Leder, *My Life in Stalinist Russia*, p. 45; and Mehnert, *Youth in Soviet Russia*, p. 165.
23 Mehnert, *Youth in Soviet Russia*, p. 166.
24 Ibid., p. 168.
25 Ibid., p. 170.
26 Ibid., p. 183.
27 Stites, *Revolutionary Dreams*, p. 215.
28 Mehnert, *Youth in Soviet Russia*, p. 182.
29 Ibid., p. 173.
30 Lebina, *Povsednevnaya zhizn' Sovetskogo goroda*, p. 166.
31 A member of Moscow's Hammer and Sickle factory commune insisted that '[t]he sex question is easily settled in youth communes. We live with our girls much better than the most ideal brothers and sisters. We do not think of marriage because we are too busy, and at the same time, living together with our girls weakens our sexual desire'. Lebina, *Povsednevnaya zhizn' Sovetskogo goroda*, p. 176.
32 Ibid., p. 176.
33 Worker correspondent S. Gavrilov, 'Gde zhe stroit' doma-kommuny?', *Zhilishchnoe delo* no. 3 (1925), p. 9. See also 'Nam nuzhny doma-kommuny!', by the management of House no 145 on Ligovka, *Zhilishchnoe delo* no. 4 (1925), pp. 17–18.
34 'Rabota proletarskikh domoupravlenii: subheading 'Obraztsovaya kommuna', *Zhilishchnoe delo* no. 6–7 (1924), pp. 50–1.
35 Ibid.
36 D. Mallori, 'Bor'ba za novyi byt', *Ogonek* no. 19 (1924), pages not numbered.
37 M. Zarina, 'Revolyutsiya byta: Stroitel'stvo narodnogo pitaniya', *Rabotnitsa* no. 6 (1924), pp. 25–6.
38 E. Mikulina, 'Tri kukhni', *Ogonek* no. 47 (1929), pages not numbered.
39 M-v., 'Zhilishche i molodezh'', *Zhilishchnoe delo* no. 1 (1928), pp. 4–5.
40 K. Polinin, 'Rabochii poselok v Ivanovo-Voznesenske', *Ogonek* no. 1 (1926), p. 15.
41 'Sovetskie Farforshchiki. Bor'ba za prostornuyu zhizn'', author not named, *Ogonek* no. 43 (1925), pages not numbered.
42 M. Yunprof, 'U yartsevskikh tekstil'shchits (Smolenskaya gub.)', *Rabotnitsa* no. 12 (1925), pp. 10–12.

43 Ibid.
44 M. Karpova, 'Kul'turnyi podkhod v byt', *Rabotnitsa* no. 8 (1929), p. 13.
45 Ibid.
46 E. Chernysheva, 'Golopuzye shpiony', under rubric 'Daite detskie komnaty v kazarmakh!', *Rabotnitsa* no. 4 (1929), p. 7.
47 N. Shurina, 'Chetyre tysyachi detei begayut besprizorniki po koridoram', under rubric 'Daite detskie komnaty v kazarmakh!', *Rabotnitsa* no. 4 (1929), p. 7.

5

The 'second socialist offensive'

With Stalin firmly in power by the late 1920s, the country was plunged into a new upheaval – what has been variously termed a second revolution, a revolution from above, a second socialist offensive. This one was carried out under the banner 'Socialism in One Country'. In the early years of the Revolution the country's leaders had been convinced that the Soviet Union was insufficiently developed to be able to establish socialism by itself, and in any case, the capitalist world would not allow it to do so.[1] However, its revolution would be such an inspiration to workers in other countries that other revolutions would follow. In the new socialist community, the more advanced countries would help out the more backward. This had not happened, and the Soviet Union now found itself isolated, and in an uncomfortable impasse. The neo-capitalism of the NEP had been a tremendous disappointment to many of those who had waged the Revolution to create a better life. By insisting that the country could go it alone and establish socialism 'by our own efforts, without foreign help',[2] Stalin answered a great psychological need.

If the Soviet Union was to survive as the only socialist state, it would have to become self-sufficient. It would need to build up its industrial base so that it could meet its own production needs, increase its agricultural production so that it could feed its own population, and develop its military capability so that it could fend off foreign aggression. In Stalin's estimation the Soviet Union was fifty to a hundred years behind the industrialised countries of the West, a gap which had to be made good in ten years. A phenomenal transformation was required, something little short of a miracle.

This second revolution was characterised by a fantastically rapid industrialisation programme, the collectivisation of agriculture, and a huge expansion of the armed forces and defence industry. The transformation of the country was outlined in the first Five Year Plan (*pyatiletka*), launched in October 1928 but only officially approved at the XVI Communist Party Congress in April 1929. Initially, the launching of the plan resulted in a huge burst of optimism and a renewal of the revolutionary enthusiasm which had prevailed, alongside the chaos, during the period of War Communism. Yet there was a major difference. The enormous investment in industrial development, the promise of huge technological advances, and the extraordinary goals of the *pyatiletka* itself, made what had so clearly been a utopian dream a decade earlier now seem achievable.

In reality, the low level of technology in the Soviet Union, combined with its largely unskilled workforce, made catching up with the West a rather tall order. Ironically, it would need Western help to do so. This was not so difficult to arrange. The Depression which followed the United States' stock-market crash in 1929 made the Soviet Union's enthusiastic industrial project extremely inviting. It offered new investment opportunities for Western firms, and ensured that large numbers of newly redundant Western specialists were available to bring their expertise to the country.

These specialists included hundreds of architects. The majority were from Germany and Austria, and, while their decision to leave their homelands is likely to have been influenced by Hilter's rise to power, most of them were motivated by genuine enthusiasm for the Soviet project. The electoral success of social democrats in post-war Western Europe had ensured a prominent role for Modernist architects in the rebuilding of devastated cities, and Modernism, at least in its early years, was strongly imbued with idealistic values and a concern for social justice and equality. Many of the architects had been involved in mass social housing projects in their own countries, the building of which had been brought to a halt by the economic crisis. They shared with their Soviet counterparts a desire to use architecture to transform daily life, and a commitment to the same kind of design: streamlined, standardised, functional, mass-producable and egalitarian. These were buildings which, as Tim Benton puts it, reflected the 'politically inspired attempt to rid architecture of symbolic imagery bearing associations of class and difference'.[3] It seemed as though the Soviet Union was now the one country where this new modern architecture could take off.[4]

Repression in the first Five Year Plan

As well as genuine enthusiasm, the first Five Year Plan generated considerable fear. State imperatives to fulfil and then over-fulfil the production plan were backed up by threats. Failure to meet the increasingly unrealistic targets was likely to meet with a charge of 'wrecking' or 'sabotage', and to result in arrest.

The persecution of 'formers' had been quite arbitrary during the early 1920s, but became more acute and systematic during the first Five Year Plan. In her study of Soviet outcasts, Golfo Alexopoulos explains that previously '[m]any members of the old bourgeoisie had managed to avoid repression and even to secure a state job under the new regime'.[5] This was no longer possible. Private business was brought to an end and the disenfranchised had little chance of finding work in state enterprises. This turned them into 'non-working elements' which made them the targets of further hostility and suspicion. When rationing began in 1928, they were denied ration cards, without which they could not acquire even basic foodstuffs.[6] They were also evicted in large numbers from municipalised housing. Their lack of rights was now hereditary, with their children banned from joining the communist youth organisations and denied access to higher education.[7] Disenfranchisement meant much more than the denial of the right to vote and participate in elections, then. It amounted to poverty, homelessness, hunger and social exclusion.

Disenfranchisement ceased to be a punishment reserved for 'formers', and now spread to other social groups. Former Nepmen joined their ranks. So did *kulaks*; these were supposedly rich peasants, but the term was applied to any peasants who opposed collectivisation. People who expressed opinions which seemed to contradict official policy were also at risk.[8] So too were those deemed marginal in what was now a work-obsessed society: the disabled, sick and elderly.[9]

According to Alexopoulos, women were particularly well represented amongst the disenfranchised. This is mainly because living off 'unearned income', i.e. income derived from anything other than waged work in a state enterprise, was now one of the main reasons for disenfranchisement, and a disproportionate number of women fell into this category.[10] Those who engaged in prostitution were at particular risk, but renting out part of one's living space also brought in unearned income and was grounds for disenfranchisement, and, according to Alexopoulos, women were more likely than men to be caught doing this.[11] She offers no explanation, but we might surmise that since women were more closely associated with the home than men, they had more responsibility for finding and dealing with tenants.

Housing management (*domoupravlenie*) played a major role in identifying likely candidates for disenfranchisement during the first Five Year Plan. It was held responsible for monitoring the credentials and behaviour of people living in the housing under its jurisdiction, and was helped in this process by neighbours, who would sometimes denounce their fellow residents in the hope that they might inherit their living space.[12] As Sheila Fitzpatrick notes: '"Apartment" denunciations provide a particularly good example of the manipulative uses of denunciation. In the former Soviet Union, even now, the term "apartment denunciation" is instantly comprehensible.'[13]

Urban expansion and communal living

It was inevitable that industrialisation would be accompanied by urbanisation. However, the growth in the urban population exceeded all expectations. The industrial labour force had doubled by the end of the first Five Year Plan, when it was only expected to grow by a quarter.[14] The result was a state of chaos. To quote Ward: 'Factories and mines, towns and cities, inundated by surging tides of humanity, lost all cohesion.'[15] The new arrivals were mostly peasants escaping collectivisation. As they flooded into the towns and cities, they brought with them what the authorities considered to be 'backward' rural habits which threatened the 'cultured' norms of the more sophisticated urban population.

This huge influx of people put still more pressure on housing. This was an alarming aspect of industrialisation, which some feared could jeopardise the success of the programme as a whole. One *Zhilishchnoe delo* commentator insisted that '[t]he industrialisation of the country and the raising of productivity are unthinkable without the creation of elementary living conditions for workers.'[16] The overcrowded conditions were also hardly conducive to the development of new *byt*. *Rabotnitsa* drew attention to the discrepancy between the breakneck speed at which industrial development was taking place and the snail's pace at which daily life was being altered, and called for the launching of a Five Year Plan specifically for the reconstruction of *byt*.[17]

Against this background, communal housing and plans for the reconstruction of *byt* enjoyed a much greater level of official support. While the move to new *byt* had featured strongly in party rhetoric since the Revolution, it only became, to borrow Buchli's words, 'fully articulated and operationalized' during the first Five Year Plan.[18] There were a number of reasons for this. The country was now supposedly forging ahead towards the bright future, and the realisation of socialist ideals had to be part of this image. The industrialisation programme also required a massive number of new workers, and women would have to make up the shortfall; they could only do this if they had help with their domestic workload, and the house commune was the most obvious way of providing this. Furthermore, some two hundred new cities were to be built alongside new industrial complexes in formerly uninhabited areas, and as well as fulfilling an ideological function, communal housing would be the most cost-efficient way of accommodating their residents. As always, ideological concerns went hand in hand with economic considerations. Yuri Larin, a key figure in the Party hierarchy and one of the most committed supporters of communal housing from the time of the Revolution, declared that: 'The collectivisation of *byt* has always been an aim of our party, but now, in connection with the reconstruction of the economy, it has become the mission of the day.'[19] He was, of course, overoptimistic. With so much money needed for industrial development, financial support for the communal facilites which were a crucial feature of new *byt* remained hopelessly inadequate.

Of the journals we have looked at in this study, *Rabotnitsa* was the most consistent in its support of communal housing, largely on the grounds that this was the only way of ensuring women's liberation. So convinced was the magazine that communal living was the only way forward that it opposed any alternative attempts to make housework easier. This would only act as a palliative, and would slow down the transition to new *byt*.

In support of its position, *Rabotnitsa* reproduced part of a speech by Aleksandra Artyukhina, one of the most prominent women in the Bolshevik regime and the current head of the *Zhenotdel*, the women's section of the Communist Party. Artyukhina had rejected the proposal that the Soviet Union follow the example set by Western Europe and use technological advancements to help housewives to do their own housework more quickly.

> This is an incorrect approach. After all, our aim consists not of lightening individual *byt*. Our aim is to construct social *byt*. It is better [for women] to suffer at present from the old wisps of bast, flat irons and frying pans in order to have the means and strength to fight for the creation of socialist institutions: dining rooms, crèches, kindergartens, laundries.[20]

The American understanding of the 'ideal' family home, *Rabotnitsa* explained, was an individual apartment with its own kitchen, and a full-time housewife devoting her day to housework with the help of the latest domestic appliances. Yet this resulted in the woman being isolated and 'chained to her kitchen'. *Rabotnitsa* warned against importing to the

Soviet Union such 'improvements in family cosiness' from the capitalist countries, since they would hold back the transition to new *byt* and 'cut the family off from social life'.²¹ Communal living was the only way to freedom.

Socialist cities and house communes

The development of gigantic new factory enterprises (*zavody-giganty*) across the country, usually in areas which had no existing settlements. was one of the key features of the first Five Year Plan. The new cities built around these factories would be managed and run by them. They would, as *Rabotnitsa* declared, be 'cities of socialism',²² and would enable their residents to 'take leave of the old way of life forever.'²³ Instead of having to adapt existing cities to the requirements of socialism, architects would be able to build the new socialist cities in accordance with socialist needs. However, there was considerable disagreement over what those needs were, and what made socialist cities distinct from their capitalist counterparts. It was not even clear that cities were appropriate in a socialist society, given that Marx and Engels had called for the disappearance of the distinction between town and countryside.

Two main approaches emerged to the organisation of the population under socialism. One, the Disurbanist position, owed much to the international Garden City movement of the late nineteenth century. The population would be spread evenly throughout the countryside, in continuous ribbons of parkland, in 'mass-produced cabins'.²⁴ The housing would be built parallel to transport arteries which would get the inhabitants to work quickly and efficiently. There would be no cities, hence no concentration of power and resources. Integral to this vision was an improvement in transportation, and especially the mass production of the car.

The second approach was that of the Urbanists. They were no more enamoured of the existing city, but they still thought it was necessary to have administrative centres which would provide leadership for the country as a whole and function as repositories, in Lenin's words, of 'economic, political, and intellectual or spiritual life'.²⁵ These towns would have around 50,000–60,000 residents, all of whom would live in house communes, each of which would house around 2,000–3,000 people. The countryside would not be left to languish in backwardness and ignorance, since collectivisation would transform agricultural production into a modern, large-scale industry, and farms would become so big that they would constitute cities in their own right. This would help eradicate the difference between the city and the countryside, and would raise the countryside 'to the level of progressive urban culture'.[26]

Competitions were held in which architects submitted designs for specific new cities. The proposed living arrangements varied considerably. Nikolai Ladovskii, one of the most prominent Disurbanists, won a competition to plan a new industrial town not far from Moscow, to be called Kostino. He proposed a variety of different types of housing: individual cottages, multi-apartment housing blocks and house communes.[27] In Kuznetsk, which would house workers at a new steel works, the plan was for all single people and 60 per cent of families to live in house communes, 25 per cent of families in ordinary multi-apartment housing blocks and the remaining 15 per cent in separate one-family houses.[28] Stalingrad (formerly Volgograd) had so many new factories that a new 'socialist city' had to be built on its outskirts to accommodate the influx of workers. The winning design, by Aleksandr and Leonid Vesnin, envisaged all residents living in huge house communes. Every person would have his or her own room, and there would be separate children's sections linked to the adults' quarters by corridors, 'so that a mother can go and see her child at any time and observe his upbringing'. The living quarters for Stalingrad as a whole would be shifted to the new city, while old Stalingrad would become the cultural and administrative centre.[29]

Clearly there was no place here for the conventional family, and the old revolutionary arguments about the fate of the family came to the fore again. Some of the more uncompromising adherents of the socialist city insisted that the family had finally had its day; as V. Kuz'min put it, it was time 'to wipe out the family as an organ of oppression and exploitation'.[30] L. Sabsovich, who wanted all towns and villages throughout the country to be transformed into socialist cities, envisaged not just the end of the family, but the end of coupledom. Life would be completely socialised and standardised; there would be no kitchens for individual use, no shops selling food products, no individual child care, and no rooms in which husband and wife could carry out any semblance of family life.[31]

Ogonek and *Rabotnitsa* enthusiastically reported on the plans for socialist cities and communal housing. A. Dunacharskii, writing in *Ogonek*, described to readers in considerable detail what Magnitogorsk would look like – quite a feat, since it would be several months before the decision would be made as to which architect had won the competition to design that city.[32] We can only assume that Dunacharskii was offering his own vision of the ideal socialist city. Housing, he claimed, would consist largely of four-storey house communes, each of which would have 1,500 to 3,000 residents. Such large 'families' were necessary both for reasons of economy, and in order to ensure a broad cultural mix. This was the only form of the family which would exist in the city, since there would be no children living in the commune, and adults would have 'unprecedented freedom of choice for intimate relations'. He did feel that people should be able to make some choices about their personal living space, however: '[e]very person has the right to his own room, where he might feel himself alone, in his own space (*u sebya*)', and it should be up to the individual to decide whether to have a single room or to share one with a sexual partner or with friends.

The house communes would be grouped around large dining rooms in which all main meals would be taken, and there would be a number of large rooms for communal activities: meetings, sports, a library, a Red Corner, a cinema, etc. At the centre of the town there would be a large square for public events, and buildings housing administrative and cultural bodies such as the House of Soviets, Palace of Culture, and House for the Protection of Public Order.[33] The latter seems like a curious intrusion of reality into an otherwise utopian dream; if the citizens of Magnitogorsk were to consist of responsible, socially oriented people, it is difficult to see why an administrative body would be required to maintain public order.

Rabotnitsa embraced the idea of these 'cities of joy'[34] with particular passion, and gave readers detailed descriptions of how people would live in them. According to one of these:

> The factory with all its workshops and its auxiliary enterprises will be located outside of the town. This will protect the population from the smells and harmful gases which come from the factory chimneys. In order to get to the town one will travel along a wide boulevard, thickly planted with greenery. On both sides of this wide street, house communes, three or four storeys high, will be constructed. On the first floor [of each house] will be a dining room and communal kitchen. Dinner will be cooked in the kitchen, but will have been supplied by the factory-kitchen. Not one worker-family will have to bother about domestic work and preparing its own food. On the same floor is an information office and a hairdresser ... On the second floor there will be rooms where the residents of the house will rest and study in their free time. There will be rooms for all kinds of clubs, and an auditorium for lectures and meetings. Scientific laboratories will be located here, where every worker can occupy himself with whatever interests him. On the second floor there will be everything essential for cultural education, popular and scientific work. The upper floor is set aside for bedrooms. Here, absolute quiet reigns. In the rooms of this floor everything is done only so as to ensure rest.[35]

The socialist city would also contain an abattoir, a bread factory, and a range of other factories producing foodstuffs, grouped together in one section of the town. The centre of the town would be taken up by theatres, a central club, and local government offices. Initially the plan had been to house children in special villages several kilometres from the socialist city, the author continued. However, mothers had generally been opposed to this. Nadezhda Krupskaya had supported their position, insisting that '[o]ne cannot deprive the mother of the right to see her child whenever she is free from her current work. One also cannot deprive children of engagement in the social life of the socialist city.' Children would still 'live in their own world', separately from adults, but they would live within the city, so there would be plenty of opportunity for contact between parents and children.[36]

The question of where children would live continued to be the most thorny issue. In fact, Krupskaya herself had changed her position. At the start of the Five Year Plan she had supported the idea of placing children in separate villages some fifteen to twenty miles from the city, but had backed down in the face of opposition from mothers.[37]

A. Tamarova insisted in *Rabotnitsa* that mothers were becoming increasingly aware that adults and children had different needs, and that it was better for everyone if they were housed separately; hence, 'children who at present disturb the residents in tiny apartments will be looked after round the clock in crèches and kindergartens'.[38] She conceded, however, that it would be up to the residents of individual house communes to decide whether children would live in completely separate apartment blocks, or be accommodated in a special children's section within the house commune. They would also need to determine whether mothers would play a role in rearing their own children, or whether this would be carried out entirely by pedagogical specialists.

Another issue residents would need to decide, Tamarova continued, was whether they would do their daily physical exercises in their own rooms, or in communal halls. This was clearly a less pressing issue than the housing and the upbringing of children, but it was mentioned virtually in the same breath. This reflects the importance attributed to health and fitness in the Soviet Union at this time, a subject we will discuss in more detail later in this chapter. It could also be seen as an indication of Tamarova's determination to consider a communal approach to virtually every aspect of daily life, however trifling.

As always, *Rabotnitsa* stressed the particular benefits of communal living to women. Crucially, they would no longer have to stay in unhappy marriages. If their husbands beat them, or just forced them to stay at home all the time with the children instead of engaging in social life, they now had an escape route. As one reporter told readers: 'I advise wives not to whimper and do nothing, and not to be afraid of divorce ... In the USSR new workers' hostels and house communes are being built which will make it possible to live a collective life – there is a collective kitchen, children's corner, laundry. And this is just the beginning.'[39]

Conversely, other writers suggested that house communes might save marriages. Women in conventional family set-ups had to spend so much time doing housework that they were unable to take advantage of the new educational and cultural opportunities which were available, and their husbands were likely to outgrow them and become bored. If women wanted to save their marriages, they would have to find time to improve themselves, and this could only happen if housework became a communal matter.[40]

The first custom-built house commune appeared in Moscow in 1929. *Rabotnitsa* enthused about its communal kitchen, with the latest in domestic equipment, the separate dining room overlooking what would soon become a garden-courtyard, and the steps leading out to a veranda; about its crèche and kindergarten, its mother and child corner, its consulting room where children would be regularly checked over by a visiting paediatrician. There was a laundry, a club, a stage for amateur theatre productions, a library, reading room and hairdressing salon. The living quarters consisted of a combination of individual rooms and family apartments, the latter with their own bathrooms and small kitchens. (Surprisingly, *Rabotnitsa* expressed no concern about this retention of individual housekeeping.) On the top floor there was a hall for physical exercise; finally, on the roof, 'like a talented artist's final brush stroke on a painting', was a solarium, which could be converted into an open-air cinema after dark. 'One would think', the author mused, 'that this house has been prepared for some exceptional people.' However, this was not the case; 80 per cent of the residents were manual workers, and 15 per cent ordinary office workers.[41]

Rabotnitsa reported with enthusiasm that workers were coming round to the idea of communal living. In Ivanovo-Voznesensk, plans for 400 individual apartments had been rejected by prospective residents, who 'demanded the construction instead of house communes, in which there was the maximum possibility for the collectivisation of daily life'. There had also been requests for help in building house communes in many other parts of the country. It was clear to the majority of people that self-contained family apartments resulted in the continuation of old *byt*, and were incompatible with socialism.[42]

The magazines had largely ignored the small-scale communes which had appeared throughout the 1920s. Now, however, with the renewed enthusiasm for communal living, they showed more interest. Arkardy Mlodika told *Ogonek* readers about a Leningrad commune set up by a group of factory workers in a former synagogue which the local housing union had given them. The members insisted that all money be pooled on the grounds that separate finances smacked of capitalist individualism.[43]

M. Angarova gave a detailed description in *Rabotnitsa* of a commune set up in 1928 in a four-room apartment by ten Komsomol members, whose number gradually increased to eighteen. At first they contributed just 40 per cent of their earnings to a food kitty, but after a while they agreed to put their entire salaries into the communal fund. Money for small expenditures was left in an open box: '[y]ou take what you need, and leave a note: "I took money for the tram, the cinema, the theatre". And if someone wants to go to the theatre or cinema with someone [who does not live in the commune], the commune isn't against this, and you can pay for your comrade's ticket from the communal purse. You only have to observe the rules that the commune's money is accounted for, and that everyone has the chance to go to the theatre or cinema a certain number of times.' A special fund of 250 rubles was set aside each month to help any needy relatives of the communards. Things had not always gone smoothly, however. Angarova acknowledged that some of the original members had either dropped out or been evicted. 'There was one lad who one could not say a word to: "Don't poke your noses into *my* life!" [he would say.] They had to part company with him. He himself acknowledged at the meeting: "I can't fit into the commune". And they had to evict one girl from the commune … for slovenliness. She would come home from work and grab bread with dirty, unwashed hands; she would lie on the bed in her boots; she did not clean up after herself. The commune adheres to cultural norms and takes a hygienic line. They talked to the girl, but it didn't help. They had to part company.' Some commune members were resistant to the idea of pooling everything; they were not able to let go of the notion of '"my money, my earnings, my dress." It is still difficult at present to change these individualistic words to the word more appropriate to the collective – "our"'. Worst of all, money had been stolen from the fund for relatives in need and 'spent on drinking and carousing. There is, of course, no place for this in the commune.' Yet, despite its failings, Angarova felt that the commune was generally a success, and could be used as an example to those who were still clinging to 'the old way of life'.[44]

The campaign against 'domestic trash'

The revolutionary enthusiasm which characterised the start of the first Five Year Plan also set itself against 'the old way of life' in the domestic interior. The socialist home should be a model of functionalism and modernism rather than 'a fetishistic refuge of bourgeois cosiness'.[45] Accordingly, a campaign against 'domestic trash' was launched in the summer of 1928 by a group of artists, art critics and journalists, using the newspaper *Komsomol'skaya pravda* (Komsomol Truth) as their forum. Among their inspirations were the poems by Mayakovskii on bad taste: lace curtains, porcelain ornaments, portraits of Marx in crimson frames and a 'frantic little canary' chirping in a cage.[46] These were relics of the pre-revolutionary past, when the bourgeoisie dictated the country's cultural and artistic norms. Decoration and ornamentation which served no practical purpose had no place under socialism. Aesthetic beauty should be inseparable from function.

The campaign, using the military terminology characteristic of the first Five Year Plan, called for an all-out attack on the production and use 'of tasteless knick-knacks (*bezdelushki*)'. The department stores GUM, *Mostorg* and their filials were the principal enemy, since they were guilty of stocking these things. However, their staff could form a 'light cavalry' and refuse to sell them. Readers were also called on to purge their rooms of anything unnecessary. A letter was published by a woman called Chervyakova, who described with enthusiasm the results of her own clean-up: 'How nice it has become, how light it is in the room!' She called on other women to follow her example, explaining that: 'It is almost always the woman who decorates the room, because she is the housekeeper.'[47] Her attempt to make the room more cosy and beautiful only resulted in it being filled up with useless clutter. It was not only simple girls who did this, but also those who considered themselves progressive and cultured. 'We – women and housewives – can and must decorate our rooms more tastefully. We must protest about these disgusting objects (*gadosti*) being on sale. Do not buy any more of this heap of tasteless "beauty".'[48]

The campaign against domestic trash did not feature prominently in either *Rabotnitsa* or *Ogonek*, but it did make an appearance. *Rabotnitsa* wrote about a Moscow exhibition on daily life which included a model apartment of a middle-ranking worker. At first glance it looked pleasant and well managed, but on closer inspection it turned out to be full of 'pointless' decorations: an outsize, over-packed commode, too many pillows crammed on the bed, a geranium plant in the window, and (a direct reference to Mayakovskii's poetry) a canary in a cage. 'It is packed', the reporter complained; 'there is nowhere to turn'. The exhibition also included a model home for 'new workers', which was more tasteful; it had 'simple and modest' furniture and 'not one superfluous item, not one trinket'. The room might seem sparse, but it was healthy and easy to clean.⁴⁹

In *Ogonek*, Tat'yana Tess wrote about the same exhibition, expressing regret for the inclusion of many unnecessary items of domestic paraphernalia. These even included equipment for use in individual kitchens, which would soon be obsolete when communal living became the norm. She contrasted the great advances of the first Five Year Plan with people's failure to embrace new ways in their personal lives. She denounced '[t]he anarchic world of things [which] crowds into our daily life. We need to take a good look at things, demand a severe purge [*surova chistka*]. Things should be deprived of the right to exist in daily life; [they are] the carriers of an alien ideology.'⁵⁰

This campaign against domestic clutter can be linked to the concern with health and hygiene which formed an integral part of both the Modernist and Soviet ethos. As Christopher Wilk notes, the Modernist enterprise in all countries 'was permeated by a deep concern for health. Modernism's social agenda – one of its defining elements – was a direct response to the interrelated problems of poor health and poor housing affecting large segments of the population in the early twentieth century … The new domestic interior directly reflected the concern that people should live in well-lit, easy-to-clean spaces supplied with the most up-to-date furnishings, equipment, technology and amenities that would increase personal and communal health.'⁵¹

Health and hygiene had been seen as important issues in the Soviet Union throughout the 1920s, but became crucial after the launching of the first Five Year Plan. The country had taken off on its flight towards the glorious future, but its cities were mired in the filth and squalor resulting from overcrowding and the in-migration of hordes of 'backward' peasants. Rooms packed with the clutter of numerous occupants were impossible to dust and clean; nor would they provide the necessary space for residents to carry out the 'physical culture' which was meant to be part of the worker's daily routine.

Again, it would have to be women who dealt with the problem. This could be encouraged by the 'friendly socialist competitions' which were introduced during the first Five Year Plan. Though they were primarily concerned with boosting production, they could also encourage housewives 'to compete with each other to achieve maximum cleanliness.'⁵²

The failure to bring about communal living

Despite the enormous enthusiasm for house communes and socialist cities at the start of the first Five Year Plan, plans for communal living were largely unsuccessful. Very few house communes were actually built; according to Gradov, there were only ever ten of them,[53] and the 1931 edition of the *Great Soviet Encyclopedia* admitted that all were so flawed that none really merited the name.[54] Most people remained stubbornly unenthusiastic about communal living. Mary Leder, an American woman living in Moscow for more than three decades, had friends who lived in a custom-built house commune:

> The apartments opened up onto a long corridor and had no kitchens. It had been assumed that the residents would have their meals in a communal dining room with adjoining kitchen in the ground floor, but this idea fell apart very quickly. The communal dining room was remodeled and the residents did their cooking on primitive ceramic electric plates or on kerosene stoves in the small halls of their apartments.[55]

Timasheff claims that Stalingrad's new 'socialist suburbs' were a failure because the lack of provision for family life meant that 'nobody but bachelors' were willing to live in them.[56]

The architect Moisei Ginzburg tried to overcome resistance to communal living by means of a 'house of a transitional type' (*dom perekhodnogo tipa*), which would not impose communal life on people but would gently encourage them to engage with it in whatever way they wanted. The housing consisted of individual apartments with their own washing and toilet facilities, and small kitchen alcoves which could accommodate small stoves but were intended primarily for making tea and for heating meals brought in from elsewhere. Communal facilities and activities such as residents' meetings, child care, adult education, recreation and public dining were available in separate buildings for those who chose to make use of them.[57] Six of these 'houses of a transitional type' were actually built, the best known of which was a Moscow apartment block for employees of the People's Commissariat of Finance (*Narkomfin*). However, Greg Castillo jokes that the building 'may have entailed a transition, but it was not to a communal lifestyle'; rather, it was to a housing hierarchy which 'allowed a managerial elite to enjoy comforts unknown to the rank and file'.[58]

The socialist cities which were constructed during the first Five Year Plan bore very little resemblance to the theory. Production was prioritised above all else, and took the lion's share of the country's resources.

Housing and other social services had to make do with the crumbs which were left over. Building cities from scratch also turned out to be more problematic than anticipated; to quote Castillo again, '[t]he absence of an inherited urban infrastructure ..., rather than liberating the town planner from the impediments of capitalism, frustrated industrial management's attempts to provide residents with even the most basic public services and levels of sanitary hygiene.'[59]

The number of people who would need housing was drastically underestimated. Dneprostroi, which was built at the construction site of the Dneper dam, had a population at the end of the first Five Year Plan which was 166 per cent higher than the figure which had been calculated as the maximum. Accordingly, premises which had been set aside for kitchens, laundries and leisure activities had to be used for accommodation.[60]

Magnitogorsk, which attracted much attention in the press as a showcase socialist city in the making, is a particularly interesting case. In his detailed study of the city, Stephen Kotkin holds that the winning entry in the competition to design the city, by a Professor Chernyshev, was one of the least innovative proposals put forward; Kotkin suggests that it was chosen precisely for this reason, because it was 'a less frightening and more conventional project' that those of the more famous architects.[61] Chernyshev did not get the chance to realise his plans, however. A team of German and Austrian architects were actually given the job, since they had tried-and-tested skills which the Soviet theorists lacked, and speed was of the essence.

The Magnitogorsk team was led by Ernst May, who had been City Architect in Frankfurt and was responsible for much of the post-war residential development in that city. The team also included the Viennese architect Margarita Schutte-Lihotzky, who had started working with May in Frankfurt in 1926 and had designed the so-called 'Frankfurt Kitchen', aimed at cutting the amount of time women had to spend on housework by eliminating unnecessary movement. This was the first fitted kitchen to be mass-produced, and was incorporated into some 10,000 Frankfurt apartments.[62] The housing in Magnitogorsk, however, was to have no kitchens, since the intention was to feed people in communal dining rooms. Residential housing was to consist of a series of identical 'superblocks', served by an extensive network of social facilities.[63]

May's work was bedevilled from the outset. His initial plans proved unworkable, since they had failed to take account of local geography. He then had to contend with a local workforce which was inadequately trained and skilled, and with extraordinary indecision on the part of the authorities, who could not even decide on which bank of the river the city should be built. May was also given totally insufficient funds to do the job. The work on the city proceeded so slowly that, by the winter of 1932, when May was effectively fired, construction had begun on just one of his 'superblocks'.[64]

The thousands of workers brought in to build the steel plant and the city had to be housed somehow, and so a succession of rough-and-ready barracks were constructed. They were meant to be temporary, but remained the main form of housing in Magnitogorsk well into the 1930s. They had no washing facilities, since people were supposed to bathe in public baths; but these were so few in number that even by 1939 they could provide each inhabitant with a bath only seven or so times per year. People were also meant to take their washing to public laundries, but the clothes had to be left there for several days, and few people had enough clothes to make this an option.[65] The public dining facilities required a long wait in line, and in any case the quality of the food was so poor that, in Castillo's words, they 'specialised in serving up gastrointestinal epidemics'.[66] Self-catering communal kitchens did finally appear, but, instead of instilling in their users any communal spirit, they were the scene 'of constant feuding and episodic theft'.[67] There were some child care facilities, but far too few to accommodate all of the children in the settlement.

The inadequacies of the domestic facilities meant that most of the women living in Magnitogorsk continued to act as domestic servants. As Kotkin puts it:

> it was an open secret among male workers that whatever the collectivist rhetoric and, to some extent, practice, if they wanted to keep their living areas and clothes clean, and to improve their diet, they needed to get married. Female workers knew this 'secret' too, as well as its wider meaning for their lives.[68]

Even if the facilities had been better, the population of Magnitogorsk seemed thoroughly disinclined to embrace communal ways. Most of them had come directly from the countryside and had no experience of urban life, communal or otherwise. They were, as Stites explains, 'thoroughly unprepared for the kind of communal living ... that the utopian blueprints had conjured up'.[69]

The socialist city was meant to be 'the very opposite of the capitalist city',[70] but in some respects it was not that dissimilar from the 'company town' which had taken off in the late nineteenth century in a number of capitalist countries, most notably the United States. These had the explicit intention of retaining and controlling workers, both by buying their loyalty with material inducements like housing, and by inculcating in them a set of values appropriate to the workplace.[71] The retention and control of workers was also part of the plan in Magnitogorsk, though conditions were such that neither was successful. The lack of housing, food and amenities resulted in a huge turnover of labour, with even dedicated Komsomol members unable to survive the appalling living conditions for long.[72] These conditions, combined with the instability of the population and the large number of convicted criminals drafted into the workforce, resulted in a rough and lawless society in which fights, rapes and murders were common.[73]

Magnitogorsk would be hailed, years later, as a brave experiment which had experienced initial difficulties but had ultimately been a great success.[74] This accolade actually exposes the huge gap between the original understanding of socialism and the version which came to pass in the Soviet Union. Despite the rhetoric about communal living and its role in the development of new *byt*, production became the country's overwhelming concern, and the 'socialist city' was little more than 'a place to settle the factory and that factory's skilled workers'.[75]

While the Soviet authorities refused to acknowledge the failings of their own housing programme, they now turned against attempts made by social democratic leaders of west European cities to provide workers with basic but comfortable housing. In Vienna, for example, the collapse of the Austro-Hungarian empire had resulted in an influx of immigrants in need of housing, and the city dealt with the problem by constructing a huge number of low-cost housing blocks, the rents for which were heavily subsidised. In some of the blocks there were no individual bathrooms in the apartments, and 'kitchen alcoves' took the place of separate kitchens. The provision of social services such as kindergartens, crèches and community centres was a key feature of the project.[76] According to Benton, '[t]he housing policy of "red Vienna" became famous throughout Europe', the blocks 'were visited by housing reformers from all over the world and were compared favourably to other Modernist estates'.[77] Yet, while the project had so much in common with the Soviet Union's original plans for housing, it was now denigrated. L. Perchik, writing in the theoretical journal *Bol'shevik*, sneered at the idea that the housing needs of workers could be successfully dealt with in a country which had not had a socialist revolution. He insisted that the Viennese socialists were, in reality, social fascists, since they preferred to 'live under capitalist slavery' rather than risk the consequences of revolution. He even insisted that subsidising rents was 'a manoeuvre on the part of factory and enterprise owners and their social democratic lackeys to reduce the wages of Viennese workers, while at the same time keeping the prestige of the Viennese social democrats at a high level in the eyes of the workers who are deceived by them.'[78] The vehemence of Perchik's response to Vienna's housing project suggests, perhaps, that the real crime of the Viennese social democrats was to expose the inadequacy of Soviet housing.

Notes

1. In Trotsky's words: 'The world division of labour, the dependence of Soviet industry upon foreign technique, the dependence of the productive forces of the advanced countries of Europe upon Asiatic raw materials ... make the construction of a socialist society in any single country impossible'. L. Trotsky, from *The Permanent Revolution*; excerpted in C.W. Mills, *The Marxists* (Harmondsworth: Penguin, 1977), p. 276.
2. 'Mozhem li my postroit' sotzializm v nashei strane?', *Rabotnitsa* no. 3 (1926), no. 3, p. 2.
3. T. Benton, 'Building Utopia', in C. Wilk (ed.), *Modernism 1914–1939: Designing a New World* (London: V&A Publications, 2006), p. 159.
4. See M. Bliznakov, 'The Realisation of Utopia: Western Technology and Soviet Avant-garde Architecture', in W.C. Blumfield (ed.), *Reshaping Russian Architecture: Western Technology, Utopian Dreams* (Cambridge: Woodrow Wilson Centre and Cambridge University Press, 1990), p. 145.
5. G. Alexopoulos, *Stalin's Outcasts: Aliens, Citizens and the Soviet State, 1926–1936* (Ithaca, N.Y.: Cornell University Press, 2003), p. 15.
6. Ibid., p. 29.
7. N.S. Timasheff, *The Great Retreat: The Growth and Decline of Communism in Russia* (New York: E. P. Dutton and Co, 1946), pp. 306–7.
8. Ibid., p. 306.
9. Alexopoulos, *Stalin's Outcasts*, p. 63.
10. Ibid., p. 107.
11. Ibid., pp. 62 and 107.
12. Ibid., pp. 52 and 55.
13. S. Fitzpatrick, *Tear off the Masks! Identity and Imposture in Twentieth-Century Russia* (Princeton and Oxford: Princeton University Press, 2005), p. 228.
14. J.N. Westwood, *Endurance and Endeavour: Russian History 1812–1971* (London: Oxford University Press, 1973), p. 303.
15. C. Ward, *Stalin's Russia* (London: Arnold, 1999), p. 60.
16. A.V., 'Vypolnenie zhilishchnoiu pyatiletki i kontrol' mass', *Zhilishchnoe delo* no. 17 (1929), pp. 1–2.
17. See, for example, Ishkova, 'Nash byt perestraivaetsya slyshkom medlenno', *Rabotnitsa* no. 28 (1930), p. 17.
18. V. Buchli (1999) *An Archaeology of Socialism* (Oxford and New York: Berg, 1999), p. 33.
19. Quoted by V.I. Isaev *Kommuna ili kommunalka? – izmeneniya byta rabochykh sibiri v gody industrializatsii*, Novosibirsk: Nauka: Sibirskaya izdatel'skaya firma RAN. 1996) p. 29.
20. 'Za sotsialisticheskuyu peredelku byta: iz vystupleniya tov. Artyukhinoi na plenume MK VKP(b), *Rabotnitsa* no. 4 (1930), pages not numbered.
21. A. Tamarova, 'Gde vy khotite zhit'?', *Rabotnitsa* no. 8 (1930), pp. 19–20.

22 L-ya, 'Postroim goroda sotsializma', *Rabotnitsa* no. 1 (1930), p. 19.
23 Ibid., p. 19.
24 G. Castillo, 'Stalinist Modern: Constructivism and the Soviet Company Town', in J. Cracraft and D. Rowland (eds), *Architectures of Russian Identity, 1500 to the Present* (Ithaca and New York, Cornell University Press, 2003), p. 142.
25 Quoted by R. Stites, *Revolutionary Dreams: Utopian Vision and Experimental Life in the Russian Revolution* (Oxford and New York: Oxford University Press, 1989), p. 197.
26 L. Perchik, 'O "zhilishchnom voprose" F. Engel'sa', *Bol'shevik* no. 10 (1932), p. 58. He also cites Lazar Kaganovich in support of this position.
27 Bliznakov, 'Soviet Housing during the Experimental Years, 1918–1933', in W. C. Blumfield (ed.), *Reshaping Russian Architecture*, p. 100.
28 Isaev, *'Kommuna ili kommunalka?'*, pp. 26–7. See also G.A. Gradov, *Gorod i byt* (Moscow: Izdatel'stvo literatury po stroitel'stu, 1968), p. 55.
29 R. Fomichev, 'My nash, my novyi mir postroim: Pis'mo iz Stalinigrada', *Ogonek* no. 6 (1930), pp. 8–9.
30 Quoted by Gradov, *Gorod i byt*, p. 49.
31 Ibid., pp. 48–50.
32 See S. Kotkin, *Magnetic Mountain: Stalinism as a Civilisation* (Berkeley and London: University of California Press, 1995), p. 109 and fn. 12, p. 447.
33 A. Dunacharskii, 'Moshchnye bazy novogo byta: SSSR stroit zhizn' dostoinuyu cheloveka', *Ogonek* no. 4 (1930), pp. 4–5.
34 See the caption under a photograph of a new city under construction, *Rabotnitsa* no. 30 (1932), pp. 18–19.
35 L-ya, 'Postroim goroda sotsializma', p. 19.
36 Ibid., p. 19.
37 See N. Krupskaya, 'Gde zhit' detyam v sotsialistecheskom gorode? (V poryadke obsuzhdeniya)', in *Deti – nashe budushchee*, Moscow: Proveshchenie, 1984, pp. 52–5. Originally in *Zhenskii zhurnal* (Women's Journal), a literary and arts journal published from 1926 to 1930.
38 A. Tamarova, 'Gde vy khotite zhit'?', pp. 19–20.
39 M. Il'ina, 'Staryi byt nado bit'!', *Rabotnitsa* no. 4 (1930), pp. 12–13.
40 K. Bykova, 'Kto vinovat v semeinykh neuryaditsak", *Rabotnitsa* no. 36 (1929), p. 12.
41 B-va, 'Dom-kommuna no 1', *Rabotnitsa* no. 41 (1929), p. 12.
42 A. Tamarova, 'Gde vy khotite zhit'?', pp. 19–20.
43 See A. Mlodika, 'Udarniki byta', one of a series of short pieces on communal living arrangements under the title of 'Novaya sotsialisticheskaya pomyshlennost': Novyi sotsialisticheskii byt', in *Ogonek* no. 6 (1930), pp. 8–9.
44 M. Angarova, 'Zhizn' po novomu', *Rabotnitsa* no. 8 (1930), pp. 18–19.
45 S. Boym, *Common Places: Mythologies of Everyday Life in Russia* (Cambridge. Mass.: Harvard University Press, 1994), p. 35.
46 Ibid., pp. 8–9, 34–5.
47 Karen Kettering holds that the campaign did not specifically target women, and that men and women were seen as equally responsible for furnishing, decorating and cluttering the home. See K. Kettering, '"Ever more Cosy and Comfortable": Stalinism and the Soviet Domestic Interior, 1928–1938', *Journal of Design History* 10:2 (1997), 119–35. This is not the impression which has emerged from my own study, however.
48 These examples and quotations are taken from a series of short pieces under the

general heading 'Doloi domashhnii khlam!', *Komsomol'skaya Pravda*, 4 November (1928), p. 3.
49 E. Vesenin, 'Na perekope byta (Vystavka byta v parke kul'tury i otdikha)', *Rabotnitsa* no. 28 (1930), p. 16.
50 T. Tess, 'Veshchi i my', *Ogonek* no. 24 (1930), p. 13.
51 C. Wilk, 'The Healthy Body Culture', in Wilk (ed.), *Modernism 1914-1939*, p. 250
52 B. Pundol'tsev, 'Novyi dom – novaya zhizn', *Zhilishchnoe delo* no. 5 (1928), pp. 33-5.
53 Gradov, *Gorod i byt*, p. 43.
54 *Bol'shaya Sovetskaya Entsiklopediya* (Moscow: Izdatel'stvo Sovetskaya Entsiklopediya, 1931 edition), p. 79.
55 M. M. Leder, *My Life in Stalinist Russia, An American Woman Looks Back* (Bloomington, Ind: Indiana University Press, 2001), p. 86.
56 Timasheff, *The Great Retreat*, p. 196.
57 See Buchli, *An Archaeology of Socialism*, p. 67; and Bliznakov, 'Soviet Housing during the Experimental Years', pp. 107-8, 113.
58 Castillo, 'Stalinist Modern', pp. 144-5.
59 Ibid., p. 146.
60 Ibid., pp. 143-144.
61 Kotkin, *Magnetic Mountain*, p. 109.
62 see 'Radical and Chic', *Guardian Weekend*, 1 April (2006), pp. 74-7.
63 Kotkin, *Magnetic Mountain*, p. 116.
64 Ibid., p. 120
65 Ibid., p. 172.
66 Castillo, 'Stalinist Modern', p. 144.
67 Ibid., p. 144.
68 Kotkin, *Magnetic Mountain*, p. 173.
69 Stites, *Revolutionary Dreams*, p. 204.
70 Kotkin, p. 108.
71 Castillo, 'Stalinist Modern', pp. 139-40.
72 Kotkin, p. 96.
73 Kotkin, p. 134.
74 See, for example, T. Blazhnova, 'Magnitka – imya sobstvennoe', *Rabotnitsa* no. 10 (1977), pp. 20-2.
75 Kotkin, *Magnetic Mountain*, pp. 122-3.
76 Tim Benton puts the figure at 62,000 housing units over the course of fifteen years. See Benton, 'Building Utopia', p. 90.
77 Ibid.
78 L. Perchik, 'O "zhilishchnom voprose" F. Engel'sa', pp. 47-58.

6

The retreat from new byt

The first Five Year Plan was supposedly such a success that it was declared fulfilled by the end of 1932, after just four years – though, as Hosking puts it, the figures which were meant to confirm this claim were 'wild flights of the imagination'.[1] Those four years of astonishing upheaval had resulted in significant changes in the official understanding of new *byt*.

Most importantly, for reasons we will discuss in due course, the commitment to communal living and communal housing came to an end, and the individual family apartment was now proclaimed the ideal form of housing. In reality, with the growth in the urban population vastly exceeding expectations, the idea that ordinary workers could enjoy individual family accommodation was just as utopian as the avant-garde proposals for communal living a decade earlier. However, it was not beyond the reach of a new middle class which had emerged in the course of the Five Year Plan. As Orlando Figes explains, 'the change in policy was obviously connected to the rise of a new political and industrial elite, whose loyalty to the Stalinist regime was secured by the handing down of material rewards'.[2] This new elite was composed primarily of Party and state officials and some members of the former intelligentsia, as well as the new worker elite – shock workers (*udarniki*) and 'Stakhanovites', who consistently overfulfilled the plan and were rewarded with housing and other scarce resources for doing so. They served as role models, and as a vision of the future: their capacity for work, and the lifestyles they enjoyed on its account, would one day be the norm for all.

Accordingly, members of the new worker elite were allowed to enjoy certain aspects of what had previously been considered a bourgeois lifestyle. Indeed, they were actually encouraged to indulge in some degree of consumerism and luxury, which included wearing fashionable clothes, drinking champagne[3] and acquiring the accoutrements of domestic comfort. This constituted being 'cultured', the buzzword of the 1930s. The model Soviet home was now full of those decorative touches and functionless knick-knacks which had been so disdained just a few years before.

The understanding of women's roles and gender equality also underwent considerable change. There was no more talk of the demise of the family, or of children being removed from their parents and brought up solely by professional pedagogues. On the contrary, the family was now proclaimed to be the basic cell of Soviet society. It also acquired symbolic significance; the country itself was depicted as one enormous family, with Stalin the ultimate patriarch.

These changes had little effect on the lives of the population as a whole. The family may have been rehabilitated, and the individual family apartment proclaimed to be the ideal, but the 'masses' still had to struggle to create some semblance of family life in the increasingly cramped living space they continued to share with strangers. Few ordinary people had enough money to procure any middle-class indulgences. In fact, the growth in urban density made conditions in the cities increasingly uncomfortable. What the changes did do was alter the conception of new *byt* and redefine the principles of life under socialism.

It could be argued that the new housing policy was a feature of Socialist Realism. This was introduced in 1934 primarily as a blueprint for the arts, but it also came to dictate the way journalists reported events. Artists and writers were required to depict 'reality in its revolutionary development', and 'educate workers in the spirit of communism'. This amounted to presenting an image of life not as it was, but as it should be. Building almost nothing but individual family apartments, when there was no possibility of them actually housing individual families, was surely part of this process.

Reasons, consequences and complications

The change in official approach towards new *byt* made its first appearance in a Central Committee resolution of 16 May 1930, 'Regarding Work on the Reconstruction of *byt*' (*O rabote po perestroike byta*). Those who had advocated a rapid and total move to communal living were now castigated. The architect Sabsovich was singled out for particular blame, as was the Old Bolshevik and intellectual Yuri Larin. Both were accused of promoting

> highly unsound, semifantastical, and hence extremely harmful attempts ... to surmount 'in one leap' the obstacles that lie along the

path to a socialist transformation of way of life: obstacles rooted, on the one hand, in the economic and cultural backwardness of the country and, on the other, in the need, at our present stage of development, to concentrate most of our resources on the rapid industrialization that alone will create the necessary material basis for a radical transformation of the way of life ... The implementation of these harmful and utopian proposals, which disregard both the actual resources of the country and the degree of preparation of the population, would lead to vast expenditures of money and would seriously discredit the very idea of a socialist transformation of the way of life.[4]

The resolution highlighted the country's backwardness, and the need to concentrate its limited resources on industry. However, these were not the only issues behind the retreat. The house commune and the transformation of *byt* had been promoted largely on the grounds that they would lead to the demise of the traditional family and liberate women from domestic responsibilities, especially child care, but this had turned out to require a level of expenditure which the authorities, given their current economic priorities, would not commit. If women were willing to provide domestic services for free, they should not be discouraged from doing so, and they were more likely to provide these services for their own families. In addition, the upheavals of the first Five Year Plan had led to an alarming drop in the birth rate, and an almost equally alarming rise in antisocial behaviour, generally referred to as 'hooliganism'. What was needed now was not more experimentation, but old-fashioned families that could function, to borrow Gale Lapidus's eloquent metaphor, as 'islands of stability in a sea of social chaos'.[5] They might encourage women both to produce more children, and to rear them more efficiently.

Saddling women with more children and domestic work would make it harder for them to work outside the home. However, despite the supposed commitment on the part of leading Soviet politicians towards women's equality, attitudes towards women's work had actually remained rather ambiguous. For a combination of reasons – a low level of training and qualifications, a lack of confidence, resistance on the part of husbands and employers – women did not begin to enter the workforce in significant numbers until well into the first Five Year Plan. The People's Commissariat for Labour drew up two lists of jobs which should either be reserved for women, or in which women should predominate. For the most part, these were the types of job which reflected their traditional activities, such as child care, education and work in the service industries.[6] Some women did, nonetheless, take on 'non-traditional' jobs, but the fact that the lists existed indicates a deep-rooted perception amongst the largely male political elite that women's work outside the home was of secondary importance and should complement their family responsibilities.

In June 1931, senior Party official Lazar Kaganovich gave a speech to the Plenum of the Central Committee which echoed the Central Committee's view that the house commune was 'harmful and utopian', and also reined in the debate on the socialist city. 'People who insist that "we must build the socialist city" ... forget a trifling point', he argued: 'that from the socio-political point of view, the cities of the USSR are already socialist cities. Our city became socialist from the moment of the October revolution, when we expropriated the bourgeoisie and when we socialised the means of production.'[7] In other words, a socialist city was any city in a socialist country. According to this definition, existing cities were no less socialist than new ones. 'The person who denies the socialist character of our cities', Kaganovich continued, in terms which in those times must have sounded quite threatening, 'comes from an absolutely incorrect, Menshevik position.'[8]

Rather than breaking Moscow into smaller units, as the Disurbanists had wanted, Kaganovich announced plans for the further development of the city. This would involve the creation of more squares, parks and boulevards, and improved public transportation, most notably the construction of an underground railway system. It would also involve more housing – not in the form of communes, but single-family apartments. Kaganovich did not repudiate all aspects of communal life; he talked of the need to create more public laundries, canteens, crèches and kindergartens, which, he pointed out, were particularly important now that women were entering the workforce.[9] However, there was no longer any suggestion that the family would 'wither away'. Instead, women would have more help in performing their traditional roles so that they could take on new ones as well.

After the Central Committee resolution, *Ogonek* went quiet both about the socialist city and the house commune. Occasional articles did appear on housing, all of which promoted the single-family apartment with its own kitchen and bathroom. One article, for example, told of the Filippov family, two adults and five children, who had been given a two-room apartment with its own kitchen and bathroom in a new Moscow suburb.[10] Another article informed readers that housing for workers at the Trekhgornyi factory in Moscow was being reconstructed into single-family apartments 'with their own kitchens, gas, bathrooms'.[11] Yet, as we noted earlier, there was no chance of ordinary workers and their families enjoying 'single-family' accommodation. Even newly built 'single-family apartments' had to accommodate several families.

There was no mention in *Ogonek* that the single-family apartment was seldom actually used to house single families. There is, though, a hint that the Filippov family was part of the worker elite, and hence more likely to be allocated superior housing. Readers were told that the wife, a former factory worker, had given up her job on the grounds that 'someone had to look after things at home!' Not only could few families afford to support a full-time housewife, but unless they were members of the worker aristocracy they were accused of parasitism if they tried to do so.[12]

Rabotnitsa was less willing than *Ogonek* both to abandon the principle of communal living and to go along with the fantasy that ordinary families could really acquire single-family apartments. One of the magazine's worker-correspondents, M. Ilyushina, penned a series of articles in 1931 warning readers of the threat to the house commune and calling on them to stand up and fight for it before it was too late.[13] A well-organised house commune would 'create all the conditions for a domestic revolution, for moulding new *byt* and the new person', she argued. Unusually, she insisted that 'not only women but also men and teenage children' should do their share of the domestic work; this would only require around two hours' work every five days, she pointed out, or about six hours' work over a two-week period. This would 'completely liberate women from domestic bondage and give them the chance to be active participants in social construction, both in industry and in social life'.

Ilyushina informed readers that self-contained apartments with their own kitchens were now the main form of urban residential construction, but pointed out that most of them still had to accommodate more than one family. On the positive side, this meant that there would still be several women using each kitchen. However, the fact that individual kitchens were being promoted was alarming and had to be rejected.

Ilyushina's particular concern was the new building work in Ivanovo-Voznesensk. Here, she complained, the local authorities were appeasing the opponents of communal life to such an extent that they were even putting individual kitchens in one-room apartments. 'One room with its own kitchen!' she despaired. 'This is individualism taken to its extreme, to the point of absurdity.' Ilyushina also objected to the abandonment of the principle of separate housing for children. She insisted that it was in nobody's interests, not even the mother's, for adults and children to live together; like everyone else, the mother should be able 'to relax in her own room, away from the children's continual racket'.[14] Ivanovo-Voznesensk had not turned its back on communal life entirely, Ilyushina conceded, since space was being set aside in the new apartment blocks for kindergartens, clubs and dining rooms. However, she saw this as a 'hopeless attempt to combine the old with the new ..., the petty-bourgeois way of life with the new communist way of life'.

The new trend towards individualism would have a negative impact not only on the current generation, but on those that followed: 'A house is not built for a year or for ten years. It is built for sixty to a hundred years. That means that our children, our grandchildren, and even our great grandchildren will still live in them. They will [have to] cook in separate kitchens, live in isolated cells.' She acknowledged that communal living had not always proved popular, and that there were often quarrels and fights in communal kitchens, but she insisted that in time communist principles would take a stronger hold on daily life, and later generations would find it easier to live communally. They would then have to undo the damage now being done by planners and builders.

In February 1932, *Rabotnitsa* published another endorsement of communal living by N. Sergeeva. Sergeeva described a bizarre situation in Yaroslavl' in which a house construction cooperative had wanted a house commune, but the builders in charge of the work had 'refused to act in accordance with the plans drawn up by the committee, and built the house with individual apartments, kitchens and stoves'. The residents refused to go along with this and took down walls and removed stoves themselves, created a communal kitchen, dining room and crèche and 'prepared the house for collective living'. On 1 May 1931 they moved in and, when other workers saw how well they lived, 'they had hundreds of applications from prospective new members'. Sergeeva made a point of stressing the close relationship between the house commune and the factory collectives, which the authorities were strongly promoting at that time in order to increase productivity. Residents who did not perform to their best ability at work were expelled from the house, she explained; and commune members were able to work much better because they had a crèche in which children could be left day and night and so their sleep was not disturbed by crying infants.[15]

In July 1931, another article in *Rabotnitsa*, written by V. Zheleznov, took a rather different position. Zheleznov drew attention to the Central Committee resolution which had denounced the '"leftist" opportunistic phrase-mongers who advance all kinds of scheming proposals for the forced liquidation of individual kitchens, the artificial propagation of domestic communes, etc.', and complained that such 'incorrect proposals' had been voiced by the magazine's own worker-correspondents. This is a clear attack on Ilyushina, whose articles had only just appeared in the magazine. Zheleznov did not denounce communal living completely, but insisted it be a gradual and voluntary process which developed out of domestic cooperatives and the creation of independent domestic institutions. Most importantly, he added, the women who would benefit from these institutions would have to find ways of funding them themselves.[16]

The new approach to new *byt*: independence, self-initiative and self-funding

The reference to self-funding indicates another change in the approach to new *byt*. Women were now berated for 'waiting for someone to do something about it', for assuming that 'Soviet power [will set things up] for us'. Responsibility for developing domestic facilities was now shifted on to women themselves.[17] As one author put it: 'We must not just demand [domestic services]; we must be pioneers of the reconstruction of *byt* ourselves.'[18] The stress was now on independence, self-initiative and self-funding.

The *Zhenotdel*, the Women's Department of the Communist Party, had played a prominent role in agitating for new *byt* and establishing the domestic facilities which would help bring it about. It was disbanded in 1931. It is likely that this was at least partly because of the desire to pass responsibility for domestic services and facilities from the authorities to the people.[19] The *Zhenotdel*'s last director, Aleksandra Artyukhina, explained that:

> We must [now] approach the question of *byt* in a new way ... We cannot count on what the state supplies, on what comes out of the budget of the Finance Department. It is necessary to mobilise the mass of women workers and the wives of workers in the development of domestic institutions. In 1931 [the country is] still not sufficiently wealthy that a million women workers who have been drawn into production can be provided with domestic institutions entirely out of the state budget. These essential domestic institutions will be successfully created only when women workers take on themselves a considerable amount of the work, and if women activists are able to mobilise the resources of the population itself for the revolution in *byt*.[20]

Rabotnitsa provided a number of examples of successful 'socialist initiatives'. In Ivanovo-Voznesensk, for example, women workers were running a canteen, a laundry and a range of children's facilities themselves, each of them putting in eight hours' unpaid work per month. They received some help with funding, but provided 60 per cent of the running costs themselves.[21] A group of female activists in Kislovodsk had opened a café in which they all worked for free, and used the takings to set up child care and domestic institutions.[22]

Women who did not work outside the home were now referred to as a 'great untapped reserve' who should put their time to good use by becoming volunteer social activists (*obshchestvennitsy*) and setting up domestic services.[23] In this way they could 'free up' thousands of housewives for work in industry.[24] Articles appearing in the same magazine a few years earlier, claiming that even full-time housewives had no free time, were conveniently forgotten. Women were now expected to set up, staff and find most of the funding for the services which would 'free them up' to work for the state.

The 'anti-egalitarian' principle and housing distribution

By the end of the first Five Year Plan, Soviet society was no longer committed to the establishment of equality, at least not in the usual sense of the word. 'Egalitarianism' supposedly stood in the way of increased productivity. Differential rewards encouraged people to work harder, and this helped society as a whole. Eventually there would be such an abundance of everything that what was now possible only for the few would be available to everyone. Then the Marxist principle 'from each according to their ability, to each according to their needs' could be put into effect. Until then, while resources were still limited, they should go to those who wielded the most responsibility and worked the hardest.

One of Klaus Mehnert's friends, a former communard, had now embraced the principle of anti-egalitarianism. He explained to Mehnert that this did not go against the notion of equality, because equality did not mean everyone having the same. It meant that everyone was judged 'according to his personal output, not according to inherited rank or banking account'. The extra rewards which hard workers received could not be used to exploit others because the means of production were owned by the state and could not be acquired by private individuals. They could only use these rewards to improve their own lives.[25] This was acceptable in the new consumerist culture.

The record-breaking feat of miner Aleksei Stakhanov, who in August 1935 managed to mine fourteen times more coal than the normal quota for one shift, led to the launching of the Stakhanovite movement, and a virtual celebration of the anti-egalitarian principle. The introduction of piece-rates meant that Stakhanovites generally received more pay than lesser achievers, but they also were given a range of non-monetary rewards which, given the shortages in shops, were far more valuable. These included food hampers, bottles of wine, bicycles, clothes, cloth from which to make clothes, and so on.[26]

Anti-egalitarianism also justified huge differentials in housing provision. As Siegelbaum notes, it was the policy of factories and enterprises to give Stakhanovites preferential treatment when distributing apartments. In some cases apartments were built especially for them, and were 'magnificently furnished' at the factory's expense.[27] Some factories also paid for any necessary repairs to Stakhanovites' apartments.

Stakhanovism was primarily a male phenomenon. Protective legislation prevented women from entering many of the 'leading occupations' which produced the greatest number of Stakhanovites, and their work in the home made it difficult for them to put in the necessary extra hours. Most Stakhanovites were skilled workers, and men could study and improve their skills after work, while women needed that time to keep up with their household chores. Furthermore, female Stakhanovites tended to prioritise their careers to such an extent that many remained unmarried and childless; this went against the pro-natal ethos which developed in the 1930s, which we will discuss later. Accordingly, female activists were encouraged to make their contribution to society not so much by breaking records themselves, but by encouraging and enabling their overachieving husbands to do so by ministering to their every domestic need. The press published enthusiastic reports of conferences organised by the wives of Stakhanovites and leading figures in industry and the military, in which new ways of ensuring the well-being of their husbands were discussed and compared. Keeping the home clean and comfortable were key elements in the Stakhanovite wife's agenda. Yet she did not have an equal stake in this home. It had been assigned to her husband, and she lived in it by virtue of her relationship with him.

The homes of those people high up in the political or administrative hierarchy were particularly luxurious. Andrew Smith, an American communist who worked at the *Elektrozavod* factory in Moscow from 1932 to 1935, visited one such family, who lived in

> a gorgeous seven-room apartment equipped with its own kitchen and individual bathroom, with elevator service, telephones, steam heat, hot and cold water. My host lived there with his wife and two maid servants: the couple had no children. The apartment consisted of a salon, or sitting room, a dining room, two master bedrooms and one bedroom for the two servants, an office or workroom for the master of the house, a room for card playing and dancing and a summer porch. The apartment was sumptuously furnished with thickly upholstered chairs, soft couches and expensive antiques.[28]

Having a home, and a home life, had become a reward for those who held the most responsibility and did the most work. It was an indication of success in the new society. Accordingly, the more sumptuous, the better. In contrast, ordinary Soviet workers still had 'living space' rather than homes.

Gender and new *byt* in the 1930s

The authorities continued to insist on the importance of women's equality, but since women were entering the workforce in considerable numbers throughout the 1930s (by 1940 they constituted 39 per cent of urban workers),[29] it was now claimed that their equality had largely been achieved. However, the state's endorsement of the family meant that women were once again designated 'keepers of the family hearth', just as they had been before the Revolution. Even if they were working alongside men in the factories, they still had to do most of the work generated by the family. While the home was now presented as a place of comfort and support, women were its providers rather than recipients.

Women's 'double burden' of work in production and in the home was not helped by the fact that, on 27 June 1936, abortion was made illegal unless the pregnancy endangered the woman's life or health. The official reason was that abortions damaged women's health even if they were performed by qualified doctors in sanitary conditions, and that the country now had the resources to provide for all its children, so there was no longer any reason to put women through the risk.[30] The reality was that the first Five Year Plan had led to a pronounced drop in the birth rate, and a ban on abortion would make it harder for women to resist the state's inducements to have more children. Other attempts to strengthen the family included making divorce harder and more expensive, and increasing the amount of alimony men would have to pay if they abandoned their wives and children.

The ban on abortion was accompanied by a range of material inducements to reproduce. These included an increase in state benefits, particularly for mothers with large families; longer paid maternity leave; more maternity homes; and more crèches and kindergartens. However, as some women pointed out in the discussions on the draft law which were held in the pages of the press, little was done to improve housing, which was surely a basic necessity of family life. In an article in *Ogonek*, a number of women were invited to give their views on the new law, and several argued that abortion should be allowed in cases where housing was inadequate. 'Of course one should not force a woman to give birth if she does not have living space', said one respondent. Another echoed her: 'We still do not have good housing and living conditions. It is essential to increase living space if we are to increase family size.'³¹

With the majority of women working outside the home, with childbirth harder to avoid, and with child care and other domestic services still inadequate, it was not uncommon for a family to employ a young woman as maid and childminder, squeezing her somehow into their already cramped living space. Leder recalls that two of her friends 'had a two-year-old daughter whom they left with their live-in domestic, a peasant girl, who slept on a folding cot in the [communal] kitchen, as did most domestics. In some apartments, two or three girls slept in the small kitchen or foyer, one for each family.'³² There was no shortage of young women from the countryside who were willing to live and work in such conditions; the miseries of collectivisation ensured a constant source of domestic labour. Inevitably it was the woman's task to deal with the 'hired help', along with other household matters.³³

Even if a man was willing to do some of the housework, he was likely to be intimidated by the disapproving scrutiny of neighbours in the multi-occupancy apartment. Leder's Russian husband spent as little time as possible in the kitchen; he refused to cook, and on the odd occasions when he did the washing-up he brought bowls of hot water to their room and did it there rather than in the kitchen. He tried to disguise the fact that he did any domestic work at all, and so 'devised a camouflage' for taking out the rubbish: 'He'd make neat packages of the trash, tying strings or even ribbons around them, and would take them out when leaving the house in the morning or the evening.'³⁴ He would sweep the floor of their own room, but never the hall or the kitchen since '[h]e did not want to be seen doing "women's work".'³⁵ The rhetoric of women's equality clearly had not crossed the communal apartment's threshold.

Magazine fiction in the 1930s

Some of the short stories appearing in *Rabotnitsa* and *Ogonek* in the 1930s illustrate the confusion which surrounded both the retreat from new *byt*, and the impact this would have on gender relations. Although, as we have noted, by the end of the first Five Year Plan the family had been officially 'rehabilitated' and placed in the centre of Soviet society, in reality it still played second fiddle to work. Many of the short stories in *Rabotnitsa* and *Ogonek* reflected this hierarchy, presenting family life as subordinate to the demands of industry and making it clear that good citizens should be willing to neglect or even discard it if it interfered with work. *Rabotnitsa* seemed loath to accept the rehabilitation of the family at all, and made out that work was the essence of women's equality.

A 1930 *Rabotnitsa* story took place in the early period of industrial expansion, when the demand for greater efficiency meant that redundancies still took place. A young woman called Nadya was among those made redundant when her factory underwent rationalisation. The foreman explained his decision to her: 'Your husband works, and two people can easily live on his salary. And there are other families in which no-one has a job. So this is just.' Nadya was crestfallen, but he reminded her that this policy had been agreed at a meeting in which she had taken part, and at the time she had approved of it.

At first Nadya tried to spend her time reading and improving herself, but her mother-in-law, who lived with them in a multi-occupancy apartment, was constantly nagging her to put her book down and help with the cooking.

> The kitchen was situated at the end of the corridor. The residents of all five floors cooked in it, and the whole day the kitchen was crowded and one had to wait in a queue for a long time. [When Nadya entered the kitchen] several women in dirty house coats and greasy bonnets stood by their saucepans and cast-iron stoves, talking about something or other at the tops of their voices. Nadya washed the potatoes, filled a saucepan with water and began the wait for a free place. But the women were apparently not in a hurry. They gossiped continually, passing judgement on someone or other. All of them were talking at once ... All week, in the kitchen, in the corridor, on the benches around the house, in her neighbours' rooms, she heard the same conversations and gossip.

Eventually Nadya could bear it no longer and went to see the factory manager and local Komsomol leader to beg for her job back. She insisted, somewhat disingenuously, that she was not concerned only about herself, but had come to realise that the rationalisation policy was unfair to women and stood in the way of their emancipation. It was always women who were 'thrown back into the dismal and boring life of the family', becoming burdens on their husbands and unable to participate in work that was of benefit to society (*obshchestvennaya rabota*). 'I am not able to live without doing social[ly useful] work', she told them. 'I despise the petty-bourgeois life style, and I do my best to avoid it ... So why do you push me into it?' By automatically making women redundant, she argued, they were following an outmoded tradition which saw it as more appropriate for women to be supported by their spouses. They would not back down, however, and Nadya went home to consider her future. On the one hand there was 'her love for Nikolai, quiet family life, the kitchen, the gossip, children ... This was the life lived by thousands – no, hundreds of thousands – of women'. On the other hand there was 'the life of the collective ... the chance to live independently'. She chose the latter, and wrote a farewell note to her husband explaining that 'I am not able to just be a wife'. By the time he came home from work she had gone, leaving his mother grumbling about the flippancy of 'these Soviet marriages'.[36]

The author's own views on Nadya's actions were not entirely clear. The desire to make a contribution to society and the insistence on equal rights for women were applauded with alacrity elsewhere in the magazine, yet Nadya's sudden conversion to the cause of women's equality seems rather suspect, an attempt to justify her concern for her own plight by placing it in a broader context. However, the portrayal of 'home life' was unambiguously negative. Apart from Nadya's husband there was no mention of any male residents in the apartment, presumably since they were only there for short periods of time between work and meetings. Home was a female domain, and the housewives were trivial and uncultured because they had no life beyond its walls. The dirt, the petty gossip and the continuation of individual housekeeping in the communal kitchen were all clear examples of old *byt*.

In another *Rabotnitsa* story, appearing in 1932, about a wife refusing to subordinate her work to family life, the author's position was less ambiguous. Vera shared a room with her husband, Petr, their young son, Pavlik, and Petr's mother. Again, the mother-in-law was an unreconstructed example of old *byt*: uncouth, uncultured and insistent that women should devote themselves to domesticity. Vera insisted on her right both to work, and to study at an evening class. She sometimes came home to find Pavlik alone and unfed, but this was presented not as neglect on her part, but on that of her husband and mother-in-law. Petr was a drunken, idle womaniser, violent towards his wife and irresponsible towards his son. He eventually left Vera for another woman, explaining in his farewell note that her work and studies were clearly more important to her than he was. Vera realised she was better off without him, got help with child care from the college authorities, and successfully completed her studies.[37]

The notion that work and society were more important than the family was presented with particular force in a short story appearing in 1932.[38] Three women were cooking breakfast on their separate Primus stoves in the kitchen of a communal apartment, when one of them, Dusya, blurted out that she feared for the safety of her husband. Sergei had gone to work as usual the previous day, but had not returned home. Their daughter noticed that he had taken his bicycle, and they thought he might have been involved in an accident. The neighbours set off to scour the streets, but before joining them, Dusya went to her room and looked around in despair:

From all corners, her tasks rose up and advanced towards her in a line. There was the unfinished dress she was making; a bread ration ticket still not used; a bulging bundle of dirty clothes under the bed. Wherever she turned her head, she saw the work that she had to do. They were all trifles, but they all demanded time and strength. And she did not have the time or strength to do everything.

Sergei was eventually found at work in the factory. He had taken on extra shifts in order to break records and to make up 'a breach in the plan', the subject of many short stories and articles at this time. Dusya's anxiety turned to pride:

Involuntarily she compared her work with that of her husband, who was now a shock-worker; he could stay up all night working, and even forget about his family. He worked, and everyone knew about his work and valued it, and they might even write about him in the newspapers.

Her own work, in contrast, was apparently devoid of value: cooking, washing, shopping and dressmaking were dismissed as 'trifles'. Dusya decided it was time that she went out to work herself, but there was no mention of the fact that she would still have to find the 'time and strength' to take care of those female trifles in the evenings. Yet it is, perhaps, possible to detect some irony in this story. That Sergei was able to forget about his family to such an extent that he did not even think to tell his wife he would be working through the night, and that his wife saw this as admirable behaviour, was surely far-fetched even in the work-obsessed Stalin era.

The family was not dismissed as unimportant in all stories of this era, though the housing shortage invariably complicated conjugal life. *Ogonek* set one of its stories in a Moscow hostel which only accommodated mothers and children, regardless of the women's marital status. One of the residents sneaked her husband in every night when the hostel's female commandant was not looking. He was eventually caught, accused of immorality for sleeping with his wife in a room full of young women, and ordered to leave. He told the commandant that he had nowhere else to go, since he had just been demobilised from the army and not yet assigned his own living space. In any case, he liked to spend as much time as possible with his wife and child. He insisted that nothing immoral had happened, and that the other women had been consulted and had given their permission for him to stay. The commandant told him that his housing situation was not her concern, and that like the other husbands he could only visit his family on Thursday evenings from 6.00 p.m. to 8.30 p.m. Eventually she relented, however, and gave him permission to stay for one more week on condition that he put a screen round the bed. He went further than this and constructed a virtual house, complete with canopy.

> That night no-one was able to sleep in room no. 23; eleven women were listening to every whisper which came from behind the screen. The husband and wife also caught all the sounds and whispers, and were afraid of stirring. And the babies, as if catching the agitation of their mothers, woke up every minute and wailed all night long.[39]

The neighbours had no problem sharing the room with the couple before they hid themselves behind their screen, so it seems to have been precisely the attempt to create some semblance of privacy which disturbed them. This could be taken as a metaphor for the state of *byt* in Stalin's Russia. Any genuine private family life was impossible; it would always be overseen and overheard by the neighbours.

Notes

1 G. Hosking, *The First Socialist Society: A History of the Soviet Union from Within* (Cambridge, Mass.: Harvard University Press, 1985), p. 152.
2 O. Figes, *The Whisperers: Private Life in Stalin's Russia* (London: Allen Lane, 2007), p. 152.
3 See J. Gronow, *Caviar with Champagne: Common Luxury and the Ideals of the Good Life in Stalin's Russia* (Oxford and New York: Berg, 2003).
4 Quoted by A. Kopp, 'Foreign Architects in the Soviet Union During the First Two Five-Year Plans', in W.C. Brumfield (ed.) *Reshaping Russian Architecture: Western Technology, Utopian Dreams* (Cambridge: Woodrow Wilson Centre and Cambridge University Press, 1993), pp. 194–5. See also G.A. Gradov, *Gorod i byt* (Moscow: Izdatel'stvo literatury po stroitel'stu, 1968), p. 56.
5 G.W. Lapidus, *Women in Soviet Society: Equality, Development and Social Change* (Berkeley: University of California Press, 1979), p. 97.
6 M.S. Rumyantseva and A.I. Pergament, *Spravochnik zhenshchiny-rabotnitsy* (Moscow: Izdatel'stvo politicheskoi literatury, 1975), p. 22.
7 L. Kaganovich, *Za sotsialisticheskuyu rekonstruktsiyu Moskvy u gorodov SSSR* (Moscow and Leningrad: Moskovskii rabochii, 1931), p. 61.
8 Ibid.
9 Ibid.
10 L. Petrov, 'Zhizni filippovnoi sem'i' udivlyaetsya nechego', *Ogonek* no. 30 (1931), pp. 10–12.
11 Caption accompanying photograph in *Ogonek* no. 27 (1932), front cover.
12 For more detailed discussion, see L. Attwood, *Creating the New Soviet Woman: Women's Magazines as Engineers of Female Identity, 1922–53* (Basingstoke: Palgrave, 1999), pp. 113–14.
13 M. Ilyushina, 'Na obsuzhdenie chitatel'nits; Ya golosuyu za bytovuyu kommunu', *Rabotnitsa* no. 16 (1931), pp. 5–6, continued in no. 18, pp. 5–6; M. Ilyushina, 'Ya golosuyu

za dom-kommunu', *Rabotnitsa* no. 19 (1931), pp. 4–5; M. Ilyushina, 'Na obsuzhdenie chitatel'nits: Ya golosuyu za kommunu', *Rabotnitsa* no. 22 (1931), pp. 5–6. See also M. Ilyushina, 'Ne tol'ko golosovat', no i rabotat'', *Rabotnitsa* no. 32 (1931), p. 7, on readers' responses to the articles.
14   M. Ilyushina, 'Ya golosuyu za dom-kommunu', *Rabotnitsa* no. 19 (1931), pp. 4–5.
15   N. Sergeeva, 'Berem perekom byta', *Rabotnitsa* no. 6 (1932), pp. 16–17.
16   V. Zheleznov, 'Vzyat'sya samim za perestroiku byta!', *Rabotnitsa* no. 32 (1931), pp. 3–4.
17   M. Ancharova, 'Organizuem bytovuyu kooperatsiyu', *Rabotnitsa* no. 13 (1931), p. 10.
18   A. Kutkina, 'Govoryat rabotnitsy Magnitostroya', *Rabotnitsa* no. 1 (1931), p. 12.
19   Curiously, a *Rabotnitsa* article held that the liquidation of the *Zhenotdel* was evidence of the Party raising, not lowering, the status of new *byt* and other women's concerns. Its 'huge aims' in relation to women, which included the transformation of *byt*, were too important to be left to a separate organisation, but had to be dealt with by the Party, trade unions and soviets as a whole. F. Yurina, 'Million – ot kukhni k stanku', *Rabotnitsa* no. 4 (1931), pp. 3–4.
20   A. Artyukhina, 'Million rabotnits – na proizvodstvo', *Rabotnitsa* no. 5 (1931), p. 6.
21   V. A., 'Ravnyaites' po Ivanovtsam!', *Rabotnitsa* no. 32 (1931), pp. 4–5.
22   'Bol'she samodeyatel'nosti v perestroike byta', *Rabotnitsa* no 3 (1931), p. 12.
23   Letter from Gavva, from a brick factory in Magnitogorsk, one of a series of letters in L. Shaks, 'Detei – na obshchestvennoe vospitanie, a svoi sily – na stroitel'stvo (po pis'mam domashnikh khozyaek)', *Rabotnitsa* no. 1 (1931), p. 8.
24   V.A., 'Ravnyaites po Ivanovtsam!', pp. 4–5.
25   See K. Mehnert, *Youth in Soviet Russia*, translated by Michael Davidson (London: George Allen and Unwin, 1933), pp. 264–5.
26   L.W. Siegelbaum, *Stakhanovism and the Politics of Productivity, 1935–1941* (Cambridge: Cambridge University Press, 1988), pp. 187–8.
27   Ibid., p. 187.
28   A. Smith, *I Was a Soviet Worker* (London: Robert Hale and Co, 1937), p. 45.
29   Lapidus, *Women in Soviet Society*, p. 166.
30   For more detailed discussion, see Attwood, *Creating the New Soviet Woman*, pp. 115–25.
31   See comments by O.I. Vlasova and M.P. Maksakova in *Ogonek* no. 17 (1936), pp. 1–2.
32   Leder, *My Life in Stalinist Russia*, p. 158.
33   Ibid., p. 168.
34   Ibid., p. 168.
35   Ibid., p. 167.
36   S. Ptistsyn, 'Razglad', serialised in *Rabotnitsa* no. 8 (1930), pp. 13–14; no. 9 (1930), pp. 8–10; and no. 10 (1930), pp. 11–13.
37   'Eksamen'. author not known, serialised in *Rabotnitsa* no. 25 (1931), pp. 14–16; no. 26 (1931), pp. 14–15; no. 27 (1931), pp. 14–5; no. 28 (1931), pp. 14–15; and no. 29 (1931), pp. 14–15.
38   Anna Zemnaya, 'Zmeevich', serialised in *Rabotnitsa* no. 26 (1932), pp. 14–15; and no. 27 (1932), pp. 28–9.
39   Iv. Kataev, 'V odnoi komnate', *Ogonek* no. 26 (1933), pp. 3–4.

7

Communal living by default

Even if the Soviet authorities had abandoned their commitment to communal living, in practice it remained the norm. Industrialisation and collectivisation resulted in a flood of additional people migrating from the countryside to the cities, and these had grossly insufficient housing for those already living there. In this chapter we will look at the various forms of housing available in the cities in the 1930s.

Workplace housing

An increasing amount of housing was now controlled by the workplace and allocated to its workers. If the workplace did not have housing of its own, it would be allotted a certain amount by the city council. Workplace housing was not an exclusively post-revolutionary phenomenon, but had become more common, especially once the industrialisation campaign was under way. Between 1924 and 1928, 52 per cent of housing was distributed through the workplace; by 1937 this proportion this had grown to 76 per cent.[1] Workplace housing often took the form of barracks and hostels, but this was not necessarily the case; a worker and his or her family might be assigned a room or part of a room in a communal apartment, or even, in the case of the new middle class, an entire apartment.

Attaching housing to the workplace further eroded the distinction between private and public life. It made the recipients' living space dependent on their jobs, and could be used as a means of controlling them, since the threat of eviction might dissuade them from 'violating labour discipline' – that is, arriving late for work, taking time off, or flitting from one job to another. Whether they were fired or left the job of their own volition, they would not only lose the housing they had been assigned by their workplace, but the local soviet would be under no obligation to provide them with alternative accommodation. Even barracks and hostels, however appalling, were preferable to the streets.

Barracks were the main form of urban factory housing in the new cities. These generally consisted of large dormitories in which dozens of people were crammed, irrespective of age, sex or family status. Some families attempted to carve out some private space by means of curtains and sheets,[2] but most did not bother. Barracks were not uncommon even in the capital. Andrew Smith reports that 11,000 of his fellow workers at Elektrozavod lived in them. One of these consisted of a wooden building, around 800 feet long and 15 feet wide, housing 550 people of both sexes and all ages in one huge room.

> The room contained approximately 500 narrow beds, covered with mattresses filled with straw or dried leaves. There were no pillows, or blankets. Coats and other garments were being utilized for covering, Some of the residents had no beds and slept on the floor or in wooden boxes. In some cases beds were used by one shift during the day and by others at night. There were no screens or walls to give any privacy to the occupants of the barracks. There were no closets or wardrobes, because each one owned only the clothes on his back.[3]

A row of kerosene stoves provided boiling water, as well as serving as the only form of heating. The washing facility was an outside pump. The lack of hygiene inevitably resulted in an infestation of lice and bedbugs, and there was a pervasive stench 'of kerosene and unwashed bodies'.[4]

Hostels generally offered a higher standard of living, but even those which were newly built lacked anything more than rudimentary facilities. Smith paid a visit to a hostel which was only three years old 'but of slip-shod construction', housing around 150 families over four storeys. Residents were divided into groups, each consisting of fifteen families; each group had one room, plus a kitchen and a toilet. The kitchen had a coal- and wood-burning stove, but the families preferred to cook on their own kerosene or Primus stoves: 'With a dozen of the latter in full blast, there was a roar like that of a huge furnace, in which no conversation could be heard.' Again, these stoves provided the only form of heating. There was always a long queue at each toilet.[5]

The Soviet media sometimes acknowledged the inadequacies of factory barracks and hostels. For example, the barracks and hostels provided by construction company Mosremont for its workers and their families were said to be extremely dirty, and the air heavy with the smell of felt boots drying on stoves. The toilets and washbasins were never cleaned and many were broken. There were no laundry facilities, so sheets and clothes had to be washed in the dormitories. Some of the rooms were infested with bedbugs, and the residents had to sleep with the lights on all night in an attempt to avoid being bitten. There were no entertainment facilities, not even functioning Red Corners or radios. The rooms were so dark that schoolchildren had difficulty doing their homework.[6]

Student hostels were little better. Some had around thirty students to a room, and the noise was so great that '[i]t was almost impossible to think, concentrate, read or write.'[7] There was often a shortage of mattresses, with the result that some students had to share beds, while others slept on the floor. Married couples and single people were housed together in the same dormitories.[8]

The conditions in barracks and hostels were hardly conducive to 'cultured' living. A commission found that drunkenness, fighting and acts of 'hooliganism' were common; there was a passive acceptance of dirt; and in the absence of any other form of entertainment, residents spent their free time playing cards and drinking vodka. Thefts were common.[9] *Rabotnitsa* insisted that the residents could be motivated to improve conditions themselves, and suggested that 'socialist competitions' would be one way of doing this. One such competition had been held to identify the best and the worst residents of a Moscow barracks. The winning family had six members – husband, wife and four children – but managed to keep its living space clean, tidy and well ventilated; the bedlinen was regularly washed, and the kitchen utensils cleaned after every use. The family kept itself well informed by means of a radio, newspapers and attendance at meetings. The worst family also consisted of six members, four adults and two children, but this one took no pride in its living space. The room was dirty, the sheets unwashed and the beds unmade. Everyone ate out of a single communal tureen, and food slops were left in the room. The adults paid no attention to the children, and did not attend meetings. The author expressed surprise that this family lived in such a state when 'two of the adults are women.'[10] As always, women were held responsible for domestic conditions.

The communal apartment

Given the conditions in barracks and hostels, it was comparative luxury for a family to have a room of its own in a 'communal apartment' or *kommunalka*. As we have seen, the term was used in the early years of the Revolution to denote an apartment which was under the control of its residents as a whole, rather than a single apartment manager. Now it was applied to any multiple-occupancy apartment in which the kitchen and washing facilities were shared by all of the residents. Lebina points out that this was the only type of accommodation in which the residents had no particular reason to be living together: they were 'not connected by a common type of work activity, as in a hostel, nor by illness, as in a hospital, nor age, as in a children's home, nor even crime, as in a prison'. Instead, they were placed together 'by order'.[11]

While the name seems to suggest some commitment to communal living, this rarely existed in real life. To quote Lebina again, 'even the most unbridled supporters of socialism never considered the communal apartment to be a prototype cell of the new *byt*'.[12] It was simply the result of urban overcrowding, combined with the commitment of insufficient resources to provide adequate housing.[13] Yet whatever the reasons for its existence, the communal apartment represents a peculiarly Soviet approach to housing. It has been referred to as 'a metaphor for the distinctive Soviet mentality'[14] and 'a major stone in the foundation [of] "the Soviet person"'.[15] This was not the new type of person envisaged by the revolutionaries, however. As Fitzpatrick notes, 'a whole folklore exists about the humiliations, petty vindictiveness, fights and resentments associated with involuntary communal living.'[16]

The communal apartment facilitated state control over citizens, and even persuaded them to participate in the process. As Boym notes, it was 'a breeding ground of police informants'.[17] Figes talks of the '[e]avesdropping, spying and informing [which] were all rampant in the communal apartment of the 1930s, when people were encouraged to be vigilant'.[18] In 1933, the Senior Tenant (or 'Elder', to use Figes' preferred term) – i.e. the person who had responsibility for the smooth running of the apartment – had his or her links with the police reinforced: 'Through the elders and yardmen [*dvorniki*], the household management became the basic operational unit of the police system of surveillance and control.'[19]

Gerasimova has suggested that the communal apartment was also used 'as an experiment in changing the social structure on a micro level, by uniting different social groups in one physical space'.[20] Certainly people from different educational and social backgrounds, with different opinions and tastes, were 'thrown together by the local Housing Committee'.[21] However, if this was a conscious experiment rather than bureaucratic indifference, it would have been complicated by the high turnover of residents. Exchanging a room in one communal apartment for a room in another was quite common, as indicated by the large number of such cases reported in *Zhilishchnoe khozyaistvo*. This would have hindered any carefully planned assigning of people to particular apartments.

Residents were forced to adhere to a detailed list of rules. For the most part these were designed to reduce the likelihood of conflict between residents. However, their cumulative effect was to limit personal autonomy. Residents were not allowed to play musical instruments, sing, dance, play the radio loudly or talk loudly on the phone between the hours of midnight and 6.00 a.m. Their own living space had to be kept in a sanitary condition, as well as the areas of common use. Cooking could only be done in the kitchen. Laundry could also only be done in the kitchen, or in the bath when this was not in use. It was to be done in accordance with a rota, with each family assigned a laundry day, apart from those with newborn babies, who were allowed to do their laundry whenever necessary. It was permitted for tenants to have dogs and cats, provided the neighbours did not object, and on condition that they did not foul the apartment or the staircases. It was forbidden to keep caged birds in the apartment.[22]

These rules did not prevent arguments and fights from breaking out between residents. In August 1940, a new law gave the state the right to intervene if order was breached in any place of common use, which specifically included the communal apartment. The penalty was a year's imprisonment.[23] The communal apartment had now officially been designated 'public' space, then.

Housing cooperatives

Housing cooperatives had been hailed as the solution to the housing crisis in the 1920s, and survived well into the Stalin era. The house-leasing cooperatives, ZhAKTy, had been considered the best and most economical way of ensuring that the municipalised housing stock was kept in good condition, while the house-building cooperatives, RZhSKTy, were seen as a way of using the capital of the population to help build more accommodation. However, a decree of October 1937 effectively brought them to an end by abolishing all credits and investments from state institutions and enterprises and forcing them to become completely self-financing.[24] They could not survive in such conditions.

The house-leasing cooperatives were accused of having failed to provide effective management of the housing under their control, and of not keeping it in an adequate state of repair. They had sometimes carried out 'irresponsible large-scale reconstruction work' on the buildings, the most notable example being the conversion of communal kitchens into living space. This had resulted in the use of stoves in the living quarters, leading to a deterioration of living conditions as well as creating a fire risk. There had been little interest in maintaining places of common use, and basic sanitary requirements had often not been observed. Some cooperatives had failed to adhere to laws concerning the setting and collecting of rents, and so had derived inadequate income from their properties. Others had engaged in speculation in living space. As for the house-building cooperatives, a significant portion of the money they had taken from their shareholders had been required to offset losses resulting from a poor financial approach to housing construction,[25] and so, instead of mobilising the finances of the population in building and improving housing, they had required an increasing amount of support from the state.

Indeed, house construction cooperatives had not been a great success. Few workers had proved ready or able to commit their earnings to the scheme; the sums involved were probably too high for many prospective members, even though the state was willing to provide 90 per cent of the building costs in the form of long-term, low-interest credit. There was rarely any indication as to when the housing would be completed, and it sometimes took years.

Most crucially, people had good reason to doubt that they would actually get the housing they were paying for. Housing cooperatives whose members were unable to find sufficient funds themselves sometimes accepted investment from various state enterprises and other organisations, which then claimed the right to a portion of the housing, often distributing it to people who were not members of the cooperative.[26] Even amongst members, housing was not distributed fairly. Having a highly placed contact – as DiMaio puts it, 'the right "know-who"' – would usually result in a much shorter wait, while 'the less fortunate cooperative members might have to sit it out for several years.'[27] Smith reported that some of his co-workers had been making regular payments to house-building cooperatives for more than six years before the building work had even started, and that when a building was finally completed it was generally 'the administration favourites [who] received first call'.[28]

Forcing housing cooperatives into liquidation was not prompted by concern for their members, however. The cooperatives were now out of step with the regime and its increased desire for centralisation, state ownership and control. As Andrusz explains: 'on an ideological plane [the cooperatives'] objective of "educating the mass of the population to participate in the democratic administration of housing" was no longer congruent with the new political policy which emphasised administrative and political centralisation at the expense of the individual and institutional autonomy to which the leasing co-operative had given rise and encouraged.'[29] House-building cooperatives were even wider off the mark, since shareholders who had been lucky enough to actually receive accommodation were rather like private home-owners, even though most of the money for the construction of the buildings had been provided by the state.[30] By cutting off credits to the cooperatives, the authorities ensured that the ownership of residential property, as well as the responsibility for building and managing it, was now firmly in the hands of the state.

Private arrangements

Despite the increased involvement of the authorities in distributing living space, private arrangements did take place. They often took the form of renting a 'corner' of someone else's room. As Leder explains: 'This was perfectly legal so long as the room was larger than the minimum required size ... and the renter was a registered resident of [the city]. "For rent" notices were posted ... at information booths around the city. A set fee was charged for a notice, depending on its length and the amount of time it was to remain posted.'[31] Leder herself lived for a while in a 'corner' of a room in a communal apartment, though her relationship with her ostensible landlady soured when the latter began to bring men home to their shared room to supplement her wages.[32]

The housing shortage and personal relations

The housing crisis inevitably had a major impact on personal relations. An article in a 1936 edition of the journal *Bol'shevik* discussed a number of court cases which supposedly indicated a need to inculcate appropriate socialist family values in Soviet citizens. Although the author did not draw attention to this fact, the housing crisis was a major issue in all but one of the cases.[33]

One couple was brought to court by their housekeeper when they decided they no longer needed her services, and tried to evict her from the apartment she had shared with them for eight years. She insisted that she could not be fired since she had entered into a sexual relationship with the husband, which meant that she was no longer an employee but an unregistered wife and dependant. The court accepted her claim to be a dependant and prevented her eviction, though it would not recognise her as an unregistered wife because it would then be acknowledging that the man had two wives, which was against the law, even if only one was registered.

In another case, a small child was turned onto the streets when her parents separated, the father took up with a new woman and started a new family, and neither of her parents wanted the girl to take up any of their living space. She ended up in a children's home, and both the mother and father were given prison terms for child abandonment.

In a third case, a factory worker seduced a series of female co-workers with the promise of marriage but abandoned them after a few days. One of them took him to court for deception, but the court accepted his argument that he was not in a position to marry any of them, since he did not have his own apartment. The judge pronounced that the women all knew of his living conditions, and must have realised that he was not a serious marriage prospect.

Similar stories appeared in the Moscow journal *Zhilishchnoe khozyaistvo*, which was published from 1935 up to Russia's entry into the war in 1941. Its aim, as declared in its first issue, was to report on the reconstruction of Moscow, which had begun in 1932.[34] However, it also offered readers advice in relation to their own housing problems, and assistance in deciphering the convoluted housing laws. Glimpses of the misery resulting from the housing crisis emerge from the bland language in which questions and answers were couched.

Many queries concerned married couples who were forced to live apart, or divorced couples who were forced to live together. In one case the wife shared a room with her mother while her husband lived in a different apartment; she claimed that they carried out common housekeeping (what this meant was that he came to them to be fed), and wanted to know how this would affect the way their rent was determined.[35] In another case, a husband and wife lived in different apartments in which each had his or her own room; they wanted to know if the housing management had the right to take into consideration the earnings of the non-resident spouse when determining rent.[36] No reason was given in either of these cases as to why the couple lived separately. In the first, it is likely that the husband shared his room with someone else, or it was too small to accommodate the two of them. In the second, the pressure placed on marital life by the chaotic conditions of Stalin's Russia might have resulted in a lack of confidence in the long-term viability of the relationship and a disinclination to give up the security of separate rooms.

The perils of abandoning such caution are clear from other queries sent to the journal. One woman informed the journal that she had notified the house management that she was getting married and moving out of the room she shared with another woman in order to live with her husband. The marriage lasted only one month, and the woman then tried to move back to her old room. She was told that she had lost her right to this living space, but had acquired the right to half of her husband's living space. Despite the failure of their relationship, they had little choice but to remain together.[37]

In another case, a couple had shared two rooms, one of which was a walk-through leading to the other. After their divorce they had taken one room each. What would happen, the woman wanted to know, if her former husband decided to exchange his room, which would result in a stranger moving in? The journal assured her that it was not legally possible to exchange a walk-through room, or a room accessed by means of a walk-through room, without the agreement of the other person or people involved; similarly, it was not legally possible to exchange part of a room without the agreement of the person or persons living in the room.[38] In reality, however, these rules were constantly flouted.

Representations of housing in the popular press

The popular press gave rather less candid reports about urban housing, at least in its supposedly non-fiction articles. Even before the official introduction of Socialist Realism, the magazines had embraced its tenets. *Ogonek* offered little comment on housing in its articles, apart from an occasional mention of the building of single-family apartments. It focused instead on the development of public spaces, sports and leisure facilities. From 1932 its main concern was the reconstruction of Moscow and the city's transformation into a capital which would "'reflect the greatness and beauty of the socialist epoch'."[39] The magazine implied that home for Moscow's citizens was the city as a whole, not just a bed in a dismal dormitory or a room in a cramped apartment. They could spend their free time in huge great squares, gardens, parks and boulevards.

The Metro was the jewel in the capital's crown. *Ogonek*'s reports suggest that the spaciousness of these underground palaces was one of their principal features. Tat'yana Tess, who had previously railed against 'things' cluttering up the domestic space, wrote with particular eloquence about this vast uncluttered public space. The tunnels were 'very wide, wider than in London or even New York. This gave us the possibility of making the Metro carriages large and spacious.' The platforms were also wider than their counterparts in other cities, so that '[i]t will not be crowded for our passengers in the stations, and the journey will be conducted calmly and comfortably.'[40] In one article the Metro was virtually likened to heaven. A young female worker on the Metro construction had taken up gliding in her free time, and spent her time 'under the clouds and under the ground'.[41] She did her first solo flight on the same day that her Metro line opened. This was clearly symbolic; just as socialism would produce a heaven on earth, the Metro had produced a heaven under the earth.

By the late 1930s, articles directly relating to housing began to reappear in the magazine, but most were decidedly fanciful. One writer claimed that the greatest changes brought about by the reconstruction of Moscow had occurred in workers' districts, with workers and their families now enjoying their own apartments, bright clean clubs, and seats at the Bolshoi theatre. This is a clear example of Socialist Realism: the celebration of life as it should be, not as it was. Another commentator, after offering an idealised image of urban life for the masses, admitted that his vision belonged in the future. Every November, he explained, the shop windows in Moscow's Gor'kii Street commemorated the Revolution with a photo exhibition depicting the city in the future, showing '[a]partment blocks which look like palaces, streets as wide as squares, marble underground halls'. Every year, 'more of the fantasies depicted in the Gor'kii street shop windows turn into reality'. These miracles supposedly included housing.

Elsewhere, however, *Ogonek* quietly acknowledged that it was only exceptional workers who got to live in these new apartments. For example, Petr Konovalov, a decorated Stakhanovite, had been allocated an apartment:

> Konovalov strode briskly and cheerfully from room to room in his own apartment, he endlessly tested the gas burners in the kitchen and tried out the shining, creamy light, licked his lips in anticipation of having a bath, regretted that it was not possible right now to experience the effectiveness of the rubbish chute, turned on the radio, rang someone on the telephone, told friends his number, went up and down in the lift three times in order to master it.[42]

An *Ogonek* journalist looked through the list of residents of a new apartment block and found they consisted of : '[a] chief designer – brigade leader – soldier and hero of the Soviet Union – honoured artiste of the republic ... metal worker ... student ... No, here we have to look more closely. Pavel Vlasovich Meger, first cook [on a naval ship], recipient of the title Hero of the Soviet Union, is now studying ...' In other words, what seemed at first to be a more humble resident turned out also to be part of the worker elite.

In its fiction, *Ogonek* offered still more candid glimpses of the housing situation. Communal apartments provided a comic setting for many of its stories. In one tale, a teenaged boy called Vasya had taken up the balalaika, to the fury of his neighbours. Three of the families acquired radios to drown out the noise, while another exchanged their room for an inferior one on the outskirts of town. Yet everything changed when Vasya won an amateur talent contest and his photograph appeared in the newspaper. The status-conscious neighbours were now happy to let their golden boy practise at all hours, and even started an amateur balalaika circle in the house. The family which had moved apartment bemoaned its fate: "'Just think how things turned out for us! We gave up a room with all mod cons in the centre [of town], and with such a celebrity neighbour!'"[43]

In another *Ogonek* story, an elderly man, Aleksei Mironych, lived in an untidy room in a communal apartment. He received a phone call late one evening informing him that he was to receive an award for his work, but his first reaction was fear: the phone call might have woken Asaf Zakharovich, one of his neighbours, who clearly frightened him. Having put down the receiver, he went on tiptoe to the door of his neighbour, and ... pressed his lips to the key hole and whispered earnestly: "Excuse me, Asaf Zakharovich, for disturbing you ...". Next morning he awoke to the usual communal apartment noise: 'The neighbours were waking up. Doors slammed. Water was running into the bath. Asaf Zakharovich was yelling into the telephone.' Our hero decided to find a newspaper, since if he had received an award it would be mentioned there. He knew that the Egorov family, who lived in the apartment downstairs, had *Pravda* delivered, but when he was taking it out of their postbox he was caught by their housekeeper, Fenechka, who accused him of stealing: 'Today it's just a newspaper, but tomorrow you'll be helping yourself to the whole apartment!' Her attitude changed, however, when she learned that he had won an award. When he came home from work that evening, he found that she had cleaned his room, and all of his neighbours had gathered in it to honour him. Even Asaf Zakharovich was friendly; the director of a button factory, he promised to take them all to a button exhibition at the Tretyakov gallery and to make them buttons with their portraits on them.[44]

This story makes the hierarchical nature of Stalin's socialism clear. The Egorovs were clearly part of the elite, having their own apartment and housekeeper. Zakharovich, the button factory manager, was presumably the apartment's informer; he was able to yell into the telephone with impunity, while Mironych felt anxious about disturbing him with his own whispered conversation. The Egorovs' housekeeper cleaned Mironych's room, and the neighbours gathered in it, without anyone consulting him or showing any concern for his privacy. Again, there was no possibility of exerting any control over one's own living space.

The problem posed by a couple trying to enjoy an intimate relationship in a communal apartment was the theme of another story, told from the perspective of their embarrassed neighbour. The narrator was a single man who shared a two-room communal apartment with a married couple. One of the rooms doubled as a living room, and in the past the young woman had slept there while the two men shared the bedroom. Now they were married, the couple slept in the bedroom and the narrator in the living room. This meant he had nowhere of his own to go when his neighbours were feeling amorous: 'They have got used to my being here. They kiss each other under my very eyes. I don't approve of this. At these times I go over to the window or look under the table.' He also went walking through the streets of the city, which was the only place where he could feel alone. The relationship between public and private had, in some respects, been turned on its head. Home for the majority of the population offered no privacy, while the open spaces of the city did.[45]

Like those in *Ogonek*, from the early 1930s *Rabotnitsa*'s supposedly non-fiction articles were dominated by fantasy images of urban life. An article appearing in 1932, two years before the official introduction of Socialist Realism, displays its hallmark features. It describes a new socialist city in the making, but there is no mention of the barracks and hostels which had become such a prominent feature of the new cities, nor of the dirt, the overcrowding and the inadequate or non-existent domestic facilities. Nor is there any reference to house communes, which little more than a year before had been seen by the magazine as a defining feature of the socialist city. Communal facilities are referred to, but only as a complement to the facilities in individual apartments. Only the occasional use of the future tense hints that this is a vision of utopia.

> Houses are being built in the midst of greenery. Parks, flower beds, and vegetable gardens stretch alongside wide asphalted streets. Trams and buses connect the factory, the centre and the outskirts of town, and all of the social and cultural facilities. The apartments are built to get the sun, and have all conveniences: bathrooms, radio, electricity. Each group of houses will have a canteen, kindergarten, crèche, and food store. A library and reading room, a hall for physical culture, a canteen, hairdressers and *banya* [bath house] serve the population. A palace of culture, a cinema, a club, theatres, music and literature courses, and workers' education faculties, provide leisure activities for male and female workers. Splendidly equipped schools provide education for all of the children. In the cities, which are built around giant enterprises, the workers are not only able to rest after the working day, but spend all of their free time in a cultured and intelligent way. The old way of life has no place in the new cities. The socialist cities will be cities of joy![46]

Despite its initial attempt to support the house commune, *Rabotnitsa* ultimately had to accept the change in official approach. As the decade progressed, it presented the single-family apartment as the best form of housing, and the practice of awarding apartments to shock workers and Stakhanovites as a positive phenomenon. However, it also acknowledged that communal apartments remained the norm, and made it clear that these bore little resemblance to the original plans for communal living.

One of the problems, it turned out, was the full-time housewife. Because she did not engage with the world beyond her own family, she lacked social orientation and was unable to follow even the basic rules of socialist life. She took as a personal insult notices about keeping the communal apartment clean and making 'cultured' use of electricity, gas and the radio, and ignored them. If there was more than one such housewife in an apartment, it was torture for the other residents because they had 'nothing better to do with their time' than pick fights with each other and try to get the other residents to take sides. The pettiness of these squabbles was illustrated by a number of case studies. 'Citizen Ponkova quarrelled with her neighbour Gerasimenko over a nail in the kitchen table. Ponkova insisted that Gerasimenko had hammered it in on purpose. Having torn her dress on this ill-fated nail, Ponkova threw herself on her neighbour and beat her with her fists.' In another case, housewives Sergeeva and Chelaznova fell out over a matter so small that *Rabotnitsa* did not even bother to explain what it was, but it gave Sergeeva the excuse 'to pour dirty slops into Chelaznova's saucepan of macaroni'.[47]

Even though *Rabotnitsa*'s commentators no longer openly rejected the single-family apartment, the magazine did express some scepticism about the state's commitment or ability to provide enough of them to go round, and to ensure that they met even basic building standards. One journalist, A. Ozertsovskaya, made the shortcomings particularly obvious after inspecting a block of apartments which was supposedly nearing completion. Each apartment consisted of three rooms, and had originally been intended to house a single family. Accordingly, one of the rooms was a walk-through. However, three families had been assigned to each apartment, so one family would have to put up with a constant flow of people walking through its room. At least there would be no disputes about the use of the kitchen, however, since this seems to have been forgotten when the apartments were designed. Ozertsovskaya reported that when she asked where the kitchen would be located, the officials became confused and, after discussing the matter amongst themselves, announced that '[f]or the time being the workers will live without kitchens'.[48]

Repression, housing policy and gender

The repression, arrests and incarcerations which came to characterise the Stalin era had strong links with the housing programme and housing policy. Housing management had played a major role in identifying candidates for disenfranchisement during the first Five Year Plan, but their role diminished with the introduction in December 1932 of the so-called internal passport, an identity document which was now compulsory for all urban residents. Citizens were not automatically granted passports, and the assessment process they had to go through involved detailed checks on their social class, their work history, and so on. It was openly acknowledged that the passport was a tool in the process of extending social control. *Ogonek* explained to readers that the main aim was to organise and register the population, making it easier to 'cleanse and relieve our cities ... of parasitism and anti-social elements, to help regulate the growth of cities and relieve large-scale population points of the Soviet country'.[49] Accordingly, those who did not qualify for a passport would no longer be permitted to live in a city. As Alexopoulos points out, the introduction of the passport system meant that '[i]nstead of neighbors and communities, the gatekeepers of the Soviet polity were now in passport control.'[50] All the same, neighbours still had a role to play. *Ogonek* warned that there would be 'inevitable resistance on the part of class enemies', and called on the proletariat to join the battle to 'reliev[e] the cities of anti-social and kulak elements'.[51] In other words, they should inform on their neighbours. Many were happy to do so, in the hope that they could take over the freed-up living space of neighbours who were arrested.

Disenfranchisement was brought to an end in 1936. However, this was not due to a softening of the state's animosity towards its supposed enemies; rather, it had found more brutal and effective means of liquidating them. Enemy status was no longer confined to the former bourgeoisie, and the majority of Stalin's comrades in the revolutionary years were executed or disappeared into the country's burgeoning system of labour camps. The Government House by Kammeny Bridge, later known as 'the House on the Embankment' after the novel by Yuri Trifonov, was 'half emptied by arrests' in the late 1930s.[52] This meant that there were always apartments available for new residents – though their tenure was unlikely to be long. After Bukharin's arrest, his wife Anna was 'moved [to the Government House] from the Kremlin into an apartment vacated in this manner';[53] she lived there for only two months before she herself was arrested.

With a disproportionate number of men falling victim to the Purges and the Terror, the family became an increasingly matriarchal institution.

As Beth Holmgren explains, reflecting on the fictional accounts of Stalin's Russia by Lidiya Chukovskaia:

> Men, who dominate the ruling and intellectual elite, are shown to be more absorbed in the public domain and removed from the demands of domestic life. At the same time, because of their high public profile, they are most immediately and harshly victimized by the regime, disappearing from the public eye into the unseen, 'unreal' world of the prisons and labor camps.[54]

Women were the characters 'left behind, burdened with a seemingly unbearable responsibility' – firstly, to try to save the lives of their husbands or sons, and, when that proved impossible, to preserve their memories and, where appropriate, their creative output.[55]

Women were not always 'left behind', however. Many were arrested simply because they were the wives or mothers of men who had been powerful figures in the political hierarchy but were now considered to be enemies. It was sometimes possible to evade arrest by divorcing a disgraced husband and quickly marrying a new one; by doing this a woman was able to change her name and create 'an entirely different identity'.[56] Yet it could be argued that by forsaking her previous husband and attaching herself to a new one she had in effect acquiesced in the authorities' accusations and relieved herself of guilt by association.

This form of guilt by association does not seem to have worked in reverse. Men were not usually arrested after their wives were declared enemies of the people. Vyacheslav Molotov, for example, continued to serve as head of the Commissariat for Foreign Affairs after his wife, Polina, was arrested on the charge of maintaining criminal relations and carrying out anti-Soviet activities with Jewish nationalists.[57] This gender difference adds an ironic twist to the notion that women bore ultimate responsibility for the family. As Wetlin put it, 'the wife must answer for the sins of the husband.'[58]

Notes

1. G. Andrusz, *Housing and Urban Development in the USSR* (Basingstoke: Macmillan, 1984), p. 36.
2. See S. Kotkin, *Magnetic Mountain: Stalinism as a Civilisation* (Berkeley and London: University of California Press, 1995), p. 171.
3. A. Smith, *I Was a Soviet Worker* (London: Robert Hale and Co, 1937), p. 43.
4. Ibid., p. 44.
5. Ibid., pp. 44–5.
6. Davydov, 'Zapushchennye obshchezhitiya', *Zhilishchnoe khozyaistvo* no. 3 (1935), pp. 10–11.

7   N. Ivanova-Romanova, quoted by N.B. Lebina, *Povsednevnaya zhizn' Sovetskogo goroda: normy i anomalii. 1920–1930 gody* (St Petersburg: Zhurnal 'Neva' – izdatel'stvotorgovyi dom 'Letnii Sad', 1999), p. 171.
8   Lebina, *Povsednevnaya zhizn'*, p. 172.
9   Ibid., p. 174.
10 M. Karpova, 'Kul'turnyi podkhod v byt', *Rabotnitsa* no. 8 (1929), p. 13.
11 Lebina, *Povsednevnaya zhizn'*, p. 183.
12 Ibid.
13 See S. Fitzpatrick, 'The Good Old Days', *London Review of Books* 25:19, 9 October 2003; www.lrb.co.uk, accessed 17 February 2006.
14 S. Boym, *Common Places: Mythologies of Everyday life in Russia* (Cambridge, Mass.: Harvard University Press, 1994), p. 124.
15 Lebina, *Povsednevnaya zhizn'*, p. 184.
16 Fitzpatrick, 'The Good Old Days'.
17 Boym, *Common Places*, p. 123.
18 O. Figes, *The Whisperers: Private Life in Stalin's Russia* (London: Allen Lane, 2007), p. 180.
19 Ibid., p. 179.
20 E.Y. Gerasimova, *Sovetskaya kommunal'naya kvartira kak sotsial'nyi institut: istoriko-sotsiologicheskii analiz (na materialakh petrograda-Leningrada, 1917–1991)*, synopsis of candidate of science dissertation, defended 21 December 2000 (St Petersburg, 2000), p. 3.
21 Boym, *Common Places*, p. 124.
22 See 'Nasha konsul'tatsiya', *Zhilishchnoe khozyaistvo* no. 18 (1935), pp. 13–14; 'Nasha konsul'tatsiya', *Zhilishchnoe khozyaistvo* no. 2 (1937), pp. 11–13; 'Nasha konsul'tatsiya', *Zhilishchnoe khozyaistvo* no. 6 (1937), pp. 14–15 'Bytovoi rasporyadok v kvartire', author not named, *Zhilishchnoe khozyaistvo* no. 12 (1939), p. 11.
23 L. Veselova, 'Uvazhat' chelovecheskuyu lichnost'', *Rabotnitsa* no. 26 (1940), pp. 14–15.
24 See A.J. DiMaio, Jr, *Soviet Urban Housing: Problems and Policies* (New York and London: Praegar Publishers, 1974), p. 179.
25 'O sokhranenii zhilishchnogo fonda i uluchshenii zhilishchnogo khozyaistva v gorodakh', *Zhilishchnoe khozyaistva* no. 19–20 (1937), pp. 7–14.
26 DiMaio, Jr, *Soviet Urban Housing*, p. 177.
27 Ibid., p. 177; see also p. 179.
28 Smith, *I Was a Soviet Worker*, p. 114.
29 Andrusz, *Housing and Urban Development*, p. 40.
30 Ibid., p. 40.
31 M.M. Leder, *My Life in Stalinist Russia: An American Woman Looks Back* (Bloomington, Ind.: Indiana University Press, 2001), p. 81.
32 Ibid., p. 81.
33 K. Krylenko, 'Sotsializm i sem'ya', in *Bol'shevik* no. 18 (1936), pp. 65–78.
34 'Nashe zadachi', *Zhilishchnoe khozyaistvo* no. 1 (1935), pp. 1–3.
35 'Nasha konsul'tatsiya', *Zhilishchnoe khozyaistvo* no. 13 (1935), p. 12.
36 'Nasha konsul'tatsiya', *Zhilishchnoe khozyaistvo* no. 19–20 (1935), p. 27.
37 'Nasha konsul'tatsiya', *Zhilishchnoe khozyaistvo* no. 4–5 (1935), p. 21.
38 Ibid.
39 L. Nikulin, 'Moskva', *Ogonek* no. 15 (1938), p. 16.

40 T. Tess, 'My edem v metro!', *Ogonek* no. 3 (1935), p. 9.
41 'Rasskaz Metrostroevki V. Sukovoi', author not named, *Ogonek* no. 1 (1936), pp. 1-2.
42 G. Grigor'eva, 'Preobrazhennaya stolitsa', *Ogonek* no. 19 (1940), p. 8.
43 V. Argov, 'Talant i poklonniki', *Ogonek* no. 12 (1937), p. 5.
44 V. Kozhevnikov, 'Odnazhdy noch'yu', *Ogonek* no. 15 (1939), pp. 10-11.
45 I. Zarubin, 'Aprel'', *Ogonek* no. 14 (1937), p. 11. Since the city itself was promoted as a home to its residents, some aspects of private life were transposed to its streets in these stories. For example, a short story about a tentative love affair was set amongst the squares and boulevards of Moscow, which were described in loving detail. See Y. Vites, 'V Moskve', *Ogonek* no. 26 (1935), pages not numbered. In another story, a married couple on the brink of divorce decided to stay together after leaving the confines of their communal apartment and enjoying an evening out on the town, including a visit to the Metropol Hotel. See L. Lench, 'Klasslyasskoe nasledstvo', *Ogonek* no. 32-3 (1938), p. 31.
46 'Stroim goroda radosti!', author not named, *Rabotnitsa* no. 30 (1932), pp. 18-19.
47 Veselova, 'Uvazhat' chelovecheskuyu lichnost'', pp. 14-15.
48 A. Ozertsovskaya, 'Plokho zabotyatsya o zhilishche', *Rabotnitsa* no. 31 (1938), p. 13.
49 *Ogonek* no. 3 (1933), front cover and p. 1.
50 G. Alexopoulos, *Stalin's Outcasts: Aliens, Citizens and the Soviet State, 1926-1936* (Ithaca, N.Y.: Cornell University Press, 2003), p. 161.
51 *Ogonek* no. 3 (1933), front cover and p. 1.
52 A. Larina, *This I Cannot Forget* (London: Pandora, 1993), p. 167.
53 Ibid.
54 Ibid., p. 66.
55 Ibid.
56 M. Wetlin, *Fifty Russian Winters: An American Woman's Life in the Soviet Union* (New York: John Wiley and Sons, 1994), p. 130.
57 See L. Vasil'eva, *Kremlevskie zheny* (Moscow: Kantor, 1993), pp. 314-51.
58 Wetlin, *Fifty Russian Winters*, p. 128.

8

The Great Patriotic War and its aftermath

On 22 June 1941, the Nazis invaded the Soviet Union and forced the country into the Second World War – or what the Soviets referred to as the Patriotic or Fatherland War. Much has been written on the country's lack of readiness for this attack, and on Stalin's apparent surprise that Hitler had reneged on the treaty which the two countries had signed in 1939. Little attention, however, has been paid to the ways in which housing and the home were explicitly affected by the war. This chapter will look at the treatment of these topics in *Ogonek* and *Rabotnitsa* and the wartime journal *Leningrad*, which celebrated that city's extraordinary literary and cultural resilience during the 900 days in which it was under siege.

Leningrad: a special case

Moscow and Leningrad, the two cities which have been the main focus of this study, had become rivals even before the war. This had a definite impact on their wartime fate. Known as the 'two capitals', they were perceived rather differently. The poet Anna Akhmatova, a native of Leningrad, celebrated her city's pedigree in a radio broadcast shortly after the start of the siege; this, she proclaimed, was 'the city of Peter, the city of Lenin, the city of Pushkin, of Dostoevsky and Blok, the city of great culture and great achievement'.[1] Moscow, in contrast, was seen as the city of government and bureaucracy – and, furthermore, as 'Stalin's city', the showcase for his version of socialism.

This rivalry has been held at least partly responsible for Stalin's failure to protect Leningrad from the Nazi advance. Stalin is said to have been suspicious of the intentions of the city's intellectual and political elite, concerned that they might one day challenge Moscow as the country's powerhouse and even attempt to reclaim the role of capital city for

Leningrad.² Accordingly, Stalin was far more concerned about Moscow. Leningrad was forced to contribute to Moscow's defence, producing munitions which were for the most part airlifted to Moscow. As Richard Bidlack has noted, 'the emphasis put on war production destined for Moscow left Leningrad almost entirely unprepared for the coming winter under siege'.³ Censorship was so tight that the city's residents had no idea how close the enemy was, and the government itself, as Barber and Harrison point out, 'delayed recognising the seriousness of the threat to the city until it was far too late to save its inhabitants or to let them save themselves'.⁴ The order to begin evacuating the population was only given on 29 August 1941, but the next day the city's rail link with the rest of the country was cut, and a week later the city was encircled.⁵ Thereafter, there was no way out until Lake Lagoda froze sufficiently to support heavy vehicles, which did not happen till late January. In the meantime the city's trapped residents had to cope with the most appalling conditions, in one of the most bitter winters on record.

In these circumstances, the housing crisis was rendered largely irrelevant. Food was the crucial thing. It was rationed in accordance with a strict hierarchy. Workers in 'hot' workshops such as steel smelting received the largest rations; next came other workers, engineers and technicians; white-collar employees were in the third category, and non-working dependants in the fourth.⁶ Ration cards were literally a matter of life and death. Even though the rations were scarcely sufficient to ward off starvation, to lose a ration card was a disaster. This was especially the case at the beginning of the month, when it had just been issued. Loss of a card at this time meant almost certain death.⁷ Some people were murdered for their cards; those caught with stolen cards would be killed by military patrols.⁸ Pet animals and wild birds were eaten. Cannibalism became a common occurrence, with some two hundred people arrested on this charge during the course of the siege.⁹ Galina Vishnevskaya, whose memoirs of the siege were later published in the West, noted that many of the corpses abandoned in the streets had their 'buttocks carved out'.¹⁰

Housing rapidly deteriorated. Some houses simply disappeared. This was partly due to the Nazi bombing raids, but also because the central heating stopped working and the city's residents had no choice but to rip apart the city's old wooden houses for firewood. The wood was then burned in *buzhuiki* stoves (the name, meaning 'bourgeois', derived from their fat-bellied shape), which were often poorly installed and maintained, resulting in many other residential buildings being destroyed by fire.¹¹

Many people abandoned their homes and moved in with friends or relatives; they were more likely to survive if they shared stoves and firewood. This had a levelling effect. Those who had, before the war, been fortunate to live in large self-contained apartments were rather less fortunate now that there was no chance of heating them. Privacy was sacrificed for a chance of shared survival.

It was also common for people to take up residence in their place of work.[12] Here they were more likely to have access to light, heat and even, in the early months of the siege, additional food; some institutions managed to continue providing canteen food to their staff outside of the ration card system until the practice was brought to a halt by the authorities.

Although the evacuation of the Leningrad population was slow, according to Harrison Salisbury some 539,400 people did leave the city by means of Lake Lagoda's 'ice road' between January and April 1942.[13] This, combined with the high death toll, meant it was no longer difficult to find an apartment which was vacant – at least, in the sense of it having no living tenants. In that first freezing winter it might be occupied by a few unburied corpses.[14] The graveyards were unable to cope with the huge number of bodies, and the ground was, in any case, too hard to dig graves. Also, the survivors were too close to death themselves to have the strength to drag their dead to the cemetery. There was one advantage to the bitter cold: it prevented the corpses from rotting. Many of the dead were left literally in their deathbeds, sharing the apartments with the living.

Leningrad became an increasingly female city. Most able-bodied men were fighting at the front, and those who had not been called up succumbed more quickly than women to hunger and cold. As Bidlack explains, 'men have less body fat and their cardiovascular systems are not as strong.'[15] Ol'ga Grechina recalled in her memoirs that men proved unable 'to adapt to the tragic conditions of life. They began to fall down in the streets, take to their beds in their apartments, to die and die and die …'[16]

It fell on women, then, to keep the city going. In the face of all the horrors that the siege forced on them, simply carrying on with daily life was an act of courage. The poet Ol'ga Berggol'ts, whose radio broadcasts earned her the sobriquet 'the voice of Leningrad', made this particularly clear. Her poem 'Conversation with a Neighbour' (*Razgovor s sosedkoi*), written in December 1941, pays homage to her 'communal apartment neighbour' (*sosedka po kvartire*), Dar'ya Vlas'evna, who, she insists, should be the model for a statue celebrating wartime heroism:

> Just like this: gaunt, brave,
> in a hurriedly tied headscarf,
> as you are when you walk,

shopping bag in hand,
under shell fire.¹⁷

Ogonek and Rabotnitsa paid less attention to the agonies of Leningrad and its citizens than might be expected. Perhaps this was due, at least in part, to the desire to sustain morale by reporting on more positive developments in the war. It might also have something to do with the fact that these were both Moscow publications.

Rabotnitsa did take up the theme of female heroism in Leningrad, reproducing the transcript of a Leningrad radio broadcast in which the female narrator talked of housewives manning barricades and running factories and sacrificing themselves and their families, sometimes quite literally, to the war effort: 'When we go to work in the morning, we do not know if our homes will still be standing when we return in the evening – and we have left [our] children at home ...'¹⁸

Ogonek also printed a few articles on the Leningrad siege, one of which described the devastation wreaked by a Nazi shell on 'a densely populated communal apartment':

> The hot fragments of the shell burn holes in the blankets covering the sleeping children. In the small room next to the bathroom, an old woman, a pensioner, is killed. A piece of the brick wall falls onto the bed of a plumber who is sleeping deeply after working overtime. The shell has brought death and destruction. The house has woken up. They phone the ashen-faced porter [dezhurnaya] downstairs, and the house office.¹⁹

Just as Ol'ga Berggol'ts' 'Conversation with a Neighbour' presents a positive image of relations between communal apartment neighbours, this article also gives the impression that the old irritations brought about by too close proximity had ceased. Enmity between neighbours had been replaced by unity in the face of a common enemy. As well as making the communal apartment seem almost homely, this same article likened the beloved city itself to a room in a communal apartment: 'During the day your attention is focused on the huge emptiness of the streets, squares and bridges. At night, however, it is as if the buildings somehow push closer together and Leningrad becomes more cosy, like the room in which you live, in which you know every corner.'²⁰

The Leningrad artistic and literary community produced its own journal throughout the war years, Leningrad, which discussed the city's horrors, to a large extent through poetry. Again, domestic life loomed large in these works. As the poet and diarist Vera Inber wrote, this was a city of 'housing without light, stoves without heat'.²¹ One article told of the deaths of an entire family, one by one. First the two teenaged brothers died. Their older sister moved in with her father to help him cope 'in the now empty apartment which had previously been filled with young voices'. Then a German shell took her life, and he abandoned the apartment, so full of tragic memories, and started sleeping at his workplace 'on the floor under his quilted jacket'.[22]

Housing and the home

In Leningrad accommodation was pushed into the background by the more pressing problems of food and cold. In other cities it remained a major issue. Elena Kononenko took up the subject of factory housing in *Rabotnitsa*, insisting that, even if the country was at war, housing was crucial. She wrote with anger about factory hostels in which the walls were black with mould, there was no hot water either for washing or for making tea, and no cultural and educational facilities: 'the Red Corner seems to be permanently under lock and key'. She pointed out that articles in the newspapers were 'constantly saying that more attention should be paid to the domestic (*bytovye*) needs of workers; Stalin himself has made this point.' It was surely, then, 'not too much to ask, to have a cup of hot tea when you get up, and a clean bed to sleep in at the end of a long shift.' In any case, if workers had good home environments they were able to work more productively. Living space should still be a priority, she concluded, even when the country was at war.[23]

The understanding of living space had become rather broader during the war, at least according to an article in *Ogonek*. The district housing departments in Moscow were now responsible not only for the maintenance of housing, it reported, but also of air-raid shelters, since they had become a second home to the city's inhabitants: 'Many Muscovites have adjusted to resting and reading in the air-raid shelters.'[24]

Conversely, some people chose to imprison themselves in their apartments for protection. V. Ardamatskii described in *Ogonek* an encounter with an elderly man of his acquaintance in the Ukrainian capital, Kiev. The city had just been liberated after twenty-five months of German occupation, and the old man 'was walking slowly and deliberately. I asked: "Are you taking a stroll?" he replied: "No. I am teaching myself how to walk along the street again"'. He had been too terrified to leave his apartment during the occupation for fear of being shot by the Nazi soldiers.[25]

The family and the war

As we saw from the writings on Leningrad, the war annihilated whole families. The large number of children left without parental care, either because their parents had died 'at the hands of the fascist barbarians'[26] or because they had been evacuated from the occupied territories, was a growing problem. Readers were encouraged to take in the waifs, either temporarily or permanently. Samarkhand, like other parts of Central Asia, had received a particularly large number of evacuees, and *Rabotnitsa* reported that residents of all nationalities and professions, some childless and some with many children of their own, had taken in homeless children. In addition, 'many collective farm workers have taken on the upbringing of whole collectives of children.'[27]

Not all of the evacuated children were orphans, but in an age of poor communications, reuniting families which had been separated by the war was not an easy task. *Ogonek* published a series of photographs of newly liberated cities in which people were trying to track down members of their families by means of notes placed or painted on what was left of their old apartment blocks. In Voronezh, one lucky soldier was pictured taking down the new address of his wife, who had painted it on a wall in the ruins of their old home.[28] A young child, Slava, was still trying to find his mother: 'Mama!', his note read, 'I come here with Papa every day at 10.00 a.m. and wait for you.' It is noteworthy that people used the walls of their old apartment blocks as their message board, not their place of work or their children's school. 'Home', such as it had been, was where the hunt for family members began.

If people could not put their old families back together, they were encouraged to create new ones. This was a process which sometimes formed the story line in the magazines' fiction. In one *Ogonek* tale, a young Leningrad war widow adopted a child from an orphanage. He turned out not to be an orphan after all, however; his father had been reported dead by mistake, and he was now back in Leningrad to reclaim his child. The story consisted of the child's efforts to make his father and his adoptive mother fall in love and become his new family.[29] A story in *Rabotnitsa* told of a young woman who wanted to adopt her dead sister's son, Petr, but all of the orphanage records had been destroyed in a bombing raid and there were three boys of the same name and age and of similar appearance. She took on all three, and subsequently found a prospective father for them in the form of a young soldier, who fell in love with her 'splendid maternal eyes'.[30]

It was not enough to adopt other people's children. The war had had a catastrophic impact on the country's population, and it was women's task to replenish it. Those who responded to the call were portrayed as heroes, serving their country no less than male soldiers at the front. To bring home this point, a series of military-style medals was introduced in the summer of 1944 for women who showed particular valour in the battle of the birth rate. Those who produced and reared five children received the Medal of Maternity Class II. A sixth child earned them the Medal of Maternity Class I. The seventh, eighth and ninth child were acknowledged with the Order of Maternal Glory. The greatest accolade went to the mother of ten or more children, who was given the title 'Hero Mother'.[31] Given the housing shortage, it is difficult to imagine where these children would be accommodated, and how the neighbours in a communal apartment would have reacted to having such an enormous family in their midst.

Construction and reconstruction during and after the war

Much was made of the fact that construction work continued on the Moscow Metro throughout the war, with lines extended and new stations opened. In the 1930s, the Metro had been a symbol of the capital's grandeur and its status as the first Socialist City. Now it was a symbol of the country's determination and invincibility.[32]

Housing, however, was in a terrible state. While there is some inconsistency in the figures on the extent of housing destruction, one source cited by Steven Harris puts it at one third of the country's entire housing stock, rendering 25 million people without accommodation.[33] Donald Filtzer holds that the urban housing stock had consisted of some 270 million square metres in 1940, but that this had fallen to 200 million square metres during the war. By 1950, he continues, the total stock has risen to 513 million square metres; but, although this was around 90 per cent more than in 1940, the urban population had continued to grow, so that average living space per resident fell from 5.1 square metres per person to 4.67 square metres.[34]

Whichever figures were the most accurate, the reality was that thousands of people had been rendered homeless and had to live in whatever makeshift shelter they could find. This included dugouts, ruined buildings, basements, barns, bath houses or train carriages.

Many of those citizens who had relocated during the war found that returning to their old homes was not an option, even if their building had survived the wartime destruction. As Rebecca Manley tells us, in some cases the room or apartment, along with the personal possessions which had been left in it, had been taken over by the former occupants' neighbours. In other cases it had been reassigned to new tenants by the housing authorities.[35]

The official ruling was that if someone had been absent for more than six months, or had not paid rent for three months, he or she would lose the right to the accommodation. However, the war clearly complicated the situation and in many cases made it impossible to adhere to these rules. Sometimes the authorities acknowledged this problem, and upheld the request of supplicants to return to their old accommodation even though they had no official right to do so. Some groups of people were treated more sympathetically than others. Servicemen and their families had the most chance of reclaiming their old accommodation. People who had been evacuated and had spent the war working in factories in Central Asia or Siberia had rather less chance; even though the work they had done had been essential and the conditions they had lived under had been horrendous, there was a widespread perception that they had managed to get through the war years in relative safety. To some they were perceived as little better than deserters.[36]

Jews seem to have faced particular discrimination. Manley quotes from a number of letters sent to the Jewish Anti-Fascist Committee which make it clear that even those Jews who had served in the armed forces sometimes had difficulties reclaiming their old homes. She also cites the memoirs of a Jewish resident of Odessa, S. Ia. Borovoi, who insisted that he was prevented from returning to his old home largely by, as Manley puts it, 'officially sanctioned and popularly endorsed anti-semitism'.[37] She is cautious about attributing the problems encountered by these people solely to anti-Semitism, however. Nothing was that clear-cut in this chaotic era. Different decisions were made by officials in different cities; central government and local authorities were often at loggerheads; and official decisions were often thwarted by ordinary people refusing to abide by them. All the same, Manley acknowledges that Jews did experience more difficulties than others. There was, she tells us, a widespread perception that Jews formed a large proportion of those evacuees who supposedly 'sat out' the war well away from the front. Furthermore,

> While the obstacles encountered by Jews do not seem to have been the result of a systematic policy of exclusion elaborated by central or even regional authorities they were shaped, at least in part, by central policies. The period of re-evacuation corresponded with the onset of a series of initiatives divesting Jews of their responsibilities in a variety of fields, namely in the arts, in academia, and in party and government organizations ... The individuals who had taken over their apartments,

moreover, were more likely to feel emboldened to remain there, and to feel justified in doing so.[38]

People who did manage to reclaim their old homes, or were given long-term alternative accommodation, were still likely to find themselves in pretty basic accommodation. Filtzer notes that, even in Moscow, in 1947 over half of all dwellings lacked running water, sewerage or central heating.[39] The situation was still worse in other cities, particularly those which had received large numbers of evacuees during the war or were in areas earmarked for further development.[40] The desperate need to provide some kind of accommodation for the post-war influx of new workers meant that even new-build residential property often lacked water and sewerage. To quote Filtzer once more:

> enterprises built dormitories and barracks anywhere they could, irrespective of whether or not they could provide safe drinking water, roads, pavements, or even transportation to allow workers to travel to work. In Kospash, a mining town in Molotov *oblast'*, if workers wanted water for drinking or washing they had to use snow or scoop water out of contaminated puddles lying on the ground.[41]

At least the housing problem was now so acute that it could not be ignored, even by the magazines we have been exploring. As we have seen, before the war, the Soviet city, with its great parks, wide boulevards and public gardens, had been portrayed as one big home to its residents. This had made it possible to minimise the importance of individual living space. That was no longer possible.

According to the magazines, housing reconstruction began even before the end of the war. The cities which had been occupied had suffered particularly heavy destruction and, as soon as the Germans were forced into retreat, residents got to work.[42] *Ogonek* claimed that in the city of Stalingrad, where hardly any buildings remained intact, virtually all of the inhabitants had become builders: 'After work and on Sundays they go out to the forest to build homes for themselves and their neighbours.' Out of necessity they learned the required skills. For example, blacksmith Lyuba Chegvintseva 'mastered the work of stonemasons, concrete workers and plasterers in a short time', and her efforts soon compared well with those of the professionals who worked alongside her, such as stonemason Nadya Nazarova.[43]

Curiously, the article made no comment on the fact that the blacksmith and stonemason were both women. With men still fighting at the front, much of the building work was down to them. As *Ogonek* explained in a caption accompanying a photograph of building work in Orel:

'Special brigades of women work at dismantling ruined buildings, they carefully place blocks and other materials nearby.'[44] Women were not only responsible for preserving their cities during the war, then, but now for rebuilding them.

When the war finally came to an end, new housing was presented as a vital part of the post-war renaissance. Cities would emerge Phoenix-like from the rubble and proudly parade their 'new housing blocks, schools, palaces of culture, trolleybuses and cars running along asphalt roads, squares and boulevards.'[45] In addition to a huge state housing programme, almost every factory and enterprise was said to be building homes for its workers.[46] New residential suburbs were appearing,[47] and additional storeys were being added to existing buildings in city centres to provide extra accommodation.[48]

So desperate was the need for housing that private building was encouraged. A new law introduced in 1948 required local authorities to provide plots of land to people willing to construct their own houses, which could be one or two storeys high and contain up to five rooms. Between the years 1946 and 1949, around 30 per cent of all new and renovated urban housing was built – and owned – by private individuals.[49]

Prefabrication was also promoted. *Ogonek* explained that the use of factory-produced panels would make it possible for amateur builders to put together a 'cottage' in just two days.

> The putting up of such a house is characterised by ease and simplicity. A house which has been prepared in the workshop of the *kombinat* can be assembled without much difficulty by women, teenagers and 'invalids of the Patriotic War'. Experience shows that six people, who have no building qualifications, can assemble a one-storey house in thirty hours.[50]

Anticipating the objection that these hastily built buildings would be too flimsy to withstand the cold, the author explained that shavings, sawdust and other building by-products would be turned into insulation which would be soaked in special substances to make it resistant both to rot and to fire. 'The mass construction of houses built in accordance with the factory method is a matter of great social significance', the author concluded, 'which promises to give the country millions of square metres of living space.'[51]

The interest in the construction of homes led logically to an interest in home life. In the pre-war years, images of public leisure activities abounded in the popular press. Now people could be depicted enjoying their free time in their homes. A typical photograph in *Sovetskaya zhenshchina*, a glossy new post-war women's magazine, showed a family 'spending Sunday together', seated cosily round a large dining table in the centre of a room surrounded by homely decorative touches: lace curtains, house plants, a reproduction of a Russian still life.[52]

Yet the home still did not constitute private space. Many of the articles told of inspection visits on the part of Soviet officials concerned either with quality control of the building work or with ensuring that the conditions for 'the workers' daily life' were adequate.[53] Women's magazines also felt obliged to offer their readers guidance on how to decorate and furnish their homes in accordance with a prescribed notion of 'good taste'. In the supposedly typical apartment, 'everything sparkles with cleanliness. On the windows there are tulle curtains, and there are tubs of flowers. There is a cupboard with a mirror, a sofa-bed covered with a white cover, books, reproductions of paintings by Russian artists – in everything one feels order and good taste.'[54]

In reality, housing construction proceeded at a snail's pace in the last years of the Stalin regime. By the time of Stalin's death in 1953, tens of thousands of Soviet citizens, including demobilised veterans, were still living in makeshift shelters unfit for human habitation,[55] or wooden barracks and hostels which had been built in the immediate aftermath of the war as a supposedly short-term measure.

A room in a communal apartment constituted one of the better forms of housing for these times. Yet the residents of communal apartments, particularly the women, who had to spend more of their time in the 'areas of communal use', remained as antagonistic to communal living as ever, making some sad if humorous attempts to achieve a measure of independence and privacy. The newspaper *Trud*, reviewing a play set in a communal apartment, noted that one female character insisted on securing all her saucepans with chains and locks.[56] In an article in *Rabotnitsa*, G. Rykin complained that each resident in one communal apartment he visited 'has her [sic] personal light bulb and personal switch in the kitchen, the corridor, the bathroom, and other places of general use ... Everything has to be separate.'[57]

Despite the laws introduced to stamp out so-called 'apartment hooliganism', tensions between female neighbours continued to explode into physical fights. Rykin did concede that '[m]en can also ... kindle rows in apartments', but the examples he gave were all of women, and the article was illustrated by a sketch of a woman wielding a soup ladle as a weapon.[58] That 'apartment hooliganism' was largely a female phenomenon is hardly surprising given that the conflicts generally took place in the kitchen, which was firmly identified as a female domain.

The housing shortage had important demographic implications. A *Rabotnitsa* commentator pointed out that many young couples were forced to live separately in single-sex hostels, which was hardly conducive to starting a family.[59] This was particularly worrying in view of the demographic catastrophe created by the war. In 1946 there were almost 13 million more women than men in the crucial 20 to 44 age group.[60] Those who had husbands had to have children. This could only happen if they had more appropriate housing.

Yet the single-family apartment remained a pleasure for the privileged few. Despite greater interest in cheap pre-fabricated housing, the extravagant architectural styles which had characterised construction in the 1930s were not abandoned, and reached their zenith in the form of seven new Moscow skyscrapers resembling wedding cakes. Only two of these were given over to residential space, none of which was available to 'ordinary' Russians.[61]

For Soviet Jews, communal living was particularly unpleasant in the post-war years. As we have seen, there was a widespread perception that Jews had, on the whole, managed to keep themselves safe during the war by avoiding active service. The creation of Israel in 1948 added to the negative attitude towards Jews and led to a wave of officially sanctioned anti-Semitism. This culminated, in January 1953, in the so-called 'Doctor's Plot', in which a group of predominantly Jewish doctors were arrested on the charge of attempting to poison the country's leaders, including Stalin himself. Stalin died two months later – clearly not at the hands of these doctors, since they were all in prison – after which the charges were dropped and the doctors released. In the meantime, however, as Mary Leder recounted from personal experience, '[I]nsulting Jews became a national pastime ... For many Jewish families living in communal apartments with non-Jewish neighbors, each day was a nightmare.'[62]

Notes

1 H. Salisbury, *The Siege of Leningrad* (London: Secker and Warburg, 1969), p. 285.
2 In fact this was not mere paranoia; Leningrad's heroism during the war did prompt some calls for the city to reclaim its old crown.
3 R. Bidlack, foreword to C. Simmons and N. Perlina, *Writing the Siege of Leningrad* (Pittsburgh: University of Pittsburgh Press, 2005), p. xiv.
4 J. Barber and M. Harrison, *The Soviet Home Front* (London: Longman, 1991), p. 66.
5 Ibid., p. 66.
6 R. Bidlack, foreword to *Writing the Siege of Leningrad*, p. xiv.
7 See Salisbury, *The Siege of Leningrad*, p. 389.
8 Ibid., p. 477.

9. Bidlack, foreword to *Writing the Siege of Leningrad*, p. xviii.
10. Ibid., p. xxxi.
11. See Salisbury, *The Siege of Leningrad*, p. 456.
12. See, for example, V. Inber, 'Leningradski zapisi', *Ogonek* no. 32 (1942), pp. 305.
13. Salisbury, *The Siege of Leningrad*, p. 498.
14. A. Adamovich and D. Granin, *A Book of the Blockade* (Moscow: Raduga, 1983), p. 79.
15. Bidlack, foreword to *Writing the Siege of Leningrad*, p. xiv.
16. Quoted in Simmons and Perlina, *Writing the Siege of Leningrad*, p. 2.
17. This translation is from K. Hodgson, *Written with the Bayonet: Soviet Russian Poetry of World War Two* (Liverpool: Liverpool University Press, 1996), p. 243. In Russian it reads: Вот такой же: исхудавшей, смелой / В наскоро повязанном платке / Вот такой, когда под артобстрелом / Ты идешь с кошелкою в руке.
18. Matveeva, 'My o tstoyali rodnoi Leningrad', *Rabotnitsa* no. 11 (1942), pp. 10–11.
19. V. Belyaev, 'Leningradskie nochi', *Ogonek* no. 3 (1941), pp. 6–7.
20. Ibid.
21. V. Manuilov, 'Novye knigi', review of Inber's 'Dusha Leningrad', *Leningrad* no. 1 (1942), p. 24.
22. V. Druzhinin, 'Oboima', *Leningrad* no. 4–5 (1942), p. 27.
23. E. Kononenko, 'Kogda obshchezhitie – rodnoi dom…', *Rabotnitsa* no. 23–4 (1942), pp. 4–5.
24. L. Beregovoi and G. Senin, 'Moskva v eti dni', *Ogonek* no. 34 (1941), pp. 3–5.
25. V. Ardamatskii, 'Gorod doblesti', *Ogonek* no. 48 (1942), pp. 3–4.
26. Caption on front cover of *Rabotnitsa* no. 9 (1942), accompanying a photo of a young woman and her adopted daughter.
27. D. Kreptyukov, 'V novykh sem'yakh', *Rabotnitsa* no. 12–18 (1942), p. 12.
28. *Ogonek* no. 36 (1943), pp. 8–9.
29. P. Pavlenko, 'Zhizn', *Ogonek* no. 43 (1942), pp. 5–6,
30. A. Preobrazhenskii, 'Tri Petra', *Rabotnitsa* no. 7 (1945), pp. 14–15.
31. See the announcement of these rewards in *Rabotnitsa* no. 8–9 (1944), pp. 4–5.
32. 'Novye stantsii Metro', *Ogonek* no. 48 (1944), p. 12.
33. S.E. Harris, 'Moving to the Separate Apartment: Building: Distributing, Furnishing, and Living in Urban Housing in Soviet Russia, 1950s–1960s', Ph.D. dissertation, University of Chicago (2003), p. 159.
34. D. Filtzer, 'Standard of Living versus Quality of Life: Struggling with the Urban Environment in Russia during the Early Years of Post-War Reconstruction', in Polly Jones (ed.), *The Dilemmas of De-Stalinization: Negotiating Cultural and Social Change in the Khrushchev Era* (London and New York: Routledge, 2006), p. 84.
35. R. Manley, 'Where Should We Resettle the Comrades Next?', in J. Fuerst (ed.), *Late Stalinist Russia: Society between Reconstruction and Reinvention* (London and New York: Routledge, 2006), pp. 233–4.
36. Ibid., pp. 239–40.
37. Ibid., p. 234.
38. Ibid., pp. 242–3.
39. Filtzer, 'Standard of Living versus Quality of Life', p. 85.
40. Ibid., pp. 87–8.
41. Ibid., p. 88.
42. 'V osvobozhdennom Gomele', *Ogonek* no. 48 (1943), pp. 1–2.

43 B. Tseitlin, 'Segodnya v Stalingrade', *Ogonek* no. 46–7 (1943), pp. 3–5.
44 'Vosstanovlenie Orla', *Ogonek* no. 40–1 (1943), p. 8.
45 B. Shatilov, 'Stalino segodnya', *Sovetskaya zhenshchina* no. 1 (1951), pp. 19–20.
46 N. Ol'shanov, 'Stroim dlya mira', *Sovetskaya zhenshchina* no. 3 (1952), pp. 18–19.
47 L. Vepritskaya, 'Novosel'e', *Sovetskaya zhenshchina* no. 1 (1950), pp. 58–9.
48 B. Shatilov, 'Stalino segodnya', pp. 19–20.
49 G. Andrusz, *Housing and Urban Development in the USSR* (Basingstoke: Macmillan, 1984), p. 99.
50 G. Sagal, 'Dom stroitsya v tsekhakh kombinata', *Ogonek* no. 48–9 (1944), p. 12.
51 Ibid.
52 *Sovetskaya zhenshchina* no. 3 (1954), p. 11.
53 See, for example, Leont'eva, 'Chas Dobryi!', *Sovetskaya zhenshchina* no. 1 (1955), pp. 25–6.
54 M. Zlatogorov, 'Zdes' zhivut tekstil'shchiki', in *Sovetskaya zhenshchina* no. 5 (1951), pp. 31–2.
55 See Zubkova, *Russia after the War: Hopes, Illusions and Disappointments, 1945–1957* (London: M.E. Sharpe, 1998), p. 102.
56 L. Novogrudskii, 'My khotim, chtoby v novykh domakh novogo stala zhizn'!', *Trud* 12 July (1961), p. 2.
57 G. Rykin, 'Skandal'nykh del masteritsa', *Rabotnitsa* no. 10 (1955), p. 29.
58 Ibid.
59 V. Karbovskaya, 'Dlya slovo – derzhis'!', *Rabotnitsa* no. 12 (1956), pp. 11–12.
60 E. Zubkova, *Russia after the War*, p. 20.
61 Khrushchev himself claimed in his memoirs that 'not a single inhabitant of Moscow could possibly afford to live in them, so Stalin decided to reduce the rent somewhat so the apartments could be assigned to certain prominent and well-paid actors, scientists and writers' See N.S. Khrushchev, *Khrushchev Remembers,* translated by Strobe Talbott (London: André Deutsch, 1974), p. 99.
62 M. Leder, *My Life in Stalinist Russia: An American Woman Looks Back* (Bloomington, Ind.: Indiana University Press, 2001), p. 327.

9

The Khrushchev era: 'To every family its own apartment'

By 1956 Khrushchev had emerged as the new leader of the country, and that same year he launched what was arguably 'the most ambitious governmental housing program in human history'.[1] The aim was to provide all families, including newly wed couples, with their own apartments within the next twelve years. The seven-year plan launched by Khrushchev in 1958[2] pledged to build 15 million new city apartments, to be distributed 'on the principle "one family, one flat"'.[3] The building programme would be characterised by the slogan 'build quickly, cheaply, and well' (*stroit' bystro, deshevo, khorosho*).[4]

This mammoth enterprise could only be achieved by radically cutting building costs. The architectural 'excess' (*izlishestvo*) of the Stalin era, with its fussy 'cornices and turrets',[5] was denounced. Not only was it expensive, but it was also presented as anti-socialist, aimed at 'outdated, petty-bourgeois tastes'.[6] Opulence was to be replaced by utilitarianism. Urban residential construction would be based on a few standardised models and would make use of new, more economical building materials such as concrete, plastic and asbestos.[7] The 'industrial method of construction' would be developed: the various elements would be produced in factories and would just have to be put together at the building site, which would drastically reduce the time spent on construction. The optimum height would be four or five storeys, which would be just low enough to make expensive lifts unnecessary.[8] Since the new apartments would each house only one family, they could be 'small-dimensioned' (*malometrazhnaya*);[9] and, although it was acknowledged that high ceilings were healthier as they allowed more air circulation, they would have to be lowered in the interests of economy.[10] In Khrushchev's view, Soviet people, brought up to appreciate 'truth and expediency', would be sure to appreciate the 'simple, logical and elegant form' of the new apartment blocks.[11]

Khrushchev admitted that the apartments would not be luxurious.

Indeed, before long they would acquire the nickname 'khrushchoby', a cross between Khrushchev's name and the word for slums, *trushchoby*. However, 'ask any housewife', he insisted, and she would tell you that the benefits outweighed the disadvantages. 'You have to decide ... do you build a thousand adequate apartments, or seven hundred very good ones? And would a citizen rather settle for an adequate apartment now, or wait ten or fifteen years for a very good one?'[12]

The standardised 'Soviet family'

Soviet planners had a distinct tendency to standardise, and the general perception was that two or three different apartment designs would accommodate all types of family.[13] This was seemingly the result of both ideological factors (an idealised image of 'the Soviet family') and economic requirements (it was cheaper to mass-produce a limited number of designs). Few concessions were made by urban planners and architects to geographical, cultural and demographic differences. Architect M.G. Barkhin later noted that: 'The country from Brest to Vladivostok was built in identical districts consisting of identical houses.'[14] While references were made to multi-child families consisting of five or more people, and the need to provide appropriate accommodation for them, the 'average family' – which apparently consisted of a married couple with two dependent children – was the main focus of the housing programme.[15]

Yet even a family which started out 'average' would inevitably change over the course of time. As Blair Ruble has pointed out: 'Grandparents die; couples divorce, remarry, grow old; preschool-aged children turn into adolescents, and eventually become adults themselves. Grown children, in turn, may marry and have children, all the while continuing to live with their parents.' This, he points out, presented inevitable problems for 'an immobile housing market with inflexible conceptions of how best to design standardised apartments'.[16]

The problem of changing family size was acknowledged by some Soviet commentators. An article in *Sovetskaya zhenshchina* noted that young people would want to marry when they reached adulthood, and 'a family of two people very quickly becomes a family of three people. Builders have to take this into consideration.'[17] Yet how were they to do so? *Arkhitektura SSSR* (Architecture in the USSR) reported approvingly on a new experimental housing project in Moscow which incorporated moveable cupboards and sliding partitions so that the apartments could be altered: 'each family will be able to modify the layout of the apartment according to its own judgement', increasing the number of rooms when necessary by reducing their size.[18] The extent to which such flimsy partitions would create genuinely separate rooms is questionable, however. Furthermore, in the 'small dimensioned' Khrushchevian apartment, any reduction in room size would have produced little more than shoeboxes.

Despite Khrushchev's insistence that newly-weds would be entitled to their own apartments, in reality there was little chance of a young married couple with no children receiving an apartment. Even when they did have children, they were unlikely to have a new apartment to themselves. Many young families continued to live with one or other set of parents, whether through choice or necessity. As their own children grew up, and had children themselves, their 'single-family' apartment, with its microscopic kitchen, could become as cramped and overcrowded as the *kommunalka* from which they had escaped. The Soviet apartment of the Khrushchev era remained in multiple occupancy, even if it was now occupied by several generations of one family. Those fortunate enough to have a reasonably large apartment might be able to exchange it in due course for two smaller ones in order to give the young family their own space, but there was a potential pitfall in this arrangement: it seems that some families were targeted by gold-diggers who wanted to marry into the family in order to get their hands on an apartment. As we shall see, this was a common theme in the short stories appearing in *Ogonek*.

A single-family apartment might also contain non-family members. Alexander Werth, visiting Moscow in the Khrushchev era, noted that the newspaper *Vechernyaya Moskva* (Evening Moscow) regularly carried advertisements for rooms to let, most of which were in new apartments: 'if a fairly large family had a three-room flat, and had only a small income, they were content to cram into two rooms, and let the third one for good money. A lifetime spent in "communal flat" conditions had largely conditioned them to sharing a flat with a stranger.'[19] Since most Soviet women worked, and there were not enough crèches and kindergartens, it was also not uncommon for a family with young children to squeeze a live-in childminder into their apartment.

If a young couple was unlikely to get assigned an apartment to itself, a single person had virtually no chance. Despite the predictions in the 1920s that the family would 'wither away' under socialism, Stalin had put it firmly back in the centre of Soviet life, and by the Khrushchev era being single was considered either a temporary phenomenon or a sad consequence of the post-war demographic crisis. There was no acknowledgement that some people may want to live alone, and no provision for them to do so. The journal *Arkhitektura SSSR* put this in a positive light, insisting that single people did not need the same type of accommodation as families, since they 'do not undertake housekeeping'[20] and that it would be more appropriate for them to live 'in specially constructed, improved hostels, with rooms for one to two people, and a semi-hotel type system: that is, their rooms will be cleaned, their sheets washed for them. There will be a canteen and some form of cultural service (reading room, room for rest and games, etc.).'[21]

If apartment design was over-standardised, there was little standardisation in distribution. City councils had some housing at their disposal, which they assigned to people whose existing accommodation was so poor that it was to be demolished. Most of the new housing, however, was under the control of factories and enterprises, and was in theory assigned to workers according to three main criteria: how productive they were in their jobs, how acute was their housing need[22] and how long they had been working at the factory or enterprise. Yet confused letters to the press make it clear that in reality these norms were constantly flouted.[23] *Trud* (Labour), the trade union newspaper, was particularly concerned about housing matters, and frequently reported on the dubious ways in which new apartments were assigned to tenants. It found that decisions were often made on the whim of an individual, and that this provided much scope for corruption. For example, it was not uncommon for apartments to be given to important officials in return for political favours.[24] Nor were apartments always assigned to appropriately sized families. One journalist reported that eighty families were moved into a new apartment block in Volgograd, but only twenty-eight of those received flats which met 'existing sanitary norms concerning living-space'. Fourteen families were given apartments with too much space for their needs, while fifty families found themselves squeezed into apartments that were too small. This happened, the journalist argued, because the housing department was concerned only with matching the appropriate number of people to the apartment block as a whole.[25]

Women suffered considerable discrimination in housing distribution. In view of the demographic peculiarities of the post-war period, they formed a disproportionate share of the long-term single, and hence of long-term, hostel residents; indeed, many single women lived in hostels for most of their lives.[26] Yet even having a family did not ensure that a woman received equal treatment. V.M. Polishchuk complained in *Rabotnitsa* in 1958 that she had been denied a new apartment, despite the fact that she met all the appropriate criteria: she was recognised as an excellent worker, she and her large family (she had four children) lived in very inadequate housing and she had worked in the same factory for eight years. The president of the factory committee justified his decision on the grounds that he only assigned apartments to heads of families and, since Polishchuk was married, he insisted that she could not be the head of her family. It was up to her husband to 'take care of the apartment situation' through his place of work.[27] Being dependent on her husband for her accommodation had inevitable repercussions for a woman if the marriage broke down. As noted in another *Rabotnitsa* article, 'It can happen that a woman wants to leave an alcoholic husband, but she has nowhere to go. It was he who was assigned the apartment, and he is not prepared to go anywhere else.'[28]

A woman who had children but no husband fared no better in obtaining an apartment. A fatherless family, of which there were inevitably many in the post-war period, seems not to have been considered a family at all when it came to apartment allocation. Although all apartments built after 1958 were supposedly intended only for single-family occupancy, some communal apartments were actually being established in the new apartment blocks. A 1962 article in *Trud* told of a mother and daughter who were allocated a room in a new apartment which already had a resident, an elderly woman. She was clearly not happy about sharing the apartment with strangers, and began by locking them out; then, when forced by the authorities to back down, she presented them with a list of draconian rules concerning their use of the common areas. Eventually they bought an electric hotplate and withdrew to their own small room. The article's author, M. Moisyuk, complained not about the fact that strangers were still being placed together in the new apartments, but that the old woman had brought 'her old norms and habits with her'. It would seem that the mere fact that the apartments were new, whether or not they were self-contained, was meant to result in improved attitudes in their residents.[29]

Private 'ownership' of single-family apartments: 'self-build' and cooperatives

The hugely ambitious plans for dealing with the housing shortage put enormous pressure on the state budget. Alternative sources of funding had to be encouraged, even if they seemed to challenge socialist housing principles. This led to an awkward compromise, with private housing being promoted alongside the new state-owned apartment blocks. Since private property clearly contradicted the social ethos, the term in official use was 'personal' rather than 'private'. The difference was supposedly, as Mark Smith explains, that personal property 'derived from a citizen's own labour, and as it was only for personal use ... by definition it could not actively exploit another citizen'.[30]

Initially, this 'personal housing' took the form of 'self-build'. This was an initiative which had begun in a fairly modest way at the end of the Stalin era,[31] but was now expanded and heavily promoted. Individual workers, or groups of workers, were encouraged to join together into amateur building brigades and construct their own small houses in their free time. The response was phenomenal. According to the journal *Novyi mir* (New World), in some towns these amateur brigades produced more than a third of the annual total of new residential housing.[32] *Trud*, attempting to explain the phenomenon in socialist terms, insisted that self-build was so successful because the Khrushchev reforms inspired a 'high socialist consciousness' in workers.[33] In reality, it seems more likely that the workers were inspired by the prospect of inhabiting, even owning, their own living space. This, as Steven Harris points out, had great psychological importance: people felt like 'masters of their worlds, ... more in control and more responsible for the spaces and things around them'.[34] As we noted at the start of this book, this sense of control over one's living space is one of the crucial aspects of feeling 'at home'.

Financial arrangements differed from city to city. The land was generally provided by the factory or enterprise, which in some cases also paid professional builders to give advice and assistance. Other expenses were shared between the builders' factories or enterprises, the local authorities, and in some cases the builders themselves, with the latter usually eligible for bank loans. As with housing construction cooperatives in the 1920s, 'self-build' was a way of using the capital and labour of the population itself to help solve the housing problem. It was not clear who actually owned the property, however. An article in *Trud*, arguing that the amateur builders should be paid for their work, justified this by explaining that 'the houses built by them belong to the enterprises and the state. And everyone who receives living space in them will have to pay rent.'[35] In reality it was not that clear-cut, and differed from city to city.

Women, as usual, were not in an equal position. While there were some references in the press to them joining building brigades, this was presented as a novelty,[36] despite the fact that they had been heavily involved in construction work in the immediate post-war period. 'Self-build' was an overwhelmingly male phenomenon. This meant that few women could acquire an apartment in their own right, and were, again, dependent on their husbands.

The encouragement of private building did not last. Concerns were expressed about the quality of the workmanship, and about the amorphous urban spread which resulted from the proliferation of one- and two-storey houses.[37] In addition, private ownership was clearly not a socialist solution to the housing problem, and sat awkwardly with Khrushchev's enthusiastic declaration that full communism would be achieved by 1980. Accordingly, there was, to quote DiMaio, 'a wave of confiscations of privately owned housing' from 1961,[38] and in January 1964 a ban on private housing construction in cities with more than 100,000 inhabitants.[39]

The housing cooperative, which Stalin had effectively brought to an end in 1937 by prohibiting access to state loans, now represented, at least to some housing officials, a more attractive way of supplementing the state housing fund. Accordingly, it was revived in 1958, but under a new name: instead of the old Workers' Housing Cooperative Association, it was now known simply as the House-Construction Cooperative (*Zhilishchno-stroitel'nyi kooperativ*, or *ZhSK*). In fact some housing cooperatives had come into being in the late Stalin era, and a few had even managed to arrange state loans, despite the official ban; rules could always be broken, even in the Stalin era.[40] The cooperative's supporters, according to Harris, promoted it 'by taking advantage of the populist approval of people's construction';[41] yet it actually catered to quite different people. Self-build had been a largely working-class phenomenon, while members of cooperatives were more often white-collar professionals who could afford to pay for their housing rather than build it themselves.[42] Some self-build houses were actually pulled down to free up plots for cooperative apartment blocks, and their owners were given little in the way of compensation.[43] Clearly cooperatives represented a challenge to equality, and made some politicians uneasy; Khrushchev himself expressed concern that the members of cooperatives were getting separate apartments out of turn.[44] All the same, the additional funds cooperatives brought to the house building programme, and the fact that they made more intensive use of available land (building multi-storey apartment blocks rather than small individual houses), outweighed such objections. Another point in their favour was that the apartments would remain under social ownership, i.e. they would be owned by the cooperative rather than its individual members. This meant that cooperative housing sounded more socialist than self-build private housing, whatever the reality.

Initially state credits were still unavailable, and members of a cooperative had to put up the entire cost of construction before the work could begin. However, this ruled out all but those with a considerable horde of savings, and hence failed to create the conditions in which cooperatives could flourish and create a genuine alternative to state housing.[45] Accordingly, in 1962 they were granted the right to apply for loans which would pay up to 60 per cent of the estimated cost of construction, to be repaid over a period of ten to fifteen years.[46] All the same, members had to contribute themselves what was for most people an enormous sum of money. Accordingly, cooperative housing developed at a slow rate. It only began to play a significant role in the housing programme from the mid-1960s, when Khrushchev was no longer in power.

'Private ownership' of state housing

It was not only residents of self-build or cooperative housing who were able to feel themselves 'masters of their world'. Tenants of the new single-family apartments in the state sector could also experience some sense of ownership. The fact that they no longer had to share their accommodation with strangers inevitably granted them greater privacy and personal control over their living space, and the housing programme was also accompanied by an increase in tenants' rights, such as greater security of tenure.[47] As Mark Smith explains, by the late Khrushchev era, residents of state housing could only be evicted if they were guilty of 'acute violation' of their obligations as tenants, and even then, they had the right to argue their case in court. Furthermore, if a family member or members moved out of the apartment it was no longer likely that a stranger would be moved in, even though the remaining residents would now have more space than the sanitary norm.[48] Tenants did not have the legal right to sell their apartments, but they were able to exchange them with people living in other state apartments. They could not officially bequeath their apartments to their offspring, but this was not actually necessary; as Smith explains, if one resident died, as long as the other family members were registered to live at the apartment they could not be evicted.[49] The result of these changes was that tenants began to develop a sense of private ownership of their homes.

The single-family apartment and new forms of socialist community

This 'privatisation' of family life was problematic for the authorities. They were not inclined to allow people to close their doors and disappear into their own private space. Accordingly, the move to single-family accommodation was accompanied by much socialist rhetoric. As Christine Varga-Harris explains, 'although the separate family apartment connoted privacy, the home was intended to be a site for the rejuvenation of the collectivist spirit and the revival of socialist activism'.[50]

One way of encouraging a new type of socialist community was to ensure the heterogeneity of residents of the new apartment blocks. Accordingly, articles in the press made much of the fact that government ministers, professors, factory workers, actors, teachers, engineers and writers apparently lived happily alongside one another, offering mutual support and friendship.[51] One article in *Sovetskaya zhenshchina* told how retired residents imparted their knowledge and skills to their new neighbours; a former dancer, for example, set up a dance circle for the children in her block and her (female) neighbours sewed the costumes for their shows, while a former gardener became 'chief gardening consultant' for his block, helping his neighbours decorate their apartments and balconies with plants.[52] An article in *Trud* urged residents to put to good use their 'variety of interesting professions' by devoting an hour or two per week to chatting with neighbours about their work, and helping younger residents make their career choices.[53] According to *Rabotnitsa*, in some cases residents had so many professional skills to put at each others' service that it was seldom necessary for anyone to call out a plumber or electrician. Neighbours also took it in turns to clean and paint the entranceways and stairwells of their buildings.[54] The 'communal apartment', then, had been replaced by the 'communal apartment block'.

There was also a revival of the *domkom* or house committee, which had played an important role in the 1920s but had since fallen into abeyance. It now took the form of a residents' group which organised communal ventures such as libraries and crèches. In Buchli's words, it 'refocus[ed] the inward looking petit-bourgeois household outwards on to socialist, public, and communal activities'.[55]

A much-lauded socialist housing innovation of the late Khrushchev era was the 'micro-district' (*mikroraion*). This was to be a complete community, built outside of the city, which would meet all of its residents' domestic and recreational needs. As Ruble put it, 'individual apartment units were merely the smallest part of an all-encompassing system.'[56] This included schools, crèches and kindergartens, shops, public dining rooms, sports and leisure facilities such as libraries and cinemas, and shaded garden areas.[57] In some apartment blocks the ground floor would accommodate an 'apartment block kitchen' [*dom khukhnya*], producing ready-prepared meals which housewives could take home to their families. In some respects the micro-district can be seen as a reincarnation, in miniaturised form, of the 'socialist city' which had assumed such importance in the first Five Year Plan.

Micro-districts had a number of defects, however, which, again, affected women in particular. Despite pledges to the contrary, few provided even basic services and amenities, at least in the early years of their existence. As Barkhin admitted, 'Social buildings were hardly even worked into the projects, and were not built.'[58] Residents had to make gruelling journeys to the nearest city just to take care of their basic domestic needs, and guests from the city had to bring huge bags full of essential items with them when they came to visit.[59] Crèches and kindergartens, which were supposed to be an integral part of the micro-district, were in reality not seen as priorities,[60] and some women were forced to give up work because they had nowhere to leave their children.[61] The laundries and other domestic facilities that were supposed to appear alongside the apartment blocks failed to materialise, while the apartment blocks themselves sometimes lacked the most basic services. One *Rabotnitsa* journalist, L. Travkin, found that women in some new districts outside Orel had no choice but to spend their one free day per week doing their family's washing, hauling the water up to their apartments from standpipes, instead of enjoying the leisure activities which were supposed to be a central part of Soviet life.[62]

The geography of the new apartment

According to an article in *Rabotnitsa*, the optimum size for a one-room apartment was 18 to 20 square metres; of a two-room apartment, 30 square metres; and a three-room apartment, 36 to 40 square metres. Accordingly, the more rooms an apartment had, the smaller each would be. These figures did not include the space required for the kitchen (which should be 6 square metres), nor the bathroom.[63] Architects L. Bumazhnyi and A. Zal'tsman proposed that room size ultimately be reduced still further, to 10 or 11 square metres. This would make it possible to have more rooms in the apartment without increasing its overall size, which would enable the family 'to save the living room of the apartment from being used as a sleeping area; [and] to have separate bedrooms for the parents and children.'[64] This would create 'more normal conditions for raising children and for leisure activities for the older members of the family'[65] – a coded suggestion, perhaps, that sexual activities could be carried out in private.

Corridors were kept to a minimum. As well as saving space, this made it easier to assemble the apartments from prefabricated sections. However, cutting down on corridor space had a major drawback. It often resulted in the largest room, which functioned as the family's living room, being directly linked to all the other rooms, so everyone had to walk through that room to get to the kitchen, the bathroom and their own sleeping quarters. According to Harris, the architects, who had no control over the distribution of the new apartments, introduced the walk-through room as a way of preventing the apartment from being assigned to more than one family,[66] though this was not always successful.[67] The architects also intended the walk-through room to be a common area in which no one would sleep, but this was a luxury few could achieve. Inevitably, the privacy of the family members who had to sleep in this room was severely compromised. As years passed, it became common for people to reconstruct their apartments and separate the walk-through room from its neighbours by creating extra corridor space, even though this made the rooms themselves even smaller.[68] In the last years of the Khrushchev era the mistake was tacitly acknowledged, and new apartments were built without walk-through rooms.

Feathering the nest: furnishing and decorating the new apartment

The single-family apartment needed furnishing and decorating, and the magazines offered copious advice on how this should be done. As one commentator put it in *Trud*, taste 'is an essential part of our world view, and it needs to be addressed seriously'.[69] This was echoed in *Rabotnitsa*, which called for a 'fight against incorrect tastes'.[70] The advice was invariably addressed to the 'housewife'.

The ideal Stalinist apartment had been portrayed as a cosy mass of furniture and furnishings, all in different colours and patterns. There was a heavy dining table; large armchairs; possibly an ornate carpet hung on the wall; chandeliers, and side-lamps with tassled shades; and an abundance of house plants and lace doilies. In contrast, good taste in the Khrushchev era was based on simplicity, modesty and utility. The magazines urged readers to ensure that curtains and drapes were in quiet tones, with no contrasting colours or designs. Furniture should have more than one function: sofas should turn into beds and incorporate hidden linen cupboards, bookcase doors should open out to form writing desks or dining tables, and crockery cupboards should be concealed beneath table tops.[71] Furniture should also be discreetly placed: 'The large dinner table, standing usually in the middle of the room and taking up a lot of space, should be replaced by a fold-away table positioned next to the wall'.[72]

If something did not serve a practical function, it should be removed. Gol'dshtein, writing in *Rabotnitsa*, chastised housewives for cluttering up their apartments with useless things which they considered beautiful, and pointed out how the very concept of beauty was linked to class and culture:

The *boyars*⁷³ wore heavy, uncomfortable fur coats; they considered that these were beautiful. Primitive men put fish bones and wooden sticks through their noses; they considered that this was beautiful. In ancient China girls bound their feet so that they would not grow; they considered that this was beautiful. We, however, consider that what is uncomfortable and inadvisable cannot be beautiful, [and] advise you to remove from the flat everything that you do not use.⁷⁴

In similar vein, Kropivnitskii complained that:

> Sometimes dining tables, bedside tables, shelves, radios, lamps, are all covered by pieces of cloth and napkins; carpets are hung on the walls, and there are chiffoniers on the doors and even on armchairs and picture frames. It goes without saying that this makes the apartment look ugly.⁷⁵

Kamenskii insisted that 'rose coloured, orange and lilac lampshades, ... "decorated" with frills and fringes', were more appropriate 'in the boudoirs of bourgeois apartments'.⁷⁶ Kropivnitskii was particularly scathing about decorative embellishments which impeded the function of an object, resulting in 'comfort in the apartment [being] sacrificed to imagined beauty'.⁷⁷ One of his acquaintances, he related, was forced to take naps in an armchair because the bed was always covered with carefully placed cushions, and his wife scolded him if the arrangement was disturbed.

The fact that the new apartments were 'small dimensioned' was a major factor in the drive for simplicity. Some authors were honest about this, advising housewives that plain colours, simple patterns and a lack of clutter would help create an illusion of space.⁷⁸ There was also no room in these miniature apartments for the large, fussy furniture which had featured in the magazines' depictions of the ideal Stalinist home.

However, there was more to it than this. Susan Reid has argued that definitions of beauty and taste were part of the battle against Stalinism, and 'became central terms in the discourse of destalinisation'.⁷⁹ This is supported by the articles looked at in this study. Excessive decoration in furnishings, as in architecture, was denounced as a throwback to the Stalin era, an indication of bourgeois or petit-bourgeois proclivities, and a primitive and uncouth understanding of beauty. In this way Stalinism was linked to both bourgeois and primitive tastes.

If the creation of a new Soviet understanding of beauty and taste was part of the de-Stalinisation campaign, then the implications, to quote Reid once more, 'reached far beyond the purely aesthetic'.⁸⁰ This would explain the fact that, while advice about domestic matters was aimed at women and appeared primarily in women's magazines, much of it was penned by men. It was clearly an issue important enough to lure men into the feminine world of curtains and carpets.

The attempt to achieve a high degree of standardisation in the self-contained apartment might also have been a way of counteracting its potential for creating a degree of privacy which was thought excessive in a socialist society. Some factories actually furnished and decorated the apartments they allocated to their workers. An article in *Trud* talked enthusiastically of residents' surprise and delight when they turned up at their new homes to find them already equipped with 'beautiful and comfortable chairs, book cases and tables, beds and other small-scale furniture', and 'even curtains and lace in the windows'.[81] There seems to have been no consultation with the residents as to what furniture and furnishings they actually wanted to have in their homes.

Some commentators accepted that people might want to stamp their own personalities on their apartments,[82] and suggested they display a small amount of their own handiwork. After all, 'the majority of girls and women love to do needlework – to embroider, sew, decorate textiles, sew on lace'.[83] Others were more nervous about encouraging dangerous individualism. *Rabotnitsa* readers were even urged by one writer to replace their handmade quilts with mass-produced alternatives imported from China, which 'are more beautiful because they are simpler and more practical'.[84]

It was the woman's task to create the nest; her husband had simply to enjoy it. As one *Trud* reader pointed out in a letter to the newspaper, much of the work that men traditionally did, such as chopping wood and fetching water, was unnecessary in a well-equipped city home.[85] The self-contained apartment created a more conducive environment for entertaining and, judging from articles and stories in the press, one of the man's principal contributions to domestic life was to invite the guests. A *Rabotnitsa* journalist, visiting a new apartment block in Leningrad, found a mother and daughter worrying about how best 'to make things cosy'; hanging up curtains would make a crucial difference but they would have to wait until 'Papa [can] help us on Sunday'. Little did they know that Papa had no intention of helping them; he was 'giving up his beloved fishing' on Sunday, but 'in order to invite friends over for a housewarming gathering'.[86]

While inviting guests was largely a male prerogative, tending to their needs was the woman's duty. An article in *Sovetskaya zhenshchina* discussed the range of beautiful table settings, cutlery and crockery which would help women entertain more elegantly: 'Every housewife wants to set the table beautifully when guests are coming ... and this wish is being satisfied now by the increased variety of beautiful things being introduced by many factories.'[87] A *Trud* commentator was less enthusiastic about this new trend for entertaining, complaining that women were expected to drop everything and produce food and drink whenever their husbands turned up with guests.[88] A short story in *Rabotnitsa* offered a particularly chilling scenario, of a man inviting friends over to celebrate International Women's Day. Although this was supposed to be the woman's special day, his wife had to cook and serve their food, and, although the guests raised their glasses to her, she could not drink herself because she did not like vodka and her husband had not thought to buy any wine. The story ended with one guest so drunk that she had to put him to bed with her husband, leaving her with nowhere to sleep.[89]

Domestic appliances and services

The housing programme was accompanied by a commitment to increase the availability of domestic appliances: washing machines, fridges, freezers, pressure cookers, irons, vacuum cleaners, floor polishers, and so on. A female journalist writing in *Trud* suggested hopefully that if the technological aspects of this new machinery were emphasised, men might be more willing to use it.[90] However, few commentators in the women's magazines followed this lead, and articles on labour-saving devices were invariably addressed at women, and illustrated by photographs of women putting them through their paces. Children's toys reflected the new interest in domesticity, and little girls were depicted earnestly gliding miniaturised irons over dolls' dresses and preparing lunch on toy ovens.

Readers were told that this expansion in the household goods industry was aimed at 'lighten[ing] the woman's domestic work, economis[ing] on the housewife's time'.[91] The same was supposedly true of the increase in domestic services now available within the community. Yet, as well as reducing the time women had to spend on housework, providing more public services can also be seen as an attempt to counteract the increasingly privatised nature of family life.

Particular attention was paid to alternatives to home cooking. Public dining rooms were strongly recommended,[92] with *Trud* claiming that the Communist Party had set itself the task of ensuring that within ten to fifteen years it would be more common for people to eat in public dining rooms than at home.[93] For those who could not be lured out of the home, takeaway meals were available from some dining rooms and 'apartment block kitchens' in the new micro-districts,[94] and ready-made meals and washed and chopped vegetables were now on sale in delicatessen sections of food shops.[95] The press also drew attention to the growth in the number of public laundries, some of which were actually located in the new apartment blocks,[96] and to 'the fairy-tale growth' in the number of child care facilities: crèches, kindergartens, prolonged-day schools, after-school play groups and boarding schools.[97]

Yet, as more candid commentators acknowledged, the supply and quality of labour-saving devices and services remained inadequate.[98] The public dining rooms, so celebrated in the press, were unpopular since 'the food is unappetising and expensive'.[99] There were too few laundries, and they had a reputation for tearing sheets and clothes.[100] Despite the supposed 'fairy-tale' growth in the number of crèches and kindergartens, in reality some women gave up their jobs to look after their children, while others left them unsupervised while they were at work.[101]

It could also be argued that in some respects the new domestic appliances, and in general the state's new interest in the domestic realm, threatened to increase women's workload by raising expectations about the quality of their housekeeping. The director of the Institute of Experimental Planning of the Academy of Builders and Architects of the USSR, Boris Rubanenko, was asked in an interview in *Rabotnitsa* about what was being done to alleviate women's domestic workload, and replied that the Institute of Residential Life (*Institut zhilishch*) was preparing a series of books and brochures full of domestic tips, in which housewives 'will find out how best to equip their workplace in the kitchen, how to create a children's corner, how to make a beautiful window display, how to select wallpaper and material for upholstery – in a word, everything that will help them to equip and beautify their apartments with taste and convenience'.[102] This seems to be aimed less at lightening the workload than turning it into a hobby.

Fictional representations of the Khrushchev housing programme

Given the pledge to provide every family with its own apartment, it is not surprising that the separate apartment now took over from the communal apartment as the predominant setting for the magazines' fiction. Yet few of the stories focused on the pleasure families derived from having their own space. As the years passed, young children turned into adults, sometimes marrying and moving their spouses into their already cramped apartments. Overcrowding resulted in fraught family relationships, and the multi-generation occupancy challenged the original definition of a 'separate' apartment. The ensuing tensions, and the attempted solutions, presented a rich new source of material for authors.

The stories generally focused on the relationships between a young man, his mother, and his new wife, who had come to live with them.[103] Greater female longevity could explain the preponderance of mother-in-laws, but the fact that it was always a young wife who moved into her husband's family apartment might be explained by the Soviet Union's unexamined patriarchal attitudes towards gender, despite its insistence on female equality. The wife was treated as her husband's new possession and, as such, she had to be installed in his home.

Although the type of housing had changed, the notion that marriages might be forged on the basis of housing need remained a common theme. In one *Ogonek* story, a young woman called Alla moved in with her new husband Boris and his mother, and tried immediately to persuade them to exchange the apartment for two smaller ones so that she and Boris could have a place of their own. When she failed to get her way, she filed for divorce on the grounds of incompatibility. Applications for divorce now had to go before a judge, and the judge presiding over this case insisted that the couple could not know yet if they were incompatible because they were still very young and their characters would go through many changes. Alla agreed to stay with her husband if 'I can wait for these changes to take place in a separate apartment'. This seemed to confuse the judge, who pointed that they were already living in a separate apartment, which they shared with Boris's mother. 'That's just the point!', Alla exploded. After she moved out, Boris's friends confessed to him that they had always found her excessively interested in his material circumstances, and in particular what kind of apartment he lived in. Alla, it turned out, had married to get an apartment; she had little interest in her husband.[104]

In another tale it was the young man who was preoccupied with improving his housing. This story is set in the countryside, but is still relevant because it reflects Khrushchev's efforts to eradicate the distinction between the city and the countryside. The protagonist is a collective farm worker called Vladimir Kharitov, who had decided to move to the city because he thought he might procure better housing there. He had a girlfriend, Vera, but although she loved him to distraction, he seemed somewhat indifferent to her; certainly their relationship was not important enough to him to keep him on the farm. His main concern was that he lived in a hostel, and had no prospect of getting anything better. However, Khrushchev's building programme had not ignored the countryside, and the farm had been sent six prefabricated houses. Vladimir helped to assemble them, and was offered one in return for his hard work. He was surprised at the offer, since he was unmarried and had no children; but the farm's director, looking significantly at Vera, assured him that would soon change. Vladimir looked round his new home with a passion lacking in his relationship with Vera:

> The house had turned out splendidly, like in a picture. The walls were white, smooth, without a single fault. The red tiled roof had been laid superbly, tile by tile. The window frames fit so precisely that not even a gnat would be able to squeeze in ... On the left was the first room. Kharitov looked at it attentively ... He would paint this room a light green, he thought. He went into the second room ... The window was open and was rattling in the wind; a bright patch of sunlight spread across the floor. Kharitov went over to the window and secured the catch on the frame. The sunny patch moved to the corner, where it sat motionless. 'Yes, pale green would be the best', Kharitov thought again, looking round the room.[105]

Vera waited quietly in the kitchen for Vladimir to complete his tour. She was delighted to be keeping her man, even though he paid more attention to his new house than to her. Indeed, the house seemed to be his real love; her function was to provide the necessary family status to secure it for him. It is significant that she waited for him in the kitchen; this seems a tacit acceptance of the fact that this was the room in which she would now spend most of her time.

The Khrushchev housing programme: successes, failures and outcomes

The Khrushchev housing programme did constitute a major turning point. For the first time in the Soviet Union's history, housing was actually placed on the country's list of priorities.[106] As we noted earlier, a third of the total Soviet population were rehoused in the course of six years, between 1957 and 1963,[107] most of whom did receive separate apartments. The pleasure people derived from finally having their own family space, and the sense of privacy, control and 'mental tranquility' which came with it, was enormous.[108]

Yet there were major flaws to the programme. Most obviously, it failed to achieve its main pledge, which was that every family would be provided with a separate apartment within twelve years. By the early 1960s it was apparent that this would not happen, and the time frame was extended; Khrushchev declared to the XXI Party Congress that every family would have its own apartment 'by the end of the next decade'.[109] This also failed to come about, but by then it was no longer Khrushchev's responsibility.

Even if a family was rehoused, it was not necessarily into a separate apartment. When the more fortunate families moved into their own apartments, others were assigned their old living space; it might have been larger and better than what they had before, but it was still communal.[110] We have also noted that some of the new apartments were actually settled as communal apartments. Indeed, as late as the 1960s, more than one family was still being moved into some 8 to 10 per cent of supposedly single-family apartments.[111] To borrow Harris's observation, then, 'by the end of the decade one could still easily end up with just more space in a communal apartment, or a communalized new separate apartment.'[112] To make matters worse, the new apartments, designed for single-family use and hence with tiny kitchens and walk-through rooms, were less appropriate for multiple occupation than the old communal apartments.

Those families who did receive their own apartments found that their initial pleasure was offset by a growing realisation of the inadequacies of their new homes. Shoddy workmanship resulted in such problems as warped door and window frames, erratic gas and electricity supplies and poor noise insulation. The latter was particularly galling; as Harris points out, if people still had to put up with their neighbours' noise when they finally had their own apartment, it seemed 'that somehow their move to the separate apartment was incomplete and that a lingering and annoying feature of communal apartment life had stuck with them.'[113]

The new single-family apartment also constituted only a temporary solution to a family's housing difficulties. As we have noted, the housing programme included no provision for the inevitable changes families underwent, and what was initially celebrated as a single-family apartment was eventually inhabited by two or more families. Adults of different ages and often irreconcilable needs had to jostle for space in the common areas, just as they had in communal apartments – and, in the 'small-dimensioned' Khrushchevian apartment, the communal areas were generally far smaller. The fact that the adults were related by blood or marriage did not always alleviate tensions.

Since this was meant to be a socialist society, families were not supposed to close their doors and disappear into their own private space but to engage in new forms of communal living. Yet neighbourliness and a strong sense of community did not figure strongly in the recollections of the former Soviet citizens interviewed for this study. More stress was placed on the pleasures of privacy, however limited. Not having to share cooking and washing facilities with strangers was a huge relief. Despite the Party's attempts to present the move to single-family housing as a new form of socialist living, in reality it did result in a more privatised form of family life. Yet there had been no genuine sense of community in the communal apartments; on the contrary, there was a determined attempt to create as much privacy as was possible. The move to single-family accommodation indulged an existing desire for private family life rather than creating it.

As we have noted, the move to single-family accommodation encouraged not only a sense of private life, but also of private ownership. We referred to a case reported in *Trud* in 1962, of an elderly woman who tried to prevent a mother and daughter being moved into the apartment she clearly saw as her own.[114] Smith reports a similar tale, in which a couple deemed to have surplus space 'behaved with vicious proprietorship over "their" state apartment' when the housing authorities attempted to move in someone else: 'People were aware, of course, that a Soviet or [workplace]-owned dwelling did not formally belong to them, but they consistently invoked different strategies to assume extended rights of possession over it.'[115]

This new sense of home and home ownership also had gender implications. Responsibility for creating a homely atmosphere and of meeting the enhanced domestic needs of their families was placed firmly on women's shoulders. Accordingly, moving to a single-family apartment was portrayed as more important to them than to their husbands. In *Trud*, one male resident of a new apartment block was quoted as saying: 'It is difficult to convey how glad we all were – especially our wives.'[116] In another article, a woman talked of the delight of feeling herself 'to be completely the boss. For a woman housekeeper, that, to speak honestly, means a lot'.[117] *Sovetskaya zhenshchina* noted that 'children and husbands are simply pleased' at the prospect of moving to their own apartment, while women took a much more active interest in details.[118] For women the home may have been a second workplace, but it also allowed them a feeling of control. Women's magazines reflected the new emphasis on home life, devoting much more space to the family and to traditional female interests such as fashion, cooking and home furnishings.

Some effort was made to challenge the idea that women should have to bear the entire domestic burden, and articles did appear, in the general press as well as women's magazines, which discussed ways in which men could be encouraged to develop a more domestic orientation.[119] Elena Kononenko, writing in *Rabotnitsa* and *Krest'yanka* [The Peasant Woman], was the most notable crusader for women's equality; she insisted that even seemingly progressive men could turn into tyrants behind the front doors of their own apartments, and that those who mistreated their wives should be publicly shamed and forced to undergo a programme of resocialisation. Women also had to learn to stand up to their men: 'We must stir up such wives, help them, teach them to use the rights granted them by Soviet power and the laws of Leninist Communist morality.'[120]

Kononeko was in a small minority, however. The majority of commentators accepted that housework would inevitably remain a female function. The lifestyle of the typical woman of the Khrushchev era, living with her family in a self-contained apartment, was summed up in one *Rabotnitsa* article as follows: 'Having come home from work, the woman puts on an apron and begins to bustle around the kitchen: she makes supper, irons, washes, mends...'[121]

The Soviet Union and the West

A new emphasis on domesticity was also a strong feature of life in the United States in the post-war era, where, according to Elaine Tyler May, the traditional family was a reassuring symbol of security in the context of the cold war and the nuclear age.[122] It also functioned as a bulwark against possible threats from within, such as the independent sexually aggressive single woman who some feared was the likely legacy of 'Rosie the Riveter'.[123]

The Soviet Union did not have the means to provide its citizens with the large suburban homes extolled in the United States, and was ideologically opposed to the private home ownership which was a prominent part of the American Dream. Yet it still felt compelled to compete with its fellow super power. In the so-called 'kitchen debate' which took place between Nixon and Khrushchev at the American National Exhibition in Moscow in 1959, as Tyler May notes, the two men 'did not discuss missiles, bombs, or even modes of government. Rather, they argued over the relative merits of American and Soviet washing machines, televisions, and electric ranges.'[124]

There was a major difference between Soviet and American 'housewives' of this era. This was that Soviet women continued to play an essential role as paid workers in social production. Indeed, Khrushchev professed his determination to tackle gender inequalities in the workplace, and women's magazines continued to stress the importance of women having a professional and public life.[125] However, within the walls of the Soviet apartment, gender roles remained almost as distinct as they were in the American surburban home. The pinafored Soviet woman portrayed in the pages of the women's magazines, smiling over her new gas cooker and vacuum cleaner, looked remarkably like her Western counterpart.

Notes

1 By the early 1960s, the time frame had extended; Khrushchev declared to the XXI Party Congress that 'by the end of the next decade' every family would have its own self-contained apartment. N.S. Khrushchev, *Khrushchev Remembers*, translated and edited by S. Talbott (London: André Deutsch, 1974), p. 2. In fact there were never enough apartments to meet demand. See K. Zhukhov, 'Bol'shoe novosel'e i bol'shie zadachi', *Novyi mir* no. 2 (1963), pp. 230–8; I. Mendzheritskii, 'Zdes' byla derevnya', *Sovetskaya zhenshchina* no. 3 (1963), pp. 9–12.
2 The seven-year plan was dropped on 13 March 1963 on the grounds that it had been rendered out of date by the new economic changes ordered by the Communist Party Central Committee in November 1962. See A. Sobel (ed.), *Russia's Rulers: The Khrushchev Period* (New York: Facts on File, 1971), p. 328.
3 A. Werth, *The Khrushchev Phase: The Soviet Union Enters the 'Decisive' Sixties* (London: Robert Hale, 1961) p. 139.
4 See, for example, two small articles in *Trud* (1 September 1957), p. 1, both entitled 'Stroit' bystro, deshevo, khorosho'.
5 See, for example, G. Gradov, 'Sovetskuyu arkhitekturu na uroven' novykh zadach', in *Arkhitektura SSSR* no. 2 (1955), p. 5; 'Zabota o cheloveke – osnova sovetskogo gradostroitel'stva', editorial article in *Arkhitektura SSSR* no. 6 (1960), pp. 1–3; and Werth, *The Khrushchev Phase*, p. 142.
6 Gradov, 'Sovetskuyu arkhitekturu na uroven' novykh zadach', pp. 4–8.
7 In fact, the use of concrete was not as widespread as was desired. Engineer M. Taub noted in *Trud* in 1957 that in 1956 only 10 to 11 per cent of Moscow buildings were made out of large concrete panels; see 'Doma iz krupnykh blokov', *Trud* (9 May 1957), p. 2. According to Ruble this had risen to just over a quarter by 1965, and to half a decade later. See B.A. Ruble, 'From Khrushcheby to Korobki', in W.C. Brumfield and B.A. Ruble (eds), *Russian Housing in the Modern Age: Design and Social History* (Cambridge: Cambridge University Press, 1993), p. 243.
8 Towards the end of Khrushchev's time in office, technological improvements reduced costs, resulting in far higher blocks.
9 See, for example, 'Pravil'no, nauchno reshat' problemy tipizatsii zhilykh domov', editorial article, *Arkhitektura SSSR* no. 5 (1956), pp. 1–4; B. Olenko, 'V novom, "malometrazhnom" dome', *Trud* (26 March 1957), p. 2; T. Druzhinina, 'Vse dlya sovetskogo cheloveka', *Rabotnitsa* no. 11 (1958), pp. 21–2.
10 Khrushchev, *Khrushchev Remembers*, p. 101.
11 Gradov, 'Sovetskuyu arkhitekturu na uroven' novykh zadach', pp. 4–8.
12 Khrushchev, *Khrushchev Remembers*, p. 102.
13 M.G. Barkhin, *Gorod 1945–1970: Praktika, proekty, teoriya* (Moscow: Stroizdat, 1974) p. 58. See also M. Kostandi and E. Kapustyan, 'Tipy zhilykh domov dlya eksperimental'nogo zhilogo raiona Moskvy', *Arkhitektura SSSR* no. 4 (1961), pp. 17–28, in which they identified three types of housing which would would meet all needs.
14 Barkhin, *Gorod 1945–1970*, p. 58.
15 See L. Lopovok, 'Gorod, dom, kvartira', *Trud* (7 October 1961), p. 2; Lopovok, an architect himself, rails against his colleagues' insistence on designing apartments for the 'average' three person family: 'It must ... be clear that a small self-contained flat, built completely in accordance with the "average" family of three people, will not suit a family of seven to eight people.'

16 Ruble, 'From Khrushcheby to Korobki', pp. 252–3.
17 Mendzheritskii, 'Zdes' byla derevnya', p. 12.
18 V. Borovoi and L. Balanovskii, 'Eksperimental'nyi krupnopanel'nyi zhiloi dom novogo tipa', *Arkhitektura SSSR* no. 5 (1963), pp. 3–7.
19 Werth, *The Khrushchev Phase*, fn., pp. 136–7.
20 Kostandi and Kapustyan, 'Tipy zhilykh domov dlya eksperimental'nogo zhilogo raiona Moskvy', pp. 17–28.
21 L. Bumazhnyi and A. Zal'tsman, 'Perspektivnye tipy zhilykh domov i kvartir', *Arkhitektura SSSR* no. 1 (1959), p. 6. This was echoed by B. Svetlichnyi, 'Zaboty gradostroitelei', *Novyi mir* no. 10 (1958), pp. 211–23, who suggested that for young and single people it might be 'more convenient to live in house communes with all services provided for their domestic needs'. E. Tsuglulieva told of one factory which turned some of its new apartments into hostels for its female workers. See 'V dom v"ekhali zhil'tsy', *Rabotnitsa* no. 10 (1954), p. 3.
22 See, for example, F. Potashnikov, 'Komu predostavit' kvartiry?', *Trud* (30 July 1959), p. 3, response to a letter from a reader about how new flats are assigned. Also K. Olechov, 'Schastlivoe novosel'e', *Trud* (7 November 1959), p. 4, extended caption accompanying a photograph of a family which had just been moved into a new flat; A. Levina, 'Order na kvartiru', *Rabotnitsa*, no. 10 (1961), pp. 15–17; and Tsuglulieva, 'V dom v"ekhali zhil'tsy', p. 3.
23 For example, Potashnikov, 'Komu predostavit' kvartiry?'.
24 See, for example, V. Sevryukov, 'Kto budet zhit' v novom dome?', *Trud* (3 December 1957), p. 1; D. Makarov, 'Novosel'e ne sostoyalos'', *Trud* (12 November 1961), p. 4; G. Sukhov, 'Kakim budet novyi dom?', *Trud* (15 December 1961), p. 5. A light-hearted short story in *Rabotnitsa* also hints that factory housing committees were not always sufficiently diligent in checking the circumstances of applicants: in this tale, a young worker had his mother and three supposedly orphaned nephews move in with him until he was assigned a new apartment, when his 'dependants' suddenly disappeared. Vasilii Kukushkin, 'Novosel'e', *Rabotnitsa* no. 12 (1954), pp. 19–21.
25 G. Sukhov, 'Kakim budet novyi dom?', *Trud* (15 December 1961), p. 5.
26 Interview with Emma Aleksandrovna (see Chapter 12).
27 L. Pozdnyakova, 'Mozhet li zhenshchina byt' glavoi sem'i'?', *Rabotnitsa* no. 10 (1958), p. 23.
28 E. Kononenko, 'Obuzdat' p'yanits! (Po pis'mam chitatelei)', *Rabotnitsa* no. 9 (1964), pp. 23–4.
29 M. Moisyuk, 'Pokhititeli radosti', *Trud* (10 May 1962), p. 4. See also R. Izmailova, 'Klub interesnykh vstrech', *Sovetskaya zhenshchina* no. 9 (1960), pp. 24–8, which refers to one new apartment which housed both a widow and her daughter, and a lathe operator from the neighbouring factory.
30 M.B. Smith, 'Individual Forms of Ownership in the Urban Housing Fund of the USSR, 1944–64', *Slavonic and East European Review* 86:2 (2008), 285.
31 See M. Guterman, 'Sobstvennyi dom rabochego', *Trud* (23 November 1957), p. 3.
32 See E. Mikulina, 'My stroim dom – svoimi silami', *Novyi mir* no. 4 (1958), p. 4.
33 M. Kryglova, 'Na narodnoi stroike', *Trud* (4 September 1957), p. 1.
34 S.E. Harris, 'Moving to the Separate Apartment: Building, Distributing, Furnishing, and Living in Urban Housing in Soviet Russia, 1950s–1960s', Ph.D. dissertation, University of Chicago 2003, p. 159.

35 'Stroitel'stvo zhilishch – vazhnoe obshchenarodnoe delo', *Trud* (6 August 1957), p. 2.
36 See, for example, A. Levina, 'Svoimi silami', *Rabotnitsa*, no. 4 (1957), pp. 9–10.
37 See E. Mikulina, 'My stroim dom – svoimi silami', p. 4.
38 A.J. DiMaio, Jr., *Soviet Urban Housing: Problems and Policies* (New York and London: Duke University Press, 1974), p. 180.
39 Ibid., p. 182.
40 Harris, 'Moving to the Separate Apartment', p. 276.
41 Ibid., p. 301.
42 Ibid., p. 339.
43 Ibid., pp. 329, 331.
44 Ibid., p. 286.
45 Harris tells us that until loans were introduced in 1962 there were only 8,990 cooperatives in the USSR as a whole, 530 of which were in the Russian Federation. Once the state agreed to provide loans the number increased significantly; by 1 November 1964 there were 2,364 cooperatives in the Russian Federation, with a total of 198,755 members. However, they always constituted only a small proportion of total housing construction; in 1966, for example, they comprised only 6.6 per cent of all housing construction. Ibid., pp. 303, 306–7.
46 Ibid., pp. 181–2; also G. Andrusz, *Housing and Urban Development in the USSR* (Basingstoke: Macmillan, 1984), p. 83.
47 Smith, 'Individual Forms of Ownership', p. 286.
48 Smith claims (Ibid., p. 302) that the soviet or department could no longer move a stranger in, but I do know of a case in the 1970s in which a young woman who found herself living alone in a two room apartment – her widowed mother had remarried and moved in with her new husband, and her brother had emigrated – did have a stranger imposed on her. They did not get on well and the other woman moved out, and the family then rallied round and managed to register an aunt at the apartment so that the authorities would not move in another stranger.
49 Ibid., p. 302.
50 C. Varga-Harris, 'Forging Citizenship on the Home Front: Reviving the Socialist Contract and Constructing Soviet Identity during the Thaw', in P. Jones (ed.), *The Dilemmas of De-Stalinization: Negotiating Cultural and Social Change in the Khrushchev Era* (London and New York: Routledge, 2006), p. 102.
51 See, for example, T. Molilevskaya and B. Pokrovskii, 'Nash dom', *Sovetskaya zhenshchina*, no. 7 (1960), pp. 14–17; and Izmailova, 'Klub interesnykh vstrech', pp. 24–8.
52 Molilevskaya and Pokrovskii, 'Nash dom', p. 16.
53 M. Akolupin, from Novosibirsk, 'Chem ogorchen novosel'', *Trud* (28 December 1960), p. 2.
54 M. Voskresenskaya, 'Dom, v kotorom ty zhivesh'', *Rabotnitsa* no. 8 (1962), p. 25.
55 V. Buchli, 'Khrushchev, Modernism, and the Fight against Petit-Bourgeois Consciousness in the Soviet Home', *Journal of Design History* 10:2 (1997), 173–4.
56 Ruble, 'From Khrushcheby to Korobki', p. 250.
57 See, for example, Druzhinina, 'Vse dlya sovetskogo cheloveka', pp. 21–2; Izmailova, 'Klub interesnykh vstrech', pp. 24–8.
58 Barkhin, *Gorod 1945–1970*, p. 60.
59 Interview with Emma Aleksandrovna.
60 L. Burmistrova, 'Trudnosti? Net, ravnodushie!', *Rabotnitsa* no. 9 (1964), pp. 26–7. See

also, in relation to poor services in micro districts, L. Voronkova et al., 'Obedy – na dom', *Trud* (12 November 1959), p. 1; L. Bernaskoni, 'Domovaya kukhnya', *Trud* (29 May 1959), p. 2; G. Voskresenskii, 'Na vykhoda iz doma', *Trud* (12 June 1960), p. 2.
61 Interview with Emma Aleksandrovna. This point is echoed by articles in the press: see, for example, L. Burmistrova and M. Buzhkevich, 'Pavlodar – gorod novostroek', *Rabotnitsa*, no. 7 (1959), pp. 9–11; and Burmistrova, 'Trudnosti? Net, ravnodushie!" pp. 26–7.
62 L. Travkin, 'Gde vystirat' bel'e?', *Rabotnitsa* no. 4 (1959), p. 26.
63 Druzhinina, 'Vse dlya sovetskogo cheloveka', pp. 21–2.
64 L. Bumazhnyi and A. Zal'tsman, 'Perspektivnye tipy zhilykh domov i kvartir', pp. 2, 3, 6, 9.
65 Ibid.
66 Harris, 'Moving to the Separate Apartment', pp. 174, 177, 268.
67 Ibid., p. 268.
68 Personal conversation with Sasha Breigin, son of Mariya Efimovna.
69 L. Kamenskii, 'O vkusakh i bezvkusitse', *Trud* (1 June 1957), p. 2.
70 A. Gol'dshtein, 'Chto takoe uyut', *Rabotnitsa* no. 1 (1959), p. 30.
71 L. Luppov, 'Mebel' dlya kvartir novogo tipa', in *Arkhitektura SSSR* no. 5 (1959), pp. 11–15; V. Viktorov, 'Inter'ery Mauimu Plees', *Sovetskaya zheshchina* no. 10 (1960), pp. 44–5; V. Delle, 'Za prostotu i udobstvo sovremmennoi mebeli', in *Arkhitektura SSSR* no. 1 (1956), pp. 33–6.
72 O. Bayar, 'Sdelaem kvartiru udobnoi i uyutnoi', *Sovetskaya zheshchina* no. 7 (1956), p. 47.
73 The *boyars* were princes in pre-revolutionary times.
74 A. Gol'dshtein, 'Chto takoe uyut', *Rabotnitsa* no. 1 (1959), p. 30.
75 Kropivnitskii, 'Khochetsya posovetovat' khozyaikam', *Sovetskaya zhenshchina* no. 4 (1957), p. 44.
76 L. Kamenskii, 'O vkusakh i bezvkusitse', *Trud* (1 June 1957), p. 2.
77 Kropivnitskii, 'Khochetsya posovetovat' khozyaikam', p. 44.
78 I. Voeikova, 'Oboi dlya kvartira, *Sovetskaya zhenshchina* no. 10 (1954), p. 43.
79 S.E. Reid, 'De-Stalinization and Taste, 1953–1963, *Journal of Design History* 10:2 (1997), 177.
80 Ibid.
81 'Novosel'e', author not named, *Trud* (1 January 1969), p. 2.
82 Architect Irina Voeikova was particularly sympathetic to the notion of personal taste. See her articles 'Oboi dlya kvartiry', *Sovetskaya Zhenzhchina*, no. 10 (1954), p. 43; 'Kak obstavit' svoyu komnatu', *Rabotnitsa* no. 9 (1955), p. 30; 'Vasha kvartira', *Rabotnitsa*, no. 9 (1962), p. 30; and 'Uyut – v prostote', *Rabotnitsa* no. 10 (1964), pp. 30–1.
83 I. Voeikova, 'Kak obstavit' svoyu komnatu', *Rabotnitsa* no. 9 (1955), p. 30. See also Z. Supishchikova, 'Chtoby bylo uyutno', *Rabotnitsa* no. 11 (1961), p. 29, who holds that embroidery is the favourite pastime of many Soviet women. See also N. Lazareva, 'Veshchi rasskazyvayut', *Rabotnitsa* no. 4 (1964), p. 27, who admitted that mass-produced factory furniture, combined with the standardised room layout in the new apartments, did make for a certain monotony. She suggested that this could be counteracted by a 'modest' display of folk art.
84 A. Gol'dshtein, 'Chto takoe uyut', *Rabotnitsa* no. 1 (1959), p. 30.
85 'Dela nashi semeinye', author not named, *Trud* (21 August 1960), p. 2.
86 I. Golovan', 'V novom dome', *Rabotnitsa* no. 5 (1953), pp. 7–8.

87 R. Chaikovskaya, 'Dlya domashnego khozyaistva', *Sovetskaya zhenshchina* no. 11 (1954), pp. 44–5.
88 A. Protopova, 'Muzh', *Trud* (19 March 1960), p. 4.
89 N. Il'ina, 'Kak ya provela prazdnik', *Rabotnitsa* no. 2 (1963), pp. 15–16.
90 Protopova, 'Muzh', p. 4.
91 Chaikovskaya, 'Dlya domashnego khozyaistva', pp. 44–5.
92 See, for example, Protopova, 'Muzh', p. 4; G. Spiridonov, 'Vkusno kormit', khorosho obsluzhivat'', *Trud* (21 February 1960), p. 4.
93 V. Zakharov, 'Chtoby luchshe, chem doma', *Trud* (9 December 1961), p. 5.
94 Ibid., p. 5; and Bernaskoni, 'Domovaya kukhnya', p. 2. According to Zakharov, in the Russian Federation these increased in number from 40 in 1956 to 600 in 1961.
95 'Dlya domashnykh khozyaek', *Trud* (5 March 1959), p. 3.
96 See, for example, A. Levina, 'Sluzhba byta, deistvui!', *Rabotnitsa* no. 9 (1962), p. 6, and M. Angarskaya, 'V domovoi prachechoi', *Rabotnitsa* no. 8 (1955), p. 5.
97 Protopova, 'Muzh', p. 4, and P.S. Ivanov, 'V tret'em godu semiletki', *Rabotnitsa* no. 10 (1961), pp. 4–5.
98 See, for example, B. Kosharovskii and E. Cherepakhova, 'Eto – delo sovnarkhozov', *Rabotnitsa* no. 7 (1958), p. 21.
99 'Dela nashi semeinye', *Trud* (21 August 1960), p. 2.
100 Ibid.
101 Ibid.
102 'Bystro, deshevo, dobrotno!', *Rabotnitsa* no. 9 (1957), pp. 1–3, interview with Rubanenko. Rubanenko also took part in a round table discussion organised by the magazine *Sovetskaya zhenshshina*; see Izmailova, 'Klub interesnykh vstrech', pp. 24–8.
103 This was certainly the pattern of all of the stories on this subject which I found in the magazines.
104 V. Karbovskaya, 'Pochemu oni pozhenilis'', *Ogonek* no. 38 (1957), pp. 28–31.
105 A. Zlovin, 'Novyi dom', *Ogonek* no. 48 (1957), pp. 10–12.
106 DiMaio, Jr, *Soviet Urban Housing*, p. 199.
107 See K. Zhukhov, 'Bol'shoe novosel'e i bol'shie zadachi', *Novyi mir* no. 2 (1963), pp. 230–8; Ivan Mendzheritskii, 'Zdes' byla derevnya', pp. 9–12.
108 Harris, 'Moving to the Separate Apartment', p. 361. This is reinforced by comments by my interviewees.
109 Khrushchev, *Khrushchev Remembers*, p. 2.
110 Harris, 'Moving to the Separate Apartment', p. 309.
111 Ibid., p. 268.
112 Ibid., p. 310.
113 Ibid., p. 357.
114 M. Moisyuk, 'Pokhititeli radosti', p. 4. See also Izmailova, 'Klub interesnykh vstrech', pp. 24–8, which refers to one new apartment which housed both a widow and her daughter, and a lathe operator from the neighbouring factory.
115 Smith, 'Individual Forms of Ownership', pp. 302–3.
116 V. Liverko, *Trud* (15 November 1957), p. 1.
117 'Dom, v kotorom my zhivem', author not named, *Trud* (1 January 1959), p. 3.
118 Mendzheritskii, 'Zdes' byla derevnya', pp. 9–12.
119 M. Romanova, 'Muzh prishel domoi', *Trud* (4 August 1959), p. 2; Protopova, 'Muzh', p. 4; 'Dela nashi semeinye', p. 2.

120 E. Kononenko, 'Otkrovennyi razgovor (Obzor pisem v redaktsiyu)', *Rabotnitsa* no. 3 (1956), p. 30.
121 A. Cherepakhina, 'Vasha domashnyaya masterskaya', *Rabotnitsa* no. 10 (1959), p. 32.
122 E. Tyler May, *Homeward Bound* (New York: Basic Books, 1988), pp. 17–18.
123 Ibid., p. 69.
124 Ibid., p. 16.
125 See L. Attwood, 'Celebrating the "Frail-Figured Welder": Gender Confusion in Women's Magazines of the Khrushchev Era', *Slavonica* 8:2 (2000), pp. 158–76.

10

The Brezhnev years

After Khrushchev was deposed in 1964, many of his reform programmes were halted or overturned. This was not the case with the housing programme. While some aspects of Khrushchev's approach to housing were now rejected – most notably, the standardised five-storey apartment block – the programme itself continued unabated.

According to the press, it was hugely successful. *Ogonek* claimed in 1970 that between 100,000 and 120,000 new apartments were being built in Moscow alone every year,[1] and that, in the country as a whole, forty-four million people were resettled in new or renovated apartments between 1966 and 1970.[2] *Rabotnitsa* put the figure even higher, insisting that more than forty-five million people were given new apartments in that same four-year period.[3] More residential construction was taking place in the Soviet Union than in any other country in the world, *Ogonek* continued,[4] and even the Americans had been forced to acknowledge the fact: the magazine *Newsweek*, it claimed, had conceded that the scale and speed of the Soviet housing programme were unprecedented, and its success almost unimaginable.[5]

Ogonek abounded with photographs and paintings glorifying the new building work. These included Yuri Pimenov's *'Pervye modnitsy novogo raiona'* (The First Fashion Girls in a New District), which depicts three teenaged girls skipping along huge pipes lying in puddles on a vast building site; a series of completed skyscrapers stand nearby, while a poster advertising a film suggests that there is already a cinema.[6] V. Zhemerikin's *Mikroraion* (Micro-district) shows happy construction workers setting off home at the end of their shift, while the fruits of their labour, huge new tower blocks, loom over them.[7]

In reality the housing shortage was far from solved and, as we shall see, it continued to have a negative impact on *byt* and other aspects of personal life, particularly those relating to gender.

The housing programme under Brezhnev

The most visible feature of the Brezhnev housing programme was the tower block, which ranged in height from nine to thirty storeys. Building this high was made possible by improved technology, which made it easier and cheaper to include elevators, and to produce prefabricated rooms and even entire apartments in factories and just assemble them on site.[8] *Ogonek* explained to its readers that small houses were inappropriate in cities as they resulted in too much sprawl,[9] while the five-storey apartment block which had characterised the Khrushchev programme had produced monotonous architectural landscapes in which the buildings all looked like 'identical twins'.[10] There would now be blocks of different heights in all districts, which would produce a more varied and attractive effect.[11] Inevitably, building on this scale necessitated considerable standardisation, but builders would be able to choose from a range of factory-produced external decorative features and incorporate these into their buildings to produce different effects.[12] One *Ogonek* writer likened this to the way in which the letters of the alphabet were put together in different ways to make different words.[13]

The housing programme was also said to be making more allowances for variations in family size and needs, with each new apartment block containing apartments of different sizes, ranging from one to five rooms.[14] More space was being set aside for kitchens and bathrooms, partly in response to complaints from residents living in apartments built in the Khrushchev years, and partly because room was needed for the large new domestic appliances which were now available, such as washing machines.[15] Living space in general was being increased. As we saw earlier, apartments built in the Khrushchev era measured from 18 to 20 square metres for a one-room, 30 square metres for a two-room, and 36 to 40 square metres for a three-room. Now, a new one-room apartment would measure 29 to 36 square metres, a two-room 41 to 50 metres, and a three-room 58 to 63 square metres.[16] No apartments would contain walk-through rooms.[17]

Much was made of the 'experimental' nature of the new housing projects. This term had been used in the Khrushchev era, but not to the same extent. Now it seemed almost to characterise the Brezhnev housing programme. It encompassed both internal and external aspects of residential building work. The supposedly experimental internal features included advances in fitted kitchens, multi-functional furniture, and other space-saving innovations. In one project, '[i]nstead of having partitions between the rooms, there are fitted wall-cupboards going up to the ceiling, with compartments for sheets, outdoor clothes, shoes, hats, suitcases'.[18] Surveys had been conducted which showed that 'everyone, in particular housewives, react positively to the idea of setting up the kitchen with built-in furniture and equipment', and the opinions of the future residents themselves were being taken into consideration, to the extent that they were 'virtual co-designers' of their apartments.[19] Externally, the increased use of prefabrication, the variation in the heights of the buildings and the added decorative details were all presented as experimental features,[20] as was the creation of integrated communities which would provide a complete range of services and facilities – though it is difficult to see how these differed from the micro-districts of the Khrushchev era.[21] The extent to which the term was banded about is indicated by a cartoon which appeared in *Ogonek* in 1968, showing a man standing up in a vertical bath, explaining to his startled wife that 'We have this kind of bath because our apartment house is "experimental"!'[22]

The magazines omitted to mention that the amount of new housing available was partly offset by the demolition of existing housing. Most of the buildings which were pulled down were small individual houses or low-rise blocks which did not fit in with the new trend for multi-storey housing, but in some cases housing was destroyed because it stood in the way of road-building or road-widening schemes.[23] From 1964 to 1980, the loss of living space each year constituted between 12.6 and an astonishing 22.1 per cent of the total amount of new living space.[24]

Another curious paradox, especially for a country which had in the past been so loath to squander money on housing, was that tower blocks were actually more expensive to build and maintain than low-rise buildings. Andrusz tells us that in the Ukraine, in 1980, the rent received from tenants in four- and five-storey blocks was sufficient to cover costs, but in buildings of nine and ten storeys the costs exceeded revenue by 15 to 20 per cent and, in buildings of sixteen and seventeen storeys, by 50 to 80 per cent.[25]

The extra cost of high-rise housing might be one factor behind the introduction of an economy drive on services in the late 1970s. *Ogonek* published a series of letters from irate tenants complaining that their heating, hot water and in some cases even cold water were only turned on for a few hours each day. Some had received schedules detailing when they would have hot water so that they could plan their baths and showers accordingly, but the times were often inconvenient for working people, and in any case they were not always adhered to. Some readers complained of cutbacks in central heating, forcing them to buy electric heaters, which they kept on all night. This, they pointed out, was hardly consistent with an economy drive.[26]

Ogonek occasionally acknowledged the shoddy workmanship of much of the new construction. It reported that heating was sometimes either inadequate or excessive, taps did not always work, walls sometimes went mouldy from damp.[27] A poem appearing in the magazine in 1976 makes a particularly sharp comparison between the quality of new buildings and what was produced in the past:

> A brick wall, the remains of a fortress,
> Stood on a ancient square
> Overlooked by the City Council
> Whose office was also there.
> The council workers were bothered
> That the wall impeded their view
> Of a smart new apartment block
> So the wall would have to go.
> The resolution was carried.
> The day and the time were agreed.
> An explosion shook the ancient square –
> But the view was not improved.
> Apart from a crack, the wall was unchanged
> But the housing block no longer stood!
> The builders had put it up any old how
> To complete it as fast as they could.[28]

Cooperative housing under Brezhnev

A greater encouragement of housing construction cooperatives was a significant feature of the Brezhnev housing programme. Not only would they take some of the pressure off the state housing programme, but, as DiMaio suggests, they would use the surplus money of the country's elite, which might prevent these people from clamouring for more consumer goods.[29]

Yet the fact that cooperatives were only serving the elite remained a cause for concern, and attempts were made to persuade a wider range of people to take up membership. Accordingly, there was an increase in the amount of credit made available to members, and an extension of the repayment period. All the same, cooperative housing remained a far more expensive option than state housing. In Moscow and Leningrad, where the housing shortage was at its most acute, cooperatives did make a significant contribution to housing supply; according to *Ogonek* the amount of living space built by cooperatives in Moscow grew from 28,000 square metres in 1962 to 650,000 in 1965,[30] and in both of these cities demand far outstripped supply. However, in the country as a whole they constituted no more than 10 per cent of new living space.[31]

One significant problem with cooperatives was that moving house was difficult. The official owner of the apartments was the cooperative, not the residents; and the decision to sell, exchange or even bequeath an apartment to a family member could only be made by the general assembly of the cooperative membership.[32] This gave individual members less control over their living space than tenants of state-owned housing. There was also no way in which a cooperative apartment could be exchanged for anything in the state sector. This had important implications for anyone who wanted to marry and set up home with someone whose accommodation was provided by the state. *Ogonek* reported the case of a young man, recently married, who had a one-room cooperative apartment, while his wife had a room in a communal apartment. They wanted to exchange these for an apartment large enough for them to live together and start a family. The man approached the Bureau for Housing Exchanges but was told that they did not deal with cooperatives. The official who dealt with him sympathised with his plight: 'Life carries on, regardless of what department one comes under. And even if you live in a cooperative, which was built with your own resources, you still might get married and have children. Why is it necessary to mark out this family? Or to condemn old people to walk up to the fifth floor for the rest of their lives? ... Should we make all of the residents sign a statement saying that they will never want to leave?'[33]

Apartment exchanges

The convoluted process of exchanging apartments became a major feature of the Brezhnev era, and provided much material for humorous articles and stories in the popular press. The case reported above was included in a comic feature on housing exchanges by E. Mushkina, who identified herself as a worker at the Moscow Bureau for Housing Exchanges.[34] She had become adept at deducing the reasons for the exchanges she was asked to arrange: '[someone wants to] change a three room apartment for two separate apartments, one with two rooms and one with one room. This is because the children have started families and want to live separately. Two separate apartments need to be exchanged for one apartment. This is clearly on account of a new marriage ... One apartment has to be exchanged for two, even if these lack conveniences: this means that a couple has divorced and finds it intolerable to go on living together.'

The Bureau, which charged a fee for its services, performed the role of an introduction agency, providing clients with details of likely matches. However, it handled only a small proportion of exchanges. According to Mushkina, 640 people changed apartments in the Moscow region in the last four months of 1964, and only thirty had done so with the help of the Bureau. Most exchanges were arranged privately, through advertisements placed on public notice boards.[35]

Exchanging even state-owned housing was not an easy business. Those with rooms in communal apartments had particularly weak bargaining power, particularly if they wanted to move because they had problems with their neighbours. One distraught client told Mushkina that she had been deceived by the people with whom she had exchanged apartments; they had not told her their neighbour was an alcoholic. They had insisted that she visit the apartment only between the hours of 5.00 p.m. and 7.00 p.m., which she now realised was because the alcoholic was never at home at that time. Now she was stuck with him, and her old room, in retrospect, seemed like paradise.

In general, smaller communal apartments were considered less abhorrent than larger ones. One family wanted to move because they had been living with only one other person, but she had moved out and a family of three had taken her place. Yet some people actually preferred to have a large number of neighbours. As one of Mushkina's clients explained, in a small apartment, 'if there are acts of hooliganism, like putting salt in the kettle, there are no witnesses. If there are a lot [of people] there are no such problems. Providing they are good people.' Asked how one could determine if potential neighbours were good people, she explained that the presence of saucepans in the kitchen was the crucial sign: 'If the women take their saucepans to their rooms, it means there are fights in the apartment. If they leave them in the kitchen, you can move in without fear.'

Apartment exchanges involving a long chain of people often made use of a broker. This could be a member of the chain, who was paid a fee by the others to work out who was moving where, or a black market 'professional'. There was always a number of these brokers standing outside the Bureau for Housing Exchanges touting for business; they were people with 'roguish appearance' known only by their nicknames, and 'are in it for themselves – but they get results. It is said that if you take on a broker, you'll be moving within a month.'

Mushkina concluded her article with an anecdote illustrating just how convoluted the exchange process could be. A group of people stood round an unkempt young man who was clearly exhausted by the complexity of the arrangements he was overseeing:

'Let's go through it all again', the lad says, waving his arms, and, as if he is playing a children's game of mental arithmetic, he goes round the circle, touching each person on the chest: 'This is how it goes. The Sergeevs move to Ul'yanovsk, to the Drykin apartment. Drykin the elder goes to Izmailovo. Drykin the younger goes to Petrovka. Bubenchik moves from Petrovka, and Ptichkin from Ordynka, to Lobachevskii Street. The Shishkins move to the Sergeevs' apartment. My wife and I go to Dmitrovskoe Highway. And Auntie? Wait a minute, where will Auntie go?! And this whole exchange started because of her! Let's go through it again from the beginning ...'

The complexity of apartment exchanges provided the backdrop to a tragicomic short story appearing in *Ogonek* in 1977, 'I Wish to Exchange my Apartment' (*Menyayu kvartiru*).[36] Irina and Sergei became the first link in an apartment exchange chain when Irina, an ambitious woman, decided their existing apartment did not reflect their professional status. They spent the next month answering phone enquiries:

'No thanks, Izmailovo doesn't suit us ...'
  'No, the ground floor won't do.'
  'Let me write that down. And the kitchen? Excellent. Kitchen – nine metres ...'
  '... All three rooms are separate, on the seventh floor ...'
  'We are two [bus] stops from the metro, but we often walk there ... 10 minutes, at a leisurely pace ...'
  'Yes, there's a kindergarten nearby, and the school is two minutes away ...
  ... 'No, Izmailovo won't do us – it's clearly written on the notice which districts we're interested in ...'

They eventually found a suitable apartment, but by then they were part of a seven-link chain which kept one of its members, a pensioner, happily occupied: 'he took the role of broker, not for the money, though he accepted it all the same, but because he enjoyed the job.'

What began as a comic tale turned into tragedy when Sergei was killed in a car crash. Irina withdrew from the chain and it collapsed, but its members now found themselves forced to re-evaluate their lives. For example, Denis, a taxi driver, had joined the chain in order to get a new room for his elderly aunt, who currently lived with him and his family. Now he wondered with horror what would happen to his children if he or his wife were to die and realised how much help they received from the aunt, though they had always resented her presence and treated her badly. He was now filled with remorse and a determination to change. Lyuba Alekseevna, a self-absorbed woman who devoted her life to trivial distractions, realised how selfish she had been, and offered to take care of her son's children so that he and his wife could further their careers. All of the members of the chain rallied round Irina offering her friendship and support. As we have seen, the communal apartment in the Stalin era and the communal apartment block in the Khrushchev era were both presented as heterogeneous socialist communities. In this story, the apartment exchange chain seemed to serve a similar function.

Living with adult offspring

One of the major types of apartment exchange was to replace a relatively large apartment for two small ones so that adult offspring could enjoy a private family life. One *Rabotnitsa* article claimed that, according to sociological data, around 50 per cent of young people actually preferred to go on living with their parents when they started their own families, since they were given so much help.[37] However, the impression which generally emerges from the magazines is that relations between parents and their adult children could be extremely fraught, particularly when the latter moved their partners into the already cramped living space.

This was a favoured subject for the magazines' fiction writers. In one typical story, a young family – Lyala, Pavel and their small daughter – lived with Pavel's mother, Katya. The two women both felt that the other's behaviour was unreasonable. Lyala was annoyed that the older woman always went to bed early, which meant that she and Pavel had to keep quiet the whole evening, while in the mornings Katya thought nothing of stomping to and from the kitchen when they still wanted to sleep. Katya, on the other hand, thought that Lyala was noisy, and resented the fact that she played the radio late into the night. Lyala suggested to Pavel that he persuade his mother to go and live with her daughter, but Pavel refused to do so on the grounds that the apartment had been assigned to her, not them. Lyala pointed out that he was also registered to live there, and as the only man he was automatically head of the family and should be able to make the important decisions. Pavel agreed that this was the case, but still refused to ask his mother to move out. Lyala's parents tried to buy the couple a cooperative apartment, but did not have sufficient funds. The marriage fell apart, and while the author made it clear that this was largely because of Lyala's selfish nature, the housing shortage was clearly a significant factor.[38]

Selfishness on the part of young women was a recurring theme in articles as well as short stories. One thirty-year-old woman complained to *Ogonek* that her mother, who lived with her and her family, was driving her mad. 'We have so little time', she explained; 'I love music and the theatre, I love to read and to dress well. I don't have time in the evenings to listen to my mother's chatter.' She received little sympathy from the magazine, however, which pointed out that she was happy enough to leave her child in her mother's care while she went out to work, and then had the nerve to 'find it irritating that she also has to chat with her. Even today, when her mother is needed in the roles of granny, economist and dress maker, they do not live in harmony and peace. It is not hard to imagine what it will be like in the future ...'[39]

What it would be like in the future was indicated by other articles in the magazine, which took up the issue of neglect of elderly relatives. Yet a couple who had finally managed to move out of their parental homes into their own apartment were unlikely to be thrilled at the prospect of one or more of those parents moving back in with them. *Ogonek* pointed out, with clear disapproval, that many young people in this situation preferred to put their elderly parents in an old people's home.[40] This prompted a number of letters from readers wanting to justify their decision to do just that.[41] Old people grumbled incessantly about nothing, they claimed. They had different ideas about child care and upbringing. Alcohol abuse could also be a problem, particularly in the case of old men.

Coping with the tensions arising between different generations in overcrowded apartments was primarily a female problem. This was because women had a greater investment in the home and domestic life, and so were bound to have more conflicts over sharing the kitchen and bringing up the children. The burden of caring for the elderly also fell on them. As an *Ogonek* commentator acknowledged: 'We spend so much time working, and daily life is so difficult, that there is not enough time left for kindness. One result of this "women's problem" is the loneliness of our grandfathers and grandmothers.'[42]

The demise of the communal apartment

The success of the housing programme was supposedly bringing involuntary communal living to an end. Communal apartments were being broken up and their residents resettled in separate apartments. Curiously, now that their days were numbered, they were written about with a trace of fondness, as in this *Rabotnitsa* story:

> The long corridor of communal apartment no. 106 had a curve in the very middle, around the kitchen, which made it look like a strange dark street in a settlement in the past, where behind every door, as if in its own home, lived a different family. Now those times have passed when it was

difficult to go out into the corridor without crashing into someone or other's trunk, the pedal of a bicycle or a protruding twig from a broken basket; when there were always yelling, quarrelling voices in the kitchen, still audible above the gushing of water from the faucet and the hissing of a tea kettle and saucepan on the cramped stove. Now the number of people in the apartment has decreased; the children who once played hide and seek in the corners behind wardrobes and trunks have grown up and gone to other towns, or been allocated apartments in distant new districts. It has become more spacious, though some consider that it is now empty and lonely. For a long time now everyone has known everything about each other that can be known after twenty-five years of shared life. The quarrels, resentments, violent outbursts, animosities and caustic comments, which were always bubbling between the walls of the apartment, have receded into the depths of time, and for the current residents they are like a dark, half-remembered history, much like the crusades for today's Europeans. On 1 May and on Revolution Day everyone gathers round one table; the men drink shots of vodka, and the women try to stop them getting too drunk by putting food on their plates and filling their glasses with colourful soft drinks. Then they start to sing.[43]

An *Ogonek* story published in 1984, two years after Brezhnev's death, was rather less positive.[44] Sima, a single woman in her forties, had lived her entire life in a communal apartment, which she currently shared with a single mother and a family of three. 'Sima may have her own room, but she has no peace,' the author declared. Every night the baby's screams could be heard through the walls, and during the day there was continual conflict over the shared spaces: 'someone is scolding someone else because the soap has been dropped on the floor, or a plate has been broken, or the areas of common use are not well cleaned, or the swaddling clothes are hanging in the kitchen over the table where they eat'. The frustrations of communal life had so worn Sima down that she had abandoned her one passion, the opera; while she once went to live performances, now she did not even listen to opera on the radio. Her dedication to high culture had been nibbled away by the mundanity of daily life. Yet even this sad tale did not portray the communal apartment as an entirely negative phenomenon. Sima was a lonely woman with no friends or family, and although she claimed to resent being 'spied on' by her neighbours, at least they took some interest in her and showed signs of genuine concern.

Corruption in housing distribution

The corruption which continued to bedevil housing distribution was another issue which was addressed, if obliquely, in the magazines' fiction. In one *Ogonek* story it provided the backdrop to a light-hearted love story. The protagonist, Dar'ya Pavlovna, was a professor of economics and head of her department at a research institute. She was a divorcee in her mid-forties who lived alone in a one-room apartment. One of the researchers in her department, Maksim Tumanov, lived in a communal apartment, and as his line manager, Dar'ya took it on herself to secure for him a separate apartment. The institute had some housing of its own but there were no one-room apartments available, and as a single man that was all Maksim was officially entitled to. Dar'ya decided to try and 'extort' (*vykolachivat'*) an apartment from the district executive committee. She made an appointment with the assistant chair, Klavdia Agafonovna, wearing a skirt for the occasion because she knew Klavdia Agafonovna was a traditional woman who forbade her female co-workers to wear trousers. She was annoyed at having to pander to these whims, but did not want something so petty to jeopardise her mission. She explained to Klavdia Agafonovna that the smallest apartment the institute had available would give Tumanov six metres of living space above the norm, but asked Klavdia Agafonovna to officially endorse his right to this extra space on the grounds that he was a very talented specialist. Klavdia Agafonovna countered this proposal with one of her own: that the city soviet gave him a one-room apartment, and took the institute's two-room apartment in exchange. Dar'ya was not happy with this solution. Tumanov would marry soon, she argued, and start a family; if he only had a one-room apartment he would have to move again. Klavdia Agafonovna wanted to know why he was not already married, and Dar'ya explained that he had been so committed to his work that there had been no time left for personal life. Klavdia Agafonovna asked Dar'ya if she herself was still single and Dar'ya immediately understood what she was implying; she was already an old woman, she joked. The meeting ended with Dar'ya suggesting that they 'don't need to approach this formally', and with Klavdia Agafonovna agreeing to consider the situation.

To Dar'ya's surprise Maksim was not grateful for her efforts. He felt uncomfortable having a woman fight his corner, he told her, and in any case he was happy where he was since his only neighbour, an elderly woman, cooked and cleaned for him. Yet he admitted that he had insufficient space for his books, and when his right to the apartment was officially approved he agreed to take it. Dar'ya joked that he would have to get married now since he would have no one to make his meals, but it turned out that he planned to bring his neighbour with him to the new apartment. Dar'ya was astonished: the institute wanted to give him a separate apartment, she told him, and yet he was determined to turn it into a communal one! By the end of the story, however, Dar'ya and Maksim had acknowledged their mutual attraction and began to plan a future together in the new apartment. There was no further mention of the poor old neighbour.[45]

Hostel accommodation

While communal apartments remained a significant feature of the urban landscape, barracks were said to be a thing of the past; as one *Rabotnitsa* commentator observed with relief, they were 'already being wiped from our memories'.[46] Hostels, however, were a different matter, and would continue to provide essential temporary accommodation for the foreseeable future. They were said to play a particularly vital function in the new towns and cities which were built around particular industries – a continuation of Stalin's 'socialist cities', though now shorn of that title. These cities had a disproportionate number of young unmarried residents, most of whom were migrants to the city and so had no local relatives they could live with. Hostels were the most cost-effective way of housing these people. In the Siberian city of Angarsk, for example, which had been built in the 1950s, there were forty-seven hostels by 1979, housing more than 9,000 people.[47]

Rabotnitsa insisted that the new hostels were a great improvement on those of the past, and were actually the most appropriate form of accommodation for single people. Instead of large dormitory rooms leading off a single long corridor, with one communal kitchen to serve all residents, most hostels were now arranged in clusters of rooms, usually four per cluster, with each room housing two or three people. Each cluster had its own entrance hall and kitchenette.[48] They were, then, more like apartments than hostels. In some respects they were even better than apartments, since they provided a range of sporting and recreational activities, and a constant supply of companions with whom to enjoy them. They were also important agents of socialisation, teaching their young residents how to relate to other people, share with them and look out for them, and this would stand them in good stead in their married lives. If all young people lived for some time in a hostel, the magazine claimed, there would be fewer divorces on the grounds of 'incompatible characters'.[49]

This socialisation function was emphasised by the fact the hostel staff included an 'upbringer' (*vospitatel'nitsa*) to promote the residents' moral and spiritual welfare and to organise social and cultural events. This post was invariably held by a woman, even in men's hostels. *Rabotnitsa* insisted that if she had the right temperament and 'a huge amount of energy, enthusiasm and understanding of young people',[50] an upbringer could turn the hostel into a congenial home, as well as teaching residents a range of life skills.[51] However, the magazine also acknowledged that some upbringers came across as tactless intruders in residents' personal lives. One who was singled out for particular rebuke was said to enjoy lecturing the hostel residents about cultured behaviour, but thought nothing of entering a room without knocking, with a cigarette in her mouth.[52]

There could also be problems with the 'commandant', the person – again, usually a woman – who had overall control of the hostel. Some commandants insisted that all excursions and outings undertaken by the residents had to be arranged through the hostel, and refused entry to any visitors of the opposite sex. Taken to extremes, this meant that a young man could not even ask a young woman out to the cinema, or visit her in her hostel to drink tea. Women were hence denied the opportunity of developing important home-making skills: 'If a girl can invite people to visit her in the hostel she gets to feel like a mistress of her own home; she'll set the table nicely and bake a special cake, and bask in the praise of her guests – what girl would not want this!'[53]

Despite these criticisms, hostel life was portrayed as a positive experience and, even after the residents had moved into their own apartments, 'the hostel, with its young people, their passions, their anticipation of the future, will always remain [in their hearts]'.[54] This view seems not to have been shared by the majority of residents, however. Many complained to *Rabotnitsa* about the inadequacies of their hostels. There was often a shortage of furniture, facilities and entertainment.[55] The Red Corner was 'closed and padlocked more often than not',[56] or was only used for watching television.[57] Overcrowding was rife; rooms intended for two people often had to accommodate four, which meant it was virtually impossible to have 'any private space to oneself'.[58] Furthermore, hostel life was pervaded by incessant 'gossip and quarrels'.[59]

While hostels were intended for single people, residents sometimes found it impossible to get alternative accommodation after they had married, and many couples had to go on living in separate hostels. In Angarsk there were 980 couples on the waiting list for an apartment in 1979. When *Rabotnitsa*'s correspondents asked the town's housing officials why married couples could not be given a room together in the same hostel, they were told that the hostel rooms had to house three or four people, and they could not squander an entire room on a couple.[60]

If a woman had a child, she was officially required to leave the hostel on the grounds that 'combined habitation in a hostel of mothers with children and single girls does not create normal conditions for either one or the other'.[61] In some cases the hostel commandant allowed a young mother to stay in the hostel in contravention of the rules, but the other residents often disapproved, complaining that they were kept awake by the baby's crying and that its swaddling clothes took up the entire drying rack.[62] Yet, if she had no local relatives who would take her in, the mother was in a very difficult position. Renting a room privately was possible, but could rarely be done legally because 'there are few people who would be willing to register a mother and child in their apartment';[63] they were worried that the young family would acquire permanent rights to their living space.

Some new towns built hostels specifically for couples. For example, Gubkin, a mining town, had fourteen family hostels, in which 'almost every young family is able to have its own room'.[64] Yet the building of family hostels challenged the Soviet pledge to provide every family with its own apartment, and was also an acknowledgement that for many families hostel accommodation would be long-term. The new-look hostels, with their clusters of rooms replacing the long institutional corridor of the past, made the family hostel something akin to a series of communal apartments. While the real communal apartments were seen largely as a thing of the past, this new version was trumpeted as a great step forward.

The new housing law of 1982

In the summer of 1980, *Rabotnitsa* announced a new law on 'The Fundamentals of Housing Legislation in the USSR and the Union Republics', which would come into effect in January 1982. The magazine invited a number of housing and legal specialists to give their views on the law.[65]

One of the stipulations of the new law was that people of different genders, with the exception of couples, could not be assigned to the same room if they were nine or more years old. Single mothers were now to be included in the list of citizens entitled to preferential treatment in housing, along with disabled veterans of the Great Patriotic War, families of those who had died in the war, people with chronic and debilitating illnesses, certain categories of disabled people,[66] Hero Mothers (those with ten or more children), multi-child families and families with twins. The law also stipulated that accommodation would be distributed, wherever possible, on the basis of one family per apartment. Accordingly, there would no longer be pressure on residents to 'compress' any surplus living space in their apartment – that is, to have a stranger imposed on them. As one of the specialists interviewed by *Rabotnitsa* pointed out, 'it is now recognised that resolving housing matters by turning a separate apartment into a communal one is not appropriate.'

There were a number of grounds on which tenants could be evicted. These included speculation in state accommodation (that is, renting it out for a higher price), trashing an apartment, not using it for its intended purpose, and continually infringing the rules of common socialist habitation, thereby making it impossible for other residents to enjoy their habitation. A man who was abusive towards his family could now be evicted on these grounds, since he made it impossible for them to enjoy their habitation He could also be deprived of his parental rights for failing to bring up his children adequately, and a person who lost his parental rights could be evicted without being offered alternative accommodation. A couple no longer able to live together could also ask the local soviet to arrange an apartment exchange. Hence abused women would no longer have to stay with their violent partners, and divorced couples would not have to go on sharing living space.

The problems which sometimes arose from a rigid application of the law entitling factories and enterprises to evict residents from factory housing if they left their jobs was also addressed. This was an issue which could have a particular effect on women, since, as we have seen, housing was more commonly allocated to the male 'head of the family'. One housing specialist related a case in which a man living in factory housing gave up his job, abandoned his wife and children, and disappeared. The factory administration started a legal case to evict the family because the wife was not an employee and had lived in the factory's housing only on account of her husband's work. The city soviet intervened and eventually persuaded the factory to wait until alternative accommodation could be found before evicting the family. This had not been easy because the law was at that time on the factory's side. Now the law stipulated that people could not be evicted from workplace housing until suitable alternative accommodation was available.[67] The new law also entitled citizens to apply for housing simultaneously at their workplace and in the local district soviet, which meant they had twice as much chance of receiving an apartment.

This law, at least in theory, addressed many of the housing problems which have featured prominently in the pages of this book. In reality, however, the situation was not much changed. Whatever the law's requirements, if the housing was not available, it could not be assigned.

The new understanding of new *byt*

Soviet society became increasingly privatised in the Brezhnev era, largely as a result of the large number of families now living in self-contained apartments. The huge crowded kitchen of the communal apartment, with its gossip, quarrels and informers, had been replaced, for many people, with the small private kitchen, a haven, at least in relative terms, of privacy and calm. They could now gather round the kitchen table with family and friends and criticise the system, confident that their views would go no further than the walls around them.[68] This increased privatisation is as a key element in the new *byt* of the Brezhnev era.

The authorities were still not entirely comfortable with the notion of private life, however, and the attempts made by Khrushchev to counteract the privatising tendency of the separate family apartment by encouraging interaction between neighbours in the new apartment blocks continued under Brezhnev. *Rabotnitsa* reported that in Yaroslavl' residents had been encouraged to join house committees to ensure that their housing was kept in good condition, and these committees had organised *subbotniki* (days of unpaid work) to clean the attics and basements of their apartment blocks, to build and repair equipment in the children's play area, and to paint staircases and clean entrance halls. Many of the residents were said to have met each other for the first time on these *subbotniki* and subsequently became good friends. Now they took an interest in each other's well-being, ensured that older neighbours were looked after, and organised clubs for the children.[69] The new *new byt*, then, involved the attempt to ensure that the privatisation of the family was combined with a sense of social responsibility.[70]

Yet in some respects there was a growing acceptance of the private family, and even a pandering to its needs. This was justified on the grounds that people with happy home lives would return to work more relaxed and rested, and work more effectively.[71]

Ogonek now explicitly linked new *byt* to the availability of domestic services and appliances. A new 'experimental' apartment block was referred to as a 'house [apartment block] of new *byt*' specifically because of the range of domestic services it provided.[72] One article even insisted that domestic appliances were a technological achievement no less significant than space travel or nuclear power.[73] The shortage of domestic goods, the wasted hours spent standing in line at shops, the surly and unhelpful attitude of some shopkeepers, should never be dismissed as trifling matters: 'there are no trifles in *byt*, even if the whole of *byt* consists primarily of "trifles".'[74]

The growing popularity of television promoted the privatisation of the family, since previous generations had been more likely to seek their entertainment en masse at the cinema. On the other hand, television could be used to bring society and socialism into the private family apartment. *Ogonek* reviewed a television programme called 'One Micro-District', which focused on the residents of an apartment block. Its pivotal character was a public-spirited young woman called Ira Agashina, who looked out for all her neighbours: 'she helps deliver newspapers and letters, rushes to the chemist for medicine and to the shop for food, cleans the apartment of a sick neighbour.' When the marriage of two residents broke down and the abandoned husband went into a deep depression, Ira turned up 'in the nick of time, understands everything, ensures that he is not left alone, helps him return to society'. The individual apartment was not a private enclave, then, but part of a social network.[75]

Another indication of the privatisation of the family was the growing popularity of the family holiday. Officially sanctioned holidays took the form of a worker applying for a pass, or being given one as a reward for hard work, for a week or two in a sanatorium or a holiday house (*dom otdikha*) which was usually owned by his or her factory or enterprise. Passes were given to individuals, not families. In the past, the only way for a family to take a holiday together had been to go 'wild', which meant arranging the illicit private rental of a room in a resort area. In February 1972, a new resolution required holiday houses to set aside a certain number of places for two, three or four people, and to admit children from the age of four to fifteen. As a *Rabotnitsa* correspondent explained, this meant that a mother could now go on holiday with her child, or both parents could go on holiday with their children, or a couple could go on holiday without their children.[76] (The one possibility that was seemingly unthinkable was for a father to go on holiday with his child.) In 1980 the magazine reported that the family holiday had really taken off, and that new blocks of holiday apartments were being built in resort areas specifically for families.[77]

The increased privatisation of family life had some negative aspects. Male violence against women was facilitated by the family's retreat behind the door of its own apartment. When *Ogonek*'s readers were invited to comment on a case in which an abused woman eventually snapped and killed her husband, one of them blamed the neighbours for not intervening: 'If just one person had dared to rebuke him – if a female neighbour ... had stood up to him in Margarita's defence – she would not have been left so alone.'[78] Yet even if they had been willing to get involved, it is quite possible that they no longer had any idea what was happening in their neighbours' lives.

Notes

1 See V. Promyslov, 'Moskva – 1970', *Ogonek* no. 12 (1970), pp. 4–5; and K. Barykin, 'Gorod, dom, kvartira', interview with Boris R. Rubanenko, *Ogonek* no. 50 (1980), pp. 16–17.
2 Yu. Mikhailov, 'Chetyre goda', *Ogonek* no. 21 (1970), p. 26.
3 N. Aleksandrovna, 'Dom, v komotorom ya zhivy', *Rabotnitsa* no. 2 (1975), pp. 10–11.
4 L. Palievskaya, 'Esli ty – novosel', interview with Gennadi Nilovich Fomin, chair of the state committee of civil construction and architecture, *Ogonek* no. 23 (1971), pp. 20–1.
5 'Dom ... obgonyaet knigu', *Ogonek* no. 5 (1971), inside front cover and pp. 1–2, photo article.
6 Yu. Pimenov, 'Pervye modnitsy novogo raiona', reproduced in *Ogonek* no. 17 (1971), p. 17.
7 V. Zhemerikin's 1974 painting *Mikroraion*, reproduced in *Ogonek* no. 9 (1976), between pp. 24–25.
8 'Dom ... obgonyaet knigu', *Ogonek* no. 5 (1971), pp. 1–2.
9 L. Kafanova, 'Zaftra', *Ogonek* no. 24 (1965), pp. 1–2.
10 L. Palievskaya, 'Esli ty – novosel', *Ogonek* no. 23 (1971), pp. 20–1.
11 Kafanova, 'Zaftra', pp. 1–2.
12 L. Palievskaya, 'Esli ty – novosel', *Ogonek* no. 23 (1971), pp. 20–1; Promyslov, 'Moskva – 1970', pp. 4–5.
13 Promyslov, 'Moskva – 1970', pp. 4–5.
14 'Kakimi stanut kvartiry?', interview with Nikolai A. Luppov of the Department of the Interior of Central Scientific Research and Design for Housing, *Rabotnitsa* no. 5 (1973), p. 28.
15 'Kakimi stanut kvartiry?', p. 28; A. Bochinin, N. Verina and Yu. Krivonosov, 'God novogo doma', *Ogonek* no. 52 (1969), p. 1.
16 L. Palievskaya, 'Esli ty – novosel', *Ogonek* no. 23 (1971), pp. 20–1.
17 'Kakimi stanut kvartiry?', p. 28; Kafanova, 'Zaftra', pp. 1–2.
18 'Dom novogo byta', interview with architect N. Osterman, *Ogonek* no 2 (1966), pp. 26–7.
19 'Kakimi stanut kvartiry?', p. 28.
20 Kafanova, 'Zaftra', pp. 1–2.
21 Ibid.; see also Dom novogo byta', *Ogonek* no. 2 (1966), pp. 26–7.
22 *Ogonek* no. 17 (1968), p. 30.
23 G. Andrusz, *Housing and Urban Development in the USSR* (Basingstoke: Macmillan, 1984), pp. 203–4.
24 Ibid., p. 205, table 8.9.
25 Ibid., p. 208.
26 'Chitatel' zhdet otveta', rubric 'Pochta ogon'ka', *Ogonek* no. 27 (1980), p. 24; 'V netoplenykh kvartirakh', rubric 'Pochta ogon'ka', *Ogonek* no. 48 (1980), p. 32.
27 'V netoplenykh kvartirakh', rubric 'Pochta ogon'ka', *Ogonek* no. 48 (1980), p. 32; 'Pochta Ogon'ka', *Ogonek* no. 52 (1980), pp. 20–1.
28 S. Mikhalkov, 'Stena i dom (k voprosu o kachestve)' (The Wall and The Apartment Block (a Question of Quality), *Ogonek* no. 12 (1976), p. 29. In Russian, the text reads as follows:

Останки крепости - кирпичная стена/ На древней площади мешала горсовету./И вот взорвать решили стену эту,/ Чтоб вид на новый дом не портила она./Решенье принято. Назначен ден и час./ И площадь древнюю однажды взрыв потряс./ Но вид на новый дом при этом не открылся – / Стена осталась как была,/ Она лишь трещину дала./А новый дом напротив – развалился!/ Я к тем строителям свой обратил упрек,/Что строят тяп да ляп чтоб только сляпать в срок.

29 A.J. DiMaio, Jr, *Soviet Urban Housing: Problems and Policies* (New York and London: Duke University Press, 1974), p. 185.
30 E.E. Mushkina, 'Kuda poedet teshcha?', *Ogonek* no. 10 (1965), pp. 22–3.
31 See DiMaio, Jr, *Soviet Urban Housing*, p.195; Andrusz, *Housing and Urban Development*, p. 94.
32 Andrusz, *Housing and Urban Development*, p. 85.
33 E.E. Mushkina, 'Kuda poedet teshcha?', *Ogonek* no. 10 (1965), pp. 22–3.
34 Ibid.
35 See Andrusz, *Housing and Urban Development*, p. 213.
36 A. Muzyrya, 'Menyayu kvartiru', *Ogonek* no. 12 (1977), pp. 10–11.
37 G. Ryabikina and T. Khizanavshili, 'Molodaya sem'ya v molodom gorode: Glava pervaya: na poroge supruszhestva', *Rabotnitsa* no. 1 (1979), pp. 20–2.
38 M. Belakova, 'Razglyad', serialised in *Ogonek* no. 19 (1967), pp. 29–31; no. 20 (1967), pp. 30–1; and no. 21 (1967), pp. 28–9.
39 Z. Zolotova, 'Stariki v dome', *Ogonek* no. 6 (1982), p. 26.
40 'Odinochestvo', *Ogonek* no. 39 (1981), p. 6.
41 Z. Zolotova, 'Stariki v dome', p. 26.
42 Ibid.
43 F. Knorre, 'Olimpiya', *Rabotnitsa* no. 1 (1967), pp. 9–13.
44 L. Shamenkova, 'Poklonnitsa', *Rabotnitsa* no. 22 (1984), pp. 22–4.
45 L. Yunina, 'Zhenshchina v odnokomnatnoi kvartire', serialised in *Ogonek* no. 2 (1979), pp. 20–2; and *Ogonek* no. 3 (1979), pp. 17–19.
46 E. Cherepakhova, 'Nash obshchii dom', *Rabotnitsa* no. 8 (1971), pp. 22–3.
47 Ryabikina and Khizanavshili, 'Molodaya sem'ya v molodom gorode', pp. 20–2.
48 T. Virkunen, 'Dom okknami na prokhodnuyu', *Rabotnitsa* no. 9 (1979), pp. 21–2.
49 See, for example, Cherepakhova, 'Nash obshchii dom', pp. 22–3.
50 L. Nemenova, 'Podruzhki', *Rabotnitsa* no. 5 (1966), pp. 20–2.
51 Ibid.
52 Ibid.
53 Ibid.
54 Ibid.
55 M. Smimova, 'Pochemy v obshchezhitii skuchno?', *Rabotnitsa* no. 1 (1966,) p. 18.
56 'A u nas v obshchezhitii', *Rabotitsa* no. 3 (1966), pp. 16–17.
57 Ibid.
58 Ibid.
59 Ibid.
60 Ryabikina and Khizanavshili, 'Molodaya sem'ya v molodom gorode', pp. 22–4.
61 Zhuravskaya, 'V obshchezhitii ne polozheno', *Rabotnitsa* no. 11 1979, p. 22.
62 Ryabikina and Khizanavshili, 'Molodaya sem'ya v molodom gorode', pp. 22–4.
63 Zhuravskaya, 'V obshchezhitii ne polozheno', *Rabotnitsa* no. 11 (1979), p. 22.
64 T. Kstygova and I. Kosheleva, 'Gubkin vzroslet', *Rabotnitsa* no. 3 (1980), pp. 12–14.

65 N. Fedorova; 'Yuridicheskaya konsul'tatsiya', *Rabotnitsa* no. 9 (1981), pp. 19-20.
66 These were 'invalids of work in Groups I and II', and 'invalids from military personnel in groups I and II'; Ibid., pp. 19-20.
67 'Nash obshchii dom: obsuzhdaem proekt Osnov zhilishchnogo zakonodatel'stva', *Rabotnitsa* no. 8 (1980), p. 14.
68 For more on this, see V. Shlapentokh, *Public and Private Life of the Soviet People: Changing Values in Post-Stalin Russia* (Oxford and New York: Oxford University Press, 1989), pp. 181-2.
69 N. Aleksandrovna, 'Dom, v kotorom ya zhivy', pp. 10-11.
70 In reality, people generally preferred to spend their free time with friends they had chosen rather than neighbours who had been imposed on them, though Shlapentokh holds that neighbours did remain important for certain categories of people, most notably elderly women and single mothers, who had limited opportunity for social contact outside the home. See Shlapentokh, *Public and Private Life of the Soviet People*, p. 181.
71 See, for example, F. Loshchenkov, 'Byt - delo sereznoe', *Ogonek* no. 2 (1965), pp. 10-11.
72 Kafanova, 'Zaftra', pp. 1-2.
73 K.S. Golovchenko, 'Dlya vsekh i dlya sebya', *Ogonek* no. 39 (1969), pp. 20-2.
74 K. Barykin, 'Byt ili ne byt?', *Ogonek* no, 40 (1973), pp. 15-16.
75 T. Troitskaya, 'V odnom mikroraione', *Ogonek* no. 14 (1976), p. 24.
76 A. Fomicheva, 'Vsei sem'ei', *Rabotnitsa* no. 6 (1975), p. 29.
77 G. Vladimirova and I. Gavrilov, 'Vsei sem'ei', *Ogonek* no. 34 (1980), pp. 31-3.
78 'Snova o "nechastnom sluchae"', *Ogonek* no. 17 (1980), pp. 20-2.

II

The Gorbachev era: the end of a socialist housing policy

Brezhnev died in November 1982. For the next two and and a half years the country was led by elderly and ailing men, first Andropov and then Chernenko. In March 1985 the relatively youthful Gorbachev came to power and launched a massive reform programme, referred to as *perestroika* or restructuring. Initially intended to make the economy more efficient, in due course it extended into all corners of Soviet life.

At the same time, the policy of *glasnost'*, or openness, made it possible to discuss the negative aspects of society much more honestly. Initially the intention had not been to introduce freedom of information for its own sake, but to illuminate certain social problems which Gorbachev wanted addressed. However, *glasnost'* soon developed its own momentum and began to expose a range of crises and catastrophes. Housing figured prominently in the reports.

The deplorable state of housing inherited by Gorbachev is clear from figures provided by Nadezhda Kosareva, Alexander Pusanov and Maria V. Tikhomirova. They claim that in 1986 every fifth family in the Soviet Union, around eight million people in total, was on a housing waiting list. This figure rose to nine million in 1987. By 1989, 17 per cent of the population still lived in communal apartments or dormitories or had no permanent place of residence.[1]

In this chapter we will explore the ways in which both the housing crisis, and the new approaches to the problem, were discussed in *Ogonek* and *Rabotnitsa* throughout the Gorbachev era, and how the socialist approach to housing which had characterised the previous seventy years was overturned.

Curiously, we will find little specific mention of gender in these articles. This could be due to the fact that private housing became a significant feature of the emerging market economy, and men were portrayed as the natural entrepreneurs. While state-owned housing had been seen largely as a female concern, the market, including the housing market, supposedly had a 'male' face.

Glasnost' and the housing crisis

As we have seen in previous chapters, journalists were able to made some reference to housing deficiencies, such as overcrowding and the poor state of repair of many buildings, before Gorbachev came to power. However, as Mary Buckley has noted, these were usually presented as temporary problems which would be eradicated as society came closer to communism. There was no suggestion that the system as a whole needed overhauling.[2]

In the early, more optimistic period of the Gorbachev reforms, the approach was not that different. The range and severity of criticisms was much greater, and included subjects which had previously only been hinted at, such as corruption and criminality in housing distribution; and the authorities now insisted they were really applying themselves to solving the problems. Yet as the Gorbachev era unfolded, this optimism declined, and the tone of reporting underwent a significant change. To quote Buckley once more, the new openness made it possible for journalists to focus more on 'the emotional results of housing conditions … *Glasnost'* enabled journalists to go beyond exposure of squalor and cramped conditions to probe their impact on individual psychology.'[3]

Housing: the most crucial '*defisitnyi*' item

The head of the Leningrad district executive committee, Vladimir Klonitskii, stated in *Ogonek* in 1987 that '[t]he biggest social problem today is [how] to give every family its own apartment.'[4] *Rabotnitsa* reported that every fifth letter it received from readers was about housing.[5] It was acknowledged that the perpetual claims of the past about the amount of new housing being brought into use had been a sham: 'Every year, and at the start of every Five Year Plan, we have been told about the colossal construction of living space, but now we are admitting that the greatest shortage in this country is precisely in this area.'[6]

Both magazines gave examples of appalling overcrowding. *Rabotnitsa* published a letter from a reader who lived with his wife and three children in a single room measuring two by five metres, in which all available space was taken up by 'beds, cots and clothes'.[7] He had only been in his current job for four years so had no hope of obtaining housing through his workplace, but had suggested to the enterprise director, only half in jest, that he would sign a contract committing himself to the company for life if it would only give him an apartment. This was a clear acknowledgement that enterprises used housing as a way of retaining and controlling their workforce, and that workers were well aware of this.

Even if a family had a self-contained apartment, this did not mean it had sufficient space to meet its needs. *Rabotnitsa* described the following as a 'typical' family (*sem'ya kak sem'ya*): a middle-aged couple, their adult son and his family, their adult daughter and her family, and an elderly grandmother, all living together in a three-room apartment.[8] In an article on the housing needs of 'multi-child' families, *Ogonek* reported that while the figures made it seem as if the situation was tolerable – in Leningrad, for example, 71 per cent of these families had their own apartments – they were often misleading. For example, one family with six children did indeed have an apartment of its own, but it measured only fifteen square metres and had to accommodate eight people.[9]

A bed in a hostel was the only home some people had ever known. It was acknowledged that women were always at the end of the queue when apartments were assigned, and that for many of them marriage was the only way out of a hostel. Yet a woman living in a hostel was less likely to get married, both because of prejudice on the part of possible spouses and their families (female hostel residents were viewed, it seems, as the Soviet equivalent of 'trailer trash') and because they had become institutionalised. Nina Rusakova related the tale of a woman who had lived in a hostel from the age of sixteen to forty. When she was finally assigned her own apartment she could not adjust to living alone and went back to the hostel every evening, using her stark apartment, with its curtainless windows and naked light-bulbs, only to sleep. While this acceptance of communal living would once have been reported as something positive, it was now depicted as a sign of mental ill-health. According to Rusakova, living in a hostel for more than three or four years resulted in permanent psychological damage.[10]

Housing remained a factor in the choice of marriage partner. The advertisements placed in 'Get Acquainted' columns made it clear that having good housing was one of a person's most vital attributes.[11] It was also not uncommon for someone migrating to a major city from a small town or the countryside to try to obtain a *propiska* (the right to stay in that city) by marrying a resident.[12]

The housing crisis was exacerbated by two new factors. One was the closure of Red Army bases in Eastern Europe, resulting in an unprecedented number of soldiers returning to the Soviet Union and requiring housing.¹³ The other was the outbreak of ethnic hostilities in the 'periphery' of the Soviet Union, resulting in a large number of refugees fleeing war zones. *Rabotnitsa* reported that some 490,000 refugees arrived in Russia in 1990, and more than 550,000 were expected by the end of 1991. The housing budget simply could not deal with this many newcomers.¹⁴

While the housing situation was worsening, people's expectations were increasing. An *Ogonek* commentator explained that housing should be more than just four walls and a roof; it should be home, a cosy place where people gathered round the family hearth. In the Soviet Union most people did not have homes, he argued, only – 'to our great misfortune – *living space*'.¹⁵ A *Rabotnitsa* journalist complained that there was no possibility of exercising personal choice over where or how one lived in the Soviet Union; one was simply assigned accommodation, and was expected to 'smile with gratitude'.¹⁶

Glasnost' resulted in increased access to information about life in the West, and inevitable comparisons. The once reviled capitalist countries were now held up as shining examples. According to S. Smelkin, writing in *Ogonek*, in the Soviet Union housing distribution was based on the formula 'n minus one': '"n" is the number of residents, and "minus one" the number of rooms. Hence four people have three rooms, three people two rooms, two people one room.' In the West, housing distribution followed a very different formula, 'n plus one': everyone would have a room to themselves, and there would be an additional room for common use. This made it possible for a person to exercise a high degree of choice over how to spend his or her time, and with whom:

> He [sic] meets with other family members only when he wants to. He watches TV only when he wants, and watches only what does not put him in a bad mood. He socialises with guests who have come to visit a family member only when they are pleasant guests. And he invites whomever he wants to visit him, without having to ask the other members of the family nest. [For this reason] people in the West irritate each other less, quarrel less, sleep better, are less tired. And, naturally, it is easier to maintain pleasure in life, a healthy atmosphere in relations both in the family and at work.

In Russia, he continued, the vast majority of people lived according to the 'n minus one' formula, which in the West would be seen as an indication of poverty.¹⁷

The new Housing Code, which we discussed in the last chapter, came into effect in 1982. This stipulated that people of different sexes should not have to share a room after the age of nine, with the exception of couples.¹⁸ Now, however, complaints were made about having to share a room at all. A group of readers complained in a letter to *Rabotnitsa* that many single mothers lived in one-room apartments with their offspring, and if the child was a boy they would be entitled to extra space once he reached the age of nine, but if it was a girl they might have to share a room for the rest of their lives. This placed severe restrictions on their activities. The mother could not watch television if her daughter had to do her homework, one of them had to be exiled to the kitchen if the other had visitors, and a young divorcee had little chance of starting a new relationship since her daughter was constantly in the same room.[19]

Housing distribution: incompetence, indifference and corruption

The magazines pointed out that the housing shortage was exacerbated by inappropriate distribution of the housing stock. While some families were crammed into apartments which could barely accommodate them, others had excess space which they did not need. In some cases this was because children had grown up and left home, and the parents were left on their own. In others, an adult child ended up living alone in a large apartment because his or her parents had died. Since 1982, in neither case did the law allow the state to reclaim the excess living space, and because the rent was so low it was not difficult for tenants to find the money. In some cases they even made a profit by renting out a room.[20]

Housing owned by factories or enterprises was sometimes inappropriately distributed due to a lack of awareness of the housing reserves they possessed, or to simple indifference on the part of those in charge. This was demonstrated by a *Rabotnitsa* reader who was so desperate to get an apartment through his workplace that he tried to determine himself whether there really was nothing available. He found that of the enterprise's three-room apartments, one hundred had only two residents and nine had only one, while of the four room apartments, twenty-four had only three residents and eight had only two. When one woman offered to exchange her large apartment for a smaller one, neither the enterprise director nor the trade union could be bothered to act on the proposal. It also transpired that some apartments were kept empty for the use of officials coming to the town on short business trips.[21]

The housing shortage inevitably encouraged speculation in the distribution of living space. Articles told of apartments assigned illegally to people in important positions, or to those who were willing to pay large bribes.[22] In some cases speculation turned into outright criminality. A *Rabotnitsa* correspondent, Irina Zhuravskaya, reported the case of a woman who had amassed a personal fortune by taking bribes for apartments which did not even exist:

> She charged 3,500 rubles for a one-room apartment, 8,000 for a two-room, 9,000 for a three-room, and 12,000 for a four-room. People had to pay up first, and were told they would get an apartment within a year. She claimed to have connections in the city and the district executive committees. This was not true; she took the money and disappeared.

People had been willing to hand over their life savings to a complete stranger engaged in a clearly criminal venture because they were so desperate. One typical victim was a divorced woman still living with her ex-husband in a one-room apartment. The institute where she worked allocated only two apartments every year, and since she was nearing retirement age she would not be in the running. Zhuravskaya refused to condone the use of criminal means to obtain apartments, but she understood what drove people to it:

> People wait for years in the queues of executive committees and enterprises, they wait for years for cooperatives ... and as with anything in deficit, sooner or later it gets engulfed in a wave of speculation.

As one reader explained in a letter to Zhuravskaya, people living in appalling housing became so desperate that they are willing to do anything to get their own homes: 'we would give as much as we could for an apartment, and to whomever it was necessary. Just to live like humans.'[23]

The legacy of short-term solutions to the housing crisis

Another issue taken up in the spirit of *glasnost'* was the poor quality and maintenance of the housing stock, and the short-term fixes which had characterised the Soviet housing programme. Articles and readers' letters talked of residents having to cope with perpetual leaks, dripping taps, broken windows in the entranceways, lifts which did not work, and fetid rubbish bins.[24] Prefabricated housing, which had been hailed as the fastest and cheapest method of solving the housing shortage in the Khrushchev and Brezhnev eras, was now denounced as a shoddy and temporary solution. According to one *Ogonek* commentator, the real principle underlying the Khrushchev programme had not been 'build quickly, cheaply, and well', but 'build quickly, and badly'. Even good-quality panel housing had a life span of only sixty to ninety years, and much of it would soon need to be demolished.[25] Another correspondent held that Moscow was losing between 55,000 and 120,000 apartments per year because they had ceased to be habitable.[26] An *Ogonek* reader claimed in a letter to the magazine that panel construction was not even the fastest form of housing construction; that only seemed to be the case because the Soviet Union had ignored Western developments in construction technology.[27]

Quick-fix solutions to the housing problem had not only resulted in housing which had a short shelf life, but in types of housing which were merely a stop-gap solution. A *Rabotnitsa* writer explained: 'There was a time when the trade unions attempted to produce a lot of housing quickly by concentrating on the so-called "small family dwellings" (*malosemeek*) – housing of a hotel type for young families' (in other words, with no cooking facilities).[28] *Ogonek* also complained that many one- and two-room apartments were still being built, although 'long term, these apartments will only be appropriate for single people'.[29]

The housing department's side of the story

Housing and government officials attempted to explain in the magazines why the housing shortage had never been solved. They pointed out that rents were too low even to provide funding for essential repairs, yet alone new housing. Economists insisted that this had to change, and Abel Aganbegyan suggested that a certain amount of space – for example, twenty square metres per person – should continue to be charged at a low rate while the rent on anything extra should be raised to reflect its real value.[30] Aleksei Poryadin, of the Committee for Housing and Communal Services (*Zhilishchno-kommunal'no khozyaistvo*), insisted that people should be charged the real price of gas, water and electricity; the fact that they currently paid so little created the illusion that these resources were cheap, and this meant they were often squandered.[31]

The problem was compounded by the fact that an increasing number of tenants failed to pay rent at all. A housing official claimed in *Ogonek* that, at the end of 1986, Moscow alone was owed more than three million rubles in unpaid rent, and that four out of five tenants were up to three months behind with their payments. The law dictated that rent and charges for utilities should be paid on a monthly basis, no later than the tenth day of each month, and that a fine of 10 per cent be imposed for late payment, to be taken directly from a person's earnings. However, this fine was too insignificant to act as a disincentive, and the housing authorities had no other means of forcing tenants to pay. If they sent someone to investigate, the tenant could simply refuse the person entry, and the housing department had no legal right to force its way in. Nor did it have the right to evict registered tenants.

Refusal to pay rent could perhaps be seen as a legitimate protest on the part of those forced to live in appalling accommodation. However, a representative from the Ministry of Finance informed *Ogonek* that the list of non-paying tenants in Moscow included thirty high-income families living in self-contained apartments.[32] It would seem that people had come to expect to have their accommodation provided by the state virtually free of charge.

Domicile 2000

The XXVII Congress of the CPSU, held in 1988, contained a resolution identical to that proclaimed by Khrushchev more than three decades earlier: that every family would have its own apartment or house within twelve years. The Gorbachev campaign went by the title '*Zhil'e* 2000' (Domicile 2000).[33] The magazines were cautiously optimistic, though they acknowledged the scale of the problem: thousands of people in every Soviet city were on a list for improved housing, and in some cities they hardly moved up the list from one year to the next. One elderly disabled man in Orel had moved from sixty-sixth place to sixty-second place in the course of eight years,[34] while a couple in their forties had been on their city's list for twelve years and had still only reached number 500.[35]

One proposal outlined in *Ogonek* was that when tenants of communal apartments were 'resettled', the freed-up rooms could be turned into kitchens and bathrooms, with the result that at least some of the remaining tenants would have self-contained apartments. These would not be as comfortable as custom-built single-family apartments, but the recipients would have avoided spending years on a waiting list. The suggestion was also made that families waiting for three-room apartments, for which demand was particularly high, could, as an interim measure, be given a one-room apartment, or a vacated room in a communal apartment, in addition to the accommodation they already had.[36]

There was one notable omission from the *Zhil'e* 2000 campaign: there was no pledge to reduce overcrowding in multi-generational single-family apartments. The resources for this were simply not available.

Privatisation

As the Gorbachev era progressed, it began to take on features which had previously been considered exclusive to capitalism. One of these was the privatisation of the housing stock. This was now presented as the only way forward. Privatisation would encourage more financial investment in the construction and maintenance of housing, relieve municipalities and enterprises of their responsibilities in relation to the housing they currently owned, and give people more choice and control over their lives. There was a new understanding of the home as a private enclave, and reference to the English expression 'my home is my castle' often appeared in these discussions. Sintsov, for example, claimed that Soviet citizens would at last also be able to 'have their own "castle".[37]

In 1988 the Council of Ministers introduced a decree allowing the registered tenants of state or workplace-owned housing to 'privatise' their apartments at very low cost. The number of people who took up the offer was very small, however; according to one official interviewed in *Ogonek*, only 0.03 per cent of apartments were privatised in 1989, and a further 0.7 per cent in 1990. To accelerate the programme, on 4 July 1991 the law was amended to give people the right to assume ownership of their apartments for free.[38] This was hardly fair on those who had already privatised their apartments, but in the words of Kosareva et al., 'the necessity of achieving an immediate transfer of a considerable part of the housing stock into private ownership to create the basis for a housing market outweighed arguments about social justice.'[39] Government assistance, in the form of legal support, credit finance and technological assistance, was also pledged to groups of families wishing to build their own houses on the outskirts of towns and cities. *Sberbank RSFSR*, set up in 1987 largely as a lending bank, offered mortgages of up to 75 per cent of building costs, with repayment over twenty-five years at a rate of 3 per cent per annum. Those wishing to buy existing apartments could get a loan of 10,000 rubles, repayable over an eight-year period at a rate of 10 per cent per annum.[40]

In 1990 *Rabotnitsa* conducted an interview with economist Larisa Piyasheva on the benefits of privatisation. This was the most detailed discussion on the subject to appear in either magazine, and is worth considering at some length.[41]

Piyasheva advocated privatisation of almost all residential property on the grounds that it gave people much more choice. At present, she argued, the state took around two thirds of its citizens' earnings to pay for rent, maintenance, utilities and social services. She acknowledged that some taxation was essential, but thought that people should be able to keep most of their earnings and decide for themselves how they used the money. For some people housing was a priority, and they should be able to choose to economise in other areas in order to afford luxurious apartments.

Responsibility for the maintenance of housing should be passed from the state to the new owners. It would be up to them to hire cleaners, workmen and porters, to collect the money for communal services, and to build up the necessary funds to pay for repairs. They would be able to choose from a range of private, state and cooperative businesses competing for work in housing maintenance and the provision of communal services and personnel.

Piyasheva acknowledged that not everyone would have sufficient money to buy their own apartments at market prices. Accordingly, those who had been on housing waiting lists for ten or more years should still be entitled to state housing. At present the state was committed to providing accommodation for certain categories of people, such as the disabled, demobilised soldiers, war veterans, veterans of labour and families on low incomes, but responsibility for these people should be transferred to other providers. For example, the workplace should help procure housing for its own veterans of labour, while local soviets would have to take care of the low-income families in their districts.

Piyasheva argued against the existence of two parallel sectors, state and private, and insisted that the organisations responsible for housing vulnerable people should not give them apartments, but help them to buy them. Otherwise speculation would be inevitable:

> Imagine that you have to pay 30,000–40,000 rubles for an apartment if you buy it on the private market, or 5,000–10,000 if you grease the palm of a functionary (*chinovnik*) who is in charge of the distribution of free state living space. Which would you prefer? The answer is clear.

In fact, the answer was not so clear. Earlier, Piyasheva had argued that people would welcome private housing since it would provide them with choice. Now she was suggesting that most of them would choose state housing if they had the chance, because they would not have to pay for it. Piyasheva went on to acknowledge that some municipal housing would always be necessary to accommodate the really impoverished (*maloimushchikh*); one can only assume that this would not lead to speculation because the housing would be of such poor quality that only the desperate would want it.

Asked about her own housing situation, Piyasheva replied that she was happy with her apartment but not with the area, which had too many drunks, 'riff raff' (*shpany*) and unemployed people. They threw litter on the streets and turned the doorways and entrance halls even of their own apartment blocks into pigsties. At present it was only possible to escape such neighbours by moving to a 'prestige settlement' on the outskirts of the city, but she was hopeful that some areas in the city centre would begin to go upmarket once apartments could be bought and sold, and then poorer people would have to move to the outskirts. Asked whether she thought they would willingly do so, Piyasheva replied that these were the harsh laws of economics; if people wanted to live in good areas they had to have the means to do so.

Piyasheva's approach to housing stands in stark contrast to that of previous eras. The communal apartment of the Stalin era and the communal apartment block of the Khrushchev era had sought to bring together people from all walks of life. Piyasheva was now proposing an 'us and them' divide, with middle-class property owners living in expensive apartments in their own enclaves, and an impoverished underclass languishing in run-down state housing or the cheapest private rental accommodation.

As privatisation evolved it went through a number of changes. Andrei Sinstsov explained the current situation to *Ogonek* readers in 1991.[42] People would be given a certain amount of space for free, and would have to pay for anything extra. In the Russian Federation the free entitlement was eighteen square metres per person, plus an additional nine square metres of 'general space' for the family as a whole. Depending on their housing resources, local authorities could increase this amount, and Moscow was proposing to increase the 'general space' entitlement to twelve square metres per family. Sintsov did not explain how a city which had always suffered such a housing shortage could afford to be so generous.

Sintsov acknowledged the unfairness of the privatisation programme when he noted that a family whose existing living space was not large enough – that is, it did not measure the requisite number of metres per resident – would not be permitted to privatise, whereas a family which lived in an apartment which exceeded the requisite number of metres would have the legal right to privatise all of that space. People would not be able to sell their apartments for three years after privatisation, but eventually there would be a free market in privatised apartments. The state would continue to provide accommodation to those who could not afford to buy their own apartments, but only in the transitional period before market relations became the norm. Then it would only be obliged to provide housing to the most vulnerable.

Until all of the apartments in a block had been privatised, the state would be obliged to continue providing services for those which had been privatised. However, in a fully privatised block responsibility would pass to the residents. They could form their own house committees, and make arrangements 'with more conscientious and accomplished repairmen and sanitary workers – if they can find them'. It is unclear whether Sintsov was acknowledging with this remark the poor-quality workmanship currently provided by state services, or expressing irritation at the arrogance of private owners. The latter is more likely, since he went on to condemn the inflated demands for repairs which were already being sent by private owners to the authorities. This, he complained, had always been the way with cooperatives, 'and it will evidently be the same with private owners'.

Sintsov acknowledged that privatisation had its drawbacks. It had resulted in a new form of speculation: 'one finds cunning people who offer money to some old lady to buy her apartment and provide her with an addition to her pension, on condition that they are named in her will as the owners of the apartment.'[43] He did not mention an even more alarming development: that these old ladies were sometimes hastened on their way by impatient and unscrupulous prospective owners.[44]

Pavel Bunich, a member of the Soviet Congress of People's Deputies, identified another problem: 'the mafia' had leapt in the moment private ownership was possible, and was 'buying up large numbers of apartments and renting them out for crazy money'.[45] Yet he felt that this was a temporary phenomenon, and that when more 'ordinary people' had privatised their apartments, some would begin to rent them out, and the cost of rental accommodation would go down.[46]

There were some distinct disincentives for 'ordinary people' to privatise, however, at least at the start of the programme. In addition to the concern about the costs of maintaining their own property, they also might have to deal with hostility on the part of neighbours. A former teacher from Leningrad told an *Ogonek* correspondent that when she tried to privatise her modest apartment, her neighbours turned against her and called her 'a *chastnitsa* (privateer), a Nepman, a capitalist.'[47]

Letters sent by readers to the magazines make it clear that there was considerable confusion about the privatisation programme, and a number of grievances. One reader revealed a lack of understanding of the real value of housing when she complained that the state was not actually giving citizens their apartments since their rent money over the years had already paid for them. Four generations of her family had lived in the same apartment for a total of seventy-four years, she continued, paying on average fifteen rubles per month in rent. She acknowledged that some of this money would have been used to pay the wages of the porter and the cleaner and for basic maintenance, but she wanted to know what had happened to the rest of it and why residents had not been made 'the owners of their own living space' years ago.[48]

The members of a house-building cooperative told *Ogonek* that they felt the cooperatives had been left out of the new arrangements, and that their members now had fewer rights than people who had lived in apartments owned by the state or the workplace which they were now entitled to privatise.

> The members of a *ZhSK* have paid in full the cost of the living space (with a percentage in the form of a loan), and have also had to pay for capital repairs and for services (the lift, the services of a porter, doorman, workmen, etc.); but we are not considered to be the owners of our apartments.

They could neither pass them on to their descendents, nor sell them when they wanted to. 'Why is there such injustice?' they wanted to know; 'Why are residents in a *ZhSK* not put on the same basis as residents of state apartments and private houses?'[49]

Other readers expressed relief that 'the great and faceless government' would no longer have 'the exclusive right to impose the rules which regulate people's lives' because of their monopoly over living space. Only when Soviet citizens were the owners of their own homes would they be able to determine themselves how they lived, and would at last be able to declare, like the English, that 'my home is my castle'.[50]

The communal apartment in the Gorbachev era

When it was first launched, the privatisation programme did not extend to residents of communal apartments. For these people, the only possibility of getting better accommodation was to be rehoused into the diminishing stock of state-owned single-family apartments, or to try to find the money to buy an apartment on the open market.

According to one *Ogonek* reader, elderly *kommunalka* residents were the least likely to be rehoused. She herself, she explained, had been born in 1917 and had lived her entire life in a *kommunalka*, and in her experience young people were always prioritised when apartments were resettled. 'The young families in the apartments yell at [the old residents], but then they receive apartments and move out, and the old people, who have been living in communal apartments for sixty to seventy years, still have to wait in line for the toilet and the bathroom, and are scared to leave their own rooms for fear they will be verbally abused.' Even as she wrote, she could hear one of her young neighbours yelling at her from the kitchen: 'it seems I have again done something I shouldn't have.' The elderly should be rehoused first, she argued, so that they could enjoy their last years 'without having to live in fear of their neighbours'.[51]

Some commentators felt that the elderly would be worse off in their own apartments, however. An *Ogonek* journalist expressed concern about the fate of an old man living in a communal apartment in Sverdlovsk. His neighbours were an elderly woman and a young single mother and her small son. The young mother looked after her elderly neighbours, in return for which they looked after her child when she wanted to go out. This mutually supportive arrangement would come to an end when the *kommunalka* was resettled. How would this old man cope, the journalist asked, in his own apartment? 'If he is taken ill, there will be no one to buy his milk or heat it up for him. And there is another terrible danger – that once he has his own four walls, he will get "eaten up" by them.'[52]

Yet if neighbours in a communal apartment could be a source of support, they were more often a source of irritation or even danger. Single women were in a particularly vulnerable position, since no attention was paid to gender when assigning people rooms in communal apartments. Although, as we saw in the last chapter, the 1982 housing reform was supposed to allow for the eviction of a person who did not adhere to the rules of 'common socialist habitation' and violated the right of other residents to live in peace, in reality this seems to have been harder to execute. One woman turned for advice to the legal section of the weekly newspaper *Nedel'ya* (The Week), explaining that she shared a two-room communal apartment with a violent alcoholic man. She had been trying to find someone willing to exchange rooms with her, but nobody else wanted such a neighbour. What could she do? *Nedel'ya*'s legal expert could offer her no assistance. The authorities had no right to remove her neighbour from the apartment in which he was registered, she was told, nor any obligation to rehouse her. All she could do was to continue trying to arrange an exchange herself.[53]

Just as the move to single-family accommodation in the Khrushchev era was accompanied by a new interest in domesticity, so too was privatisation. Residents of communal apartments were generally left out of this home-making trend, but Vladimir Stepanishchev, an interior designer taken on *Rabotnitsa* as consultant on domestic matters, made a valiant attempt to include them. He urged them not to see their room as 'a temporary shelter' in which they 'live out of cases and boxes as if they were in a railway station'. They also should not stuff the apartment with oversized pieces of furniture which they bought in the hope that they would one day have their own apartment. If they could find no appropriate mass-produced furniture, they could easily make their own to fit the dimensions of their room. In this way even the tiniest room could be turned into a comfortable home.[54]

Stepanishchev seemed to accept that the communal apartment would still be around for some time to come. However, most commentators saw it as a dying species, and the nostalgia which was already apparent in the Brezhnev era intensified under Gorbachev. A number of commentators looked back on their years in communal apartments with astonishing fondness; in retrospect, communal apartments were now portrayed as a unique and fascinating feature of Soviet life, peopled by characters who were sometimes endearing, often irritating, but never boring.

In *Ogonek*, photographer Yurii Rost published a photograph of his mother in the corridor of the *kommunalka* where she and her family had lived since the end of the Great Patriotic War. There were eight light-bulbs on the wall, each attached to its own switch. Not one of the bulbs was lit, and Rost explained that he chose to photograph his mother in shadow because he could not shake off his childish fear of their neighbours, who had constantly berated him for wasting electricity. Yet all the same, he now remembered the neighbours with pleasure. There was 'Uncle' Vasya, a driver, who woke the apartment up every morning with his accordion-playing; a middle-aged actress and her elderly husband, and the child they had adopted as a starving war orphan; a family of violinists who would often practise in the kitchen, where *borshch* was always boiling in one saucepan and sheets in another; a lift operator who had the attic room, which she reached by means of a stepladder; a mechanic who did any necessary repairs in the apartment, but set the neighbours' teeth on edge with his motorised metal grinder. These 'dear old neighbours' had managed to coexist '*tesno, no druzhno*' – cramped, but still friendly. They had all been resettled in single-family apartments on the outskirts of the city, apart from his parents; they had also been offered their own apartment, but had preferred to stay in what they saw as their true (*rodnoi*) home.[55] It is interesting to note that it was possible for the elderly couple to decide to remain alone in this enormous apartment; according to the laws of that time, registered tenants could not be forced to move. In this respect, it could be argued that some degree of choice and self-control was now possible in relation to living space.

Aleksandr Terkhov described his childhood years in a communal apartment as 'the happiest time of my life'. He wrote with particular amusement of one neighbour, who would play the same wartime song over and over again on his accordion. The same man also loved to go into the corridor first thing in the morning and phone his workplace from the communal phone, using an important tone of voice to encourage the neighbours to listen and admire him. They obliged. In fact:

> They listened in general all the time, to everything. It was a very compli-cated, tragic, unfortunate, poor, depressing, great life. This was the way

it was in our country. Everyone knew everything about each other ... And yet sometimes I regret that it is over.

The apartment had been resettled family by family, and Terkhov recalled this slow dispersal of a community as a sad process:

> Everyone began to leave, one after the other. But there was a kind of shameful sweetness to this – someone left, but the others did not. They rarely had the luck to all leave together.[56]

The *propiska* system, and the end of the Soviet era

The *propiska* or registration system remained in place up to and beyond the end of the Soviet era, and remained an impediment to the creation of a genuinely free market in housing. People still needed to be registered in a city in order to have a legal right to live there, and buying a property did not automatically give them the right to registration.

Economist Viktor Perevedentsev acknowledged that many people wanted the *propiska* system to end, but insisted that it served a vital function: it prevented uncontrolled population movement, which could place an unmanageable burden on a city's resources. The registration system ensured that, 'in order to live anywhere, it is necessary first of all to have the means to live, i.e. to receive a salary, pension or student grant.'[57]

Other commentators argued that registration could only provide limited control over migration. As we have seen, the outbreak of ethnic hostilities in some of the southern Soviet republics resulted in a flow of refugees to the European heartland, while the greater employment opportunities in the larger cities ensured a large number of economic migrants. The restrictions on registration did not stop people from coming; it just made life extremely difficult for them. At best they could become *limitchiki*, or people with limited rights. This enabled them to work, but they were forced to live in overcrowded hostels or privately rented accommodation on the city outskirts. Even this kind of accommodation was insecure. *Ogonek* related the tale of a woman who attempted to kill herself after her husband left her; she had no registration, and when she was forced to leave the privately rented apartment they had shared, she could not see how she would find any other accommodation.[58]

Some people were rendered homeless after serving time in prison, which disrupted their registration. As one ex-convict explained in *Ogonek*, half of all prisoners were divorced by their spouses in the first year of their sentence, so they were unable to move back into their old homes on release. If they did not have parents willing to take them in they would be out on the streets. Those under the age of forty could try to get *limitchik* status, which was better than nothing, since it enabled them to work. Those over forty were not eligible, however, and were caught in a vicious circle. As people of no fixed abode they could not get registration, and without registration they could not get work. He explained: 'the militia say "find a job and we'll give you registration", but prospective employers say "get registered and then we'll give you a job".' This meant it was almost impossible for these people to get registration – but not being registered was against the law, and '[i]f you have been questioned by the police three times, the fourth time you will go to prison.' If it were possible to get a job without having registration, or if organisations existed to help ex-convicts to get registration and work, there would be both fewer recidivists and fewer homeless people.[59] This suggestion, however, had not been taken up by the Soviet authorities by the time of the country's collapse.

Gorbachev announced his resignation as President of the Soviet Union on 25 December 1991. Since the country had already split into its constituent parts under the umbrella of the Commonwealth of Independent States, without Gorbachev there was no Soviet Union and by the end of the month the country officially ceased to exist. This was nine years before every family was supposed to have its own apartment and, as we will see from the interviews conducted in the final chapter of this book, post-Soviet Russia has still not delivered on that promise.

Notes

1. N.B. Kosareva, A.S. Puzanov and M.V. Tikhomirova, 'Russia: Fast Starter – Housing Sector Reform 1991–1995', in Raymond J. Struyk (ed.), *Economic Restructuring of the Former Soviet Bloc: The Case of Housing* (Avebury: Urban Institute Press, 1996), pp. 263–4.
2. M. Buckley, *Redefining Russian Society and Polity* (Boulder, Col. and Oxford: Westview Press, 1993), p. 115.
3. Ibid., p. 117.
4. Quoted by R. Likhach, 'Komnata + komnata = kvartira', *Ogonek* no. 23 (1987), p. 5.
5. L. Druzenko, 'Koren' kvadratnogo metra', *Rabotnitsa* no. 8 (1987), pp. 24–5.
6. L. Pleshakov, 'Chelovek i ekonomika' (interview with economist Abel G. Aganbegyan), *Ogonek* no. 30 (1987), p. 13.
7. Druzenko, 'Koren' kvadratnogo metra', pp. 24–5.
8. L. Ershova, 'Sem'ya kak sem'ya', *Rabotnitsa* no. 4 (1988), pp. 15–16. See also D. Akivis, 'Kak my budem zhit' zaftra', *Rabotnitsa* no. 2 (1986), p. 11.
9. Interview with S.I. Golod, of the Institute of Socio-Economic Problems, conducted by S. Sidorova, 'Mnogodetnaya sem'ya v zerkale statistiki', *Ogonek* no. 26 (1988), pp. 19–21.
10. N. Rusakova, 'Postoyal'tsy', *Rabotnitsa* no. 1 (1989), pp. 26–8.
11. A typical advertisement began by declaring: 'I live in a two-room cooperative apartment...' See N. Rusakova, 'Troe i odna', *Rabotnitsa* no. 3 (1986), pp. 26–8.

12 V. Perevedentsev, 'Bol'shie goroda', *Ogonek* no. 34 (1987), pp. 12–14; see also Y. Osilov, A. Mikhailovskii and P. Kravtsov, 'Padcheritsy bol'shogo goroda', *Ogonek* no. 41 (1987), pp. 11–15.
13 See letter from mayors V.I. Semchuk and S.N. Krasil'nikov, 'Pochta "Ogonek"', *Ogonek* no. 21 (1990), p. 4; M. Mamaev, 'Polet vo vcherashnii den'', *Ogonek* no. 24 (1989), pp. 14–17; and I. Zhuravskaya, 'Primite na postoi...', *Ogonek* no. 25 (1991), pp. 26–7.
14 N. Os'minina, 'Zhil'e, rabotu!', *Rabotnitsa* no. 8 (1991), p. 11.
15 A. Sintsov, 'Budem sobstvennikami?', *Ogonek* no. 38 (1991), pp. 12–14.
16 L. Ershova, 'Sem'ya kak sem'ya', *Rabotnitsa* no. 4 (1988), pp. 15–16.
17 S. Smelkin, 'Kommunal'noe myshlenie – nadezhno li nash zhilishche?', *Ogonek* no. 4 (1991), pp. 9–11.
18 The housing shortage meant that this rule was often flouted. My own circle of friends and acquaintances include a divorced couple who continued to live together until he emigrated in 1991, and a grown man sharing a room with his mother and stepfather.
19 Letter from T.Temnaya, A. Sarkisyan, T. Belekhova and I. Churanova, 'Pochta "Rabotnitsa"', *Rabotnitsa* no. 2 (1989), p. 18.
20 Pleshakov, 'Chelovek i ekonomika', pp. 12–14.
21 Druzenko, 'Koren' kvadratnogo metra', pp. 24–5.
22 See A. Minkin, 'Nekhoroshaya kvartira', *Ogonek* no. 48 (1990), p. 31.
23 I. Zhuravskaya, 'Igra bez vyigrisha', *Rabotnitsa* no. 4 (1986), pp. 30–1.
24 E.Mikhailovskaya, 'Nemnogo mazhora v kommunal'nom khozyaistve: O tom, kak v Kazani sozdayut komfort dlya zhil'tsa', *Rabotnitsa* no. 1 (1989), pp. 19–20; and letter from L.A. Ukhlinova and other residents of apartment house no. 27, Kolomenskaya ulitsa, Moscow, 'Pochta Ogoneka', *Ogonek* no. 45 (1990), p. 5.
25 Letter from I. Landa, chair of club 'Gorozhane' in Dnepropetrovsk, 'Pochta Ogoneka', *Ogonek* no. 8 (1990), p. 6.
26 Smelkin, 'Kommunal'noe myshlenie – nadezhno li nash zhilishche?', pp. 9–11.
27 Landa, 'Pochta Ogoneka', p. 6.
28 Akivis, 'Kak my budem zhit' zaftra', p. 11.
29 Smelkin, 'Kommunal'noe myshlenie – nadezhno li nash zhilishche?', pp. 9–11.
30 Pleshakov, 'Chelovek i ekonomika', pp. 12–14.
31 A. Poryadin, 'Podrazhaet li zhil'e posle privatizatsiya?', *Ogonek* no. 38 (1991), p. 19.
32 A. Mikhailovskii, 'Neplatel'shchiki', *Ogonek* no. 14 (1987), p. 10.
33 See Smelkin, 'Kommunal'noe myshlenie – nadezhno li nash zhilishche?', pp. 9–11; and A. Sintsov, 'Bydem sobstvennikami?', *Ogonek* no. 38 (1991), pp, 12–14.
34 O.Volodeeva, 'Prostaya istoriya', *Rabotnitsa* no. 8 (1989), pp. 11–12.
35 Sintsov, 'Bydem sobstvennikami?', pp. 12–14.
36 R. Likhach, 'Komnata + komnata = kvartira', *Ogonek* no. 23 (June 1987), p. 5.
37 Sintsov, 'Bydem sobstvennikami?', p. 14.
38 Interview with A. Krivov, of Goskomitet, conducted by S. Filippov, *Ogonek* no. 38 (1991), pp. 18–19.
39 Kosareva et al., 'Russia: Fast Starter', pp. 256–7.
40 'Kredity – novoselu', *Ogonek* no. 38 (1991), p. 19.
41 Interview with economist L. Piyasheva, conducted by N. Fedorova, 'Kuplyu kvartiru!', *Rabotnitsa* no. 10 (1990), p. 20.
42 Sintsov, 'Bydem sobstvennikami?', pp. 12–14.
43 Ibid.

44 Personal conversations. There have also been reports on the phenomenon in a range of Russian newspapers.
45 P. Bunich, 'Bar'ery privatizatsii', *Ogonek* no. 33 (1990), pp. 5–6.
46 Ibid.
47 Sintsov, 'Bydem sobstvennikami?', pp. 12–14.
48 Letter from E. Vas'kovskaya, 'Pochta "Ogonek"', *Ogonek* no. 50 (1991), p. 4.
49 Letter from members of 'Pulse' house-building cooperative, 'Slovo chitatelya', *Ogonek* no. 25 (1989), p. 5.
50 Letter from Ukhlinova et al., 'Pochta Ogoneka', p. 5.
51 Letter from veteran of labour G. Sverina, 'Chitatel' – zhurnal – chitatel'', *Ogonek* no. 31 (1987), p. 8.
52 G. Potapovskaya, 'Pomozhem drug drugy', *Ogonek* no. 46 (1986), pp. 31–2.
53 Prinuditel'nyi obmen kvariry', *Nedel'ya* no. 22 (1995), p. 12.
54 L. Shevtsova., 'Lomaite steretipy!' (interview with Vladimir Stepanishchev), 'Domashnii kaleidoskop prilozhenie k zhurnalu "Rabotnitsa"', pull-out section in *Rabotnitsa* no. 1 (1989).
55 Y. Rost, 'Mama i kommunalka', *Ogonek* no. 31 (1987), p. 30.
56 A. Terkhov, 'Kommunalka', illustrated by photographer Y. Feklistov, *Ogonek* no. 38 (1991), pp. 16–17.
57 Perevedentsev, 'Bol'shie goroda', pp. 12–14.
58 Zhuravskaya, 'Primite na postoi...', pp. 26–7.
59 Letter from N.Ya. Sobolev, 'Pochta "Ogonek"', *Ogonek* no. 44 (1990), p. 6.

12

Personal tales

The previous chapters have drawn primarily on material from Soviet magazines, journals and newspapers. Some of these publications aimed to provide information on changing housing policies for those who were engaged, in various capacities, in the construction or distribution of housing. Most, however, were intended for the 'masses': those who lived, literally, with the consequences of those policies. While they usually played down the appalling conditions in which people were housed, I have argued that a close reading can still provide numerous insights into the reality of people's lives. This chapter aims to go further down this road by asking people who lived through the various changes in housing policy to reflect on their own experiences.

Interviews were carried out in Moscow and St Petersburg between March 2002 and May 2006, with a total of sixteen people. Few of them were actually native to those cities, but had moved there from the countryside or from provincial towns. The interviewees ranged in age from thirty-eight to their late seventies. Their occupations included teaching, research, librarianship, journalism and television production. While all of them were white-collar professionals, in most cases their parents had come from more humble origins and had been beneficiaries of the increased educational opportunities and social mobility which characterised the earlier decades of Soviet power (though in the Stalin era the unfortunate reason for this social mobility was that many jobs became vacant when their previous incumbents disappeared into the jaws of the GULAG).

The interviews were organised largely in accordance with the 'snowball' effect, whereby the first people I interviewed put me in touch with others. I conducted the interviews with all but three of the respondents. Those three were carried out by Marina Anatol'evna, a friend in Moscow with whom I had discussed the project at some length and who interviewed both her parents, and a friend who she felt had a particularly interesting housing history since he had lived in a large number of communal apartments. Of the interviews I conducted myself, all but two were carried out in the respondents' own homes.

As well as offering personal tales of living with the inadequacies and absurdities of Soviet housing, the interviews provide a bridge between Soviet and post-Soviet housing experiences. In the previous chapter we discussed the privatisation of state and workplace accommodation which had been introduced in the Gorbachev era. Most of my respondents had taken advantage of this opportunity, but home ownership had proved a mixed blessing since it was accompanied by increased costs and responsibilities. By the time the interviews were conducted privatised apartments could be sold on, and a private housing market had come into being. There was, at that time, no shortage of buyers. Most of my respondents had adult children who had lived with them in the Soviet era, and so had no accommodation of their own to privatise. The huge reduction in state and workplace accommodation, and the tighter regulations on eligibility, meant that the only way these people could acquire their own apartments was to purchase them.

As Catherine Merridale has noted, 'Anyone who has collected spoken testimonies will know how they confound even the most meticulously planned research. You arrive with clear-cut questions, neatly typed; you leave with narratives, dialogues, evasions, long digressions, laughter, more phone numbers, photographs and tears.'[1] While much of this was true in relation to my own interviews, the subject matter could not have been more different. Merridale was concerned with death; I was asking my respondents to reflect on life, in the sense of daily existence or *byt*.

One thing I did not have to contend with were evasions. My respondents seemed delighted by my interest in their lives and were happy to talk at length about their experiences of Soviet housing. One had even gone to the trouble of producing from memory detailed floor plans of the apartments she had lived in. Their recollections of communal living were seasoned with sardonic humour. Yet, as we found in the articles and stories we explored in the previous chapters, there were some evident traces of nostalgia for life in the communal apartment.

I have identified the respondents by name and patronymic. One requested anonymity, and I have given her a fictitious name. I will discuss particular elements of their experiences in accordance with the themes which have emerged in the previous chapters.

Different forms of communal life: hostels, barracks and communal apartments

All but one of my respondents had experience of communal living. Many of them recalled a sense of irritation at the constant presence of others, and a desire for personal space. However, most of them looked back on their days of communal living with shrugs of acceptance. Their experiences might sound strange now, they explained, but they did not seem so at the time. This was simply how people lived in the Soviet Union.' Vladimir Nikolaevich, who was in his seventies at the time of the interview, held that people did not find it that difficult to live communally in the Soviet era because 'there was a collective psychology under socialism'. Galina Mikhailovna put it more bluntly: 'This was Russia. People were used to living all together.'

The concept of 'personal space' is relative. Reflecting on his housing history, Vladimir Borisovich, now in his sixties, felt that 'the most important thing was that we did not have to suffer life in a barracks or hostel.' Mariya Efimovna did have experience of living in a hostel, when, at the age of three, in 1930, she came to Moscow with her family to escape the famine in the Ukraine. The six of them – her parents, herself, her sister and two brothers – lived with nine other people in a room measuring sixteen square metres, which was the supposed 'sanitary norm' for two people. Four people slept in each bed. There was one large communal kitchen for the entire hostel. They were delighted when they were assigned a room in a communal apartment – 'it was a real pleasure to have a room to ourselves!' – even though there was still barely enough room for them all to stretch out to sleep. The family, if not its individual members, now had some semblance of personal space.

The industrialisation drive meant that barracks and hostels continued to be a prevalent form of housing throughout the Stalin era. As Vladimir Borisovich explained, Moscow grew enormously between the wars: 'the population doubled or even trebled, and the newcomers had to be accommodated somehow.' Emma Aleksandrovna grew up in the 1940s in Fili, a 1930s settlement on the outskirts of Moscow[2] which had been earmarked for further industrial development and which, accordingly, had a glut of post-war barracks. These were meant to provide temporary accommodation for new workers, but '"temporary" could last for a very long time', and some of her school friends lived in barracks for much of their childhood. Single women could end up living their entire adult lives in hostels, she continued; the war had wiped out an entire generation of potential husbands, which meant that many women had no chance of finding a partner. The authorities saw hostels as the most appropriate housing for them.

Communal apartments varied enormously. Those which had been converted from requisitioned bourgeois apartments at the time of the Revolution were the largest. Svetlana Ivanovna, aged forty-three at the time of the interview, continues to live in a nine-room communal apartment in St Petersburg, in a building dating from the early nineteenth century. As we have discussed in the previous chapters, communal apartments built in the Stalin era were generally much smaller. This was because by the end of the first Five Year Plan the family had been 'rehabilitated', and the single-family home declared the ideal form of housing. Yet the state was either unable or unwilling to provide sufficient resources to build enough apartments to enable each family to have one to itself, which meant that the new 'single-family apartments' became miniature communal apartments. Lyudmila Ivanovna explained that they 'were built according to the principle that one day they would be occupied by a single family, but in the meantime they had to cram people in'. She had lived as a child in the post-war years in Zhukovskii, a new socialist city built in the 1930s around an aeroplane construction enterprise, where her family shared a three-room apartment with a single man. For them it worked well, since he was quiet and, in any case, not often home. For him, however, being the only person in the apartment who was not part of the family, it might have been a less comfortable experience.

While it was rare for 'ordinary' families to have their own kitchen in the Stalin era, it was not entirely unknown. A private kitchen made the accommodation incomparably better than a communal apartment, even if the living space was just as cramped. Emma Aleksandrovna's family lived in what had been a country estate before the Revolution, consisting of a manor house and two small side-buildings which had originally housed the staff. The estate had been requisitioned and assigned to workers and their families, and her extended family had two rooms and a small kitchen in one of the side-buildings. There was no bathroom, so they had to go to the *banya* (bath house) or wash in a tub; nor were there indoor toilets, but each family had set up its own outside toilet in a wooden hut secured with a padlock. Water came from a standpipe, and heating took the form of ineffectual wood-burning stoves. Emma Aleksandrovna slept in the same room as her parents and brother. Yet the fact that they had their own kitchen meant they had some private family life, which made their accommodation exceptionally good for those times.

The neighbours in communal apartments

The neighbours were the most important and, usually, the most difficult aspect of life in the communal apartment. My respondents rejected the idea that the authorities intentionally placed people from completely different backgrounds together as an experiment in social engineering; three of them (Vladimir Nikolaevich, Lyudmila Armenakovna and Svetlana Ivanovna) pointed out that it was not difficult to change rooms and that many people chose to do so, sometimes to escape particularly unpleasant neighbours but more often for practical reasons such as the desire to live closer to their workplace. This movement between apartments meant that the original mix of people was often temporary. Vladimir Nikolaevich and Lyudmila Armenakovna also knew of communal apartments in which the residents came from quite similar social backgrounds, and developed strong friendships with one another.

All the same, some noted with amusement that it did sometimes seem as though the residents had been placed together in accordance with a pattern. Sasha Sergeevich recalled that:

> There was always one 'villain'; one exceptionally good person; one person who always picked fights; and one informer. This was usually the 'Senior Tenant' (*otvetsvennyi kvartiros'emshchik*) who would report to the chief of the housing management.

Emma Aleksandrovna claimed that all communal apartments had a 'female tyrant' who was determined to force the other residents to adhere to her notion of order. They all agreed that almost every communal apartment had a resident alcoholic.

None of my respondents described a situation as embarrassing as that experienced by Svetlana Boym's family, when the alcoholic in their communal apartment ruined their genteel gathering with foreign guests by passing out in the corridor outside their room and urinating in his sleep, sending 'a little yellow stream ... through the door of the room'.[3] Yet they acknowledged that, as Svetlana Ivanovna put it, 'the drunk is the main problem for people living in a communal apartment.' The alcoholic in Emma Aleksandrovna's apartment – in this case a woman – was always vomiting in the communal bathroom, leaving her daughter-in-law to clean up the mess. Sasha Sergeevich had more positive memories of his alcoholic neighbour, but he was just a child, and kind-hearted 'Uncle Misha' would often take him out for walks in the park. There might have been an ulterior motive on Uncle Misha's part, however: 'If there was a queue for beer, and uncle Misha turned up with me, the whole queue would say: "Let him jump the queue. He's with the boy."'

Violence, often fuelled by alcohol, was sometimes a problem in communal apartments. However, Paulina Aleksandrovna, who still lives in a communal apartment in Moscow, said that in her experience it was usually directed against family members rather than neighbours. The close proximity of other people sometimes gave women a degree of protection from domestic violence. One of Paulina's neighbours

> developed a 'survival tactic': whenever her husband attacked her she would escape from their room and stand in the corridor. When she was there, he would leave her alone. His sphere of control ended at the door of their room, but the corridor was communal territory, and the neighbours felt they had the right to get involved in what happened there.

One of the neighbours would sometimes take the woman into her own room and then 'try to reason with [the husband] in the corridor'. However, they did not feel able to cross the threshold into the family's room, whatever was happening inside. If the wife wanted their protection, she had to get herself out of her husband's sphere of control and into the communal territory.

Sexual harassment was also not uncommon, and the indiscriminate mixing of sexes made single women particularly vulnerable. As Paulina explained, 'as a married woman you would have some protection, but for a single woman it was a constant threat.' For two years in the early 1990s she herself had suffered the unwanted sexual attentions of a neighbour. He was a single man who had previously had an affair with a married woman living with her husband in the same apartment; the couple broke up because of the affair and both moved out, and when Paulina moved into their room the man transferred his attention to her. He was known as a violent man and the neighbours were afraid to intervene; all Paulina could do was try to avoid him, and when a room became vacant in the apartment next door she moved out. She later heard that the man had subsequently begun harassing another young woman whose family had moved into her old room, and they had also moved out. Paulina was now working as a researcher on gender issues and was a campaigner for women's rights, and decided to find out what legal rights a woman had if she found herself in this position. She was informed by the Ministry of Internal Affairs that the woman would be unable to get her tormentor evicted if he was registered to live in the apartment. All she could do was move out herself, as Paulina and her successor had done.

The communal areas in the apartment, especially the kitchen, constituted the main stage for disputes and arguments. Disagreements over cleanliness and order were common, but the establishment of cleaning rotas helped to deal with this. However, none of my respondents knew of apartments which had established rotas for cooking. Finding space in the kitchen to prepare their families' meals was one of the main problems women had to deal with. As Nina Borisovna pointed out, there might be three or more women cooking separately in the same kitchen, and this inevitably led to conflicts. Although neighbours might be invited to join in a special celebratory meal, my respondents agreed that it was virtually unheard of for the residents of a communal apartment to take it in turns to cook for the entire household. One of my respondents, Genrikh Pavlovich, had what in the Russian context was an unusual problem for a man: he loved to cook, but felt inhibited in the all-female environment of the communal kitchen. The other women would never leave him in peace, and constantly commented on and derided his efforts.

There could also be conflicts over the use of electricity and light bulbs. When Lyudmila Petrovna and Anatolii Aleksandrovich moved into a two-family communal apartment in 1958, their new neighbours constantly complained that they did not turn the lights off. Anatolii Aleksandrovich resolved the problem by telling them that he would pay for the light-bulbs and electricity in all of the communal areas – the bathroom, corridor and kitchen – 'so that we don't have any problems'. Relations improved so much after this that his neighbour even taught him to drive.

The desire to create some sense of privacy out of the communal apartment could be taken to extremes. It was invariably the case that each family insisted on cramming its own table into the kitchen, but Arkadii Abramovich recalled that in one of the communal apartments he lived in each family had its own toilet seat, all of which hung from hooks on the toilet wall.

Theft of foodstuffs could be an issue. Marina Anatol'evna related the following story, in which friends of hers dealt with the problem with quiet resignation: 'It was the late 1980s. There were two young families [living in a communal apartment], and they had a communal fridge. And one family repeatedly took food which belonged to the other family. The members of the other family – they were quiet, unassuming people – wrote notes and left them in the fridge, asking their neighbours to please not eat all of the *smetana*, or to leave them some potatoes. And they continued to live like this for almost a year.'

In the overcrowded conditions of a communal apartment, noise was inevitable. Arkadii Abramovich recalled a young boy who played the accordion from morning to night, though 'he had absolutely no ear for music'. Poor soundproofing contributed to what Il'ya Utekhin has referred to as the 'transparency of space', which meant that neighbours knew almost everything that went on in each other's 'private' lives. Yet, as Steven Harris has noted, while this might seem strange to an outsider, for long-term residents of communal apartments it was a 'completely normal way of life'.[4] This was confirmed by one of my respondents, Sasha Sergeevich. He claimed that as a child living in a communal apartment he was unaware of any real dividing line between an individual room and the communal corridor: 'Everyone knew everything about everyone else – who was ill, who held what opinion on what subject. Everything was seen as a matter of general interest and concern.'

Children may have been comfortable with such a complete lack of privacy, but this was not the case for most adults. For them, the desire to achieve some sense of personal space, as well as to minimise the possibility of conflict, often resulted in them having as little contact as possible with their neighbours. Genrikh Pavlovich claimed that he had always enjoyed 'reasonable' relations with his neighbours, but then added: 'well, there were no fights, which is the best one can say.' 'Reasonable' relations, then, meant that neighbours did not come to blows, nor interfere openly in each other's business.

Arkadii Abramovich and his grandmother were so detached from their neighbours in one of the communal apartments they lived in that they were unaware of the existence of one of their neighbours until he died. He recalled:

> There were two alcoholics living in the apartment, mother and son, they were around forty-five and twenty-five years old. Then it turned out that the father also lived with them, but he never left his bed and we [he and his grandmother] only found out about him when he died, when we had already been living there for two years.

In some apartments, however, neighbours offered each other considerable kindness and support when this was necessary. Svetlana Ivanovna and her neighbours helped an elderly, bedridden resident of their apartment with her shopping and cleaning in the last months of her life. For the elderly, Svetlana concluded, there were some advantages to communal living.

The stories told by most of my respondents give the impression of an 'us versus them' situation, 'our family' against 'the neighbours'. Yet the most difficult neighbour in a communal apartment could be a family member. This was Mariya Efimovna's experience when, in the mid-1950s, she moved into the apartment in which her new husband and his mother lived. They shared it with a large Tartar family, whom she remembered with fondness; they were warm, friendly people. Yet her relationship with her mother-in-law was always fraught. Mariya Efimovna and her husband had a room to themselves but enjoyed little privacy because her mother-in-law lived in the next room and was afraid that the newlyweds would literally close their door on her – if they had one. Accordingly, she insisted that their two rooms be separated only by a curtain.

Anatolii Aleksandrovich and Lyudmila Petrovna had an unusually positive experience of communal living. In the 1950s Anatolii Aleksandrovich lived in what was officially termed a hostel but was actually a three-room apartment owned by his workplace, the Institute of Atomic Energy. Eleven men from the Institute were registered to live there, though only seven or eight of them actually did at any one time. They were not much interested in domestic matters and spent most of their time at work, but they always ate together and took it in turns to shop and cook. They also shared any food parcels sent by relatives in the countryside. In 1956 Anatolii Aleksandrovich married Lyudmila Petrovna, and she moved into the apartment. One other young man slept in the same room as them, but Lyudmila Petrovna did not find this embarrassing because, as she put it, he always 'observed etiquette'. She felt more embarrassed about sharing the toilet and bathroom with all these men. The couple chose to do some things as a twosome, but their neighbours always invited them to share whatever they had cooked, and relations remained close. In due course two other men married and moved their wives in, and Lyudmila Petrovna and the woman who became known as 'wife no. 2' remain the best of friends. Yet, however congenial the relations within the apartment, Anatolii Aleksandrovich and Lyudmila Petrovna both emphasised that they did not think of it as a real home. Nor were they interested in having a real home at this point in their lives. They had different priorities back then; as new graduates and employees at a new Institute, they were thoroughly absorbed in their work, and the apartment was really just a place to sleep.

Paulina Aleksandrovna is also unusual in that she has developed a close friendship with her longstanding neighbour, a divorcee called Tanya. When people move out of a communal apartment now they are less likely to be replaced, and at the time of the interview the only people living in their apartment were Paulina, Tanya, Tanya's two children, and an elderly woman who had been offered an apartment of her own. Tanya was hoping to convince the housing authorities that her children, who were now young adults, would soon be starting families of their own and would need the freed-up space, and then she, her family and Paulina could have the apartment to themselves.

The number of residents in Svetlana Ivanovna's St Petersburg apartment had also drastically reduced in recent years. When she moved in, in 1976, there were seven families living in the apartment's nine rooms. Now there were only three. This meant that she finally had a room to herself, having shared one with her mother for twenty years. Yet she had one regret. The neighours seemed to her less tolerant of one another now that there were fewer of them: 'Perhaps when there are lots of people, they understand that they have to get on.'

Arkadii Abramovich lived his entire life in communal apartments, usually sharing a room with his grandmother, until he finally got his own apartment six years ago, at the age of thirty-two. Although at first he had been delighted to be living on his own, he was not prepared for the feeling of isolation. In the past he had always felt that there was someone he could turn to if he needed help. Now, rattling around in his empty apartment, he sometimes experienced a sense of panic.

The single-family apartment

By the end of the Khrushchev era, the communal apartment was a thing of the past for all but three of my respondents. As noted previously, the scale of the movement from communal to individual apartments was enormous. This was confirmed by my respondents. Vladimir Nikolaevich, a Leningrad resident since 1944, estimated that 90 per cent of families in that city were living in communal apartments until the Khrushchev era, but virtually every family he knew then received its own apartment.

According to Emma Aleksandrovna, most of the new apartments were distributed to workers by their trade union or workplace. Housing was an important resource, she said, and could be used to manipulate workers. People would normally only be assigned an apartment if they had worked at a factory or enterprise for some time. However, she did know of people who had taken a particular job in order to get an apartment, and subsequently gave up the job but managed to hang on to the apartment.

For unmarried people it was extremely difficult to get an apartment to themselves. For the most part they lived with their parents, in hostels, or in communal apartments. We noted earlier that some of the newly built single-family apartments were actually used as communal apartments for single people. Genrikh Pavlovich lived in one of these; he was assigned living space in a three-room apartment built in the early Khrushchev era, which he shared with five other single people. When he married, his wife moved in with him, and only when she became pregnant were they finally assigned their own apartment.

My respondent also confirmed that women who were unable to find husbands in the post-war decades might live their entire adult lives in hostel accommodation. Emma Aleksandrovna pointed out that if a single woman did somehow manage to get her own apartment, she would not remain single for long since the apartment would so improve her marriage prospects that she would soon secure herself a husband.

Even if they had not minded living communally (and Galina Mikhailovna recalled that 'life in the communal apartment could sometimes be fun'), my respondents were all delighted when they finally had their own family space. Most felt that the move to a single apartment was more important for women, because men were more focused on their work, and so their domestic situation did not matter so much. The men I interviewed generally agreed. At least in their younger years, work had been more important to them than home; as Vladimir Borisovich put it, home was where he slept. Yet there were dissenters. Elena Mikhailovna, a film critic, was extremely committed to her work and had always employed a housekeeper so that she did not have to waste her time on housework. Conversely, Genrikh Pavlovich, the keen cook, found sharing a kitchen in a communal apartment very difficult because his female neighbours resented his presence in their space. For him, the move to a single-family apartment had come as a huge relief.

Yet despite their initial pleasure at getting their own apartments, it did not take my respondents long to discover that there were significant drawbacks. The small dimensions of the Khrushchevian apartment meant that it was likely to still be overcrowded. Sasha Sergeevich's family moved into a tiny single-family apartment when he was six years old, and 'the new apartment still seemed like a communal apartment because there were so many generations living in it'.

Another problem was the ubiquitous 'walk-through' room. Almost all of the new apartments had one. According to Mariya Efimovna, the rationale was that it economised on corridor space and meant the rooms themselves could be a little larger. Her son, Sasha, thought that it also anticipated a time when space would not be at such a premium and it would be possible to have a living room in which nobody had to sleep. As yet, however, this was a utopian dream. The walk-through room might be used as the family's living room, but someone always had to sleep in it, and their privacy was severely compromised. As the years passed, many people added additional walls to close off access to the walk-through room, sacrificing room size for privacy.[5]

The size of the kitchen was also a problem. Even though they no longer had to share it with other families, some of my respondents complained that it was too small even for their own use, especially when they began to acquire the domestic appliances which were now available. The problem was exacerbated by the fact that the function of the kitchen had changed. In communal apartments it was used only for cooking, and everyone took their meals to their own rooms. However, in the single-family apartment people preferred to gather round the kitchen table to eat. This was the case even when they had guests. Galina Mikhailovna offered an entirely practical explanation for this: few families had a dining table, or enough space to put one, in any of the other rooms. Yet the private kitchen was also seen as a particularly intimate space, and the one in which guests could be made to feel most at home.[6]

For my female respondents, the kitchen had particular significance. Men's involvement in domestic work was still negligible, and so, apart from at mealtimes or when they had guests, the kitchen was a female zone, the nearest thing a woman had to her own space. Accordingly, for them the most important thing about moving to a single-family apartment was not having to share the kitchen with other women.

Yet it did not always work out this way. Mariya Efimovna had to continue sharing what she saw as her kitchen, albeit with other female family members. Firstly, her mother-in-law insisted on moving with them into the new apartment, even though she had been offered one of her own. She refused to do much housework on the grounds that she was a dentist and had to protect her hands, but she was constantly hovering over Mariya Efimovna and belittling her efforts. After her mother-in-law died, one of Mariya Efimovna's sons married and moved his new wife into the apartment. The two women did not feel comfortable with one another and would stand silently side by side in the kitchen cooking their separate meals, just like neighbours in a communal apartment.

I asked if there was resentment on the part of those who did not get their own apartments in the Khrushchev era. Opinions were divided. Anatolii Akeksandrovich and Lyudmila Petrovna insisted that people were not concerned about who had their own apartment and who did not; they just accepted that this was a feature of the times. People had different values then, they argued, and work, study and friendship were much more important than material matters. However, it could be argued that these two people were in an exceptional position. They were young, recently graduated, and were involved in particularly interesting work. Vladimir Nikolaevich had more negative memories. Before, he said, everyone had been the same; now a process of material stratification began, and those who had not been rehoused did resent those who had. This situation was not helped by the fact that some people were able to use contacts or manipulate housing distribution rules so as to get additional accommodation. It was not uncommon, he related, for elderly people who had been assigned apartments to register their adult offspring there, and then, after a respectable period of time, get themselves back on the housing list so that they would in due course be assigned another room or apartment.

Sleeping arrangements in the single-family apartment

Who slept where in the single-family apartment provides some interesting insights into attitudes towards personal space and privacy. In most cases, the married couple slept in the walk-through room. My respondents could think of no particular reason for this, save that the walk-through room doubled as the living room, and the married couple was likely to go to bed later than their young children or elderly parents.

In some cases the family calculated which of its members was most in need of privacy and organised their living space accordingly. Vladimir Borisovich's family had no walk-through room, since their apartment was built in the Stalin era (it was assigned to them in 1948, as a reward for Vladimir Borisovich's exemplary work record). However, they still had only two rooms for a family of four. Vladimir Borisovich was just starting university at the time, and it was felt that he needed his own space in order to study well. Accordingly he had the smaller of the two rooms to himself, while his teenaged sister and his parents shared the larger one.

Emma Aleksandrovna divided her time between two apartments when her daughter was small, that of her husband and her parents. Her parents' apartment was in a less polluted part of Moscow and was beside a park, which made it a better place to bring up a child, and her mother was also on hand to help her with the child care. She usually stayed there during the summer and went back to her husband's apartment in the winter: 'so I had a summer and a winter apartment!' When she was in her husband's apartment they had no fixed arrangements as to who slept where. Sometimes the child slept in the walk-through room, but if her husband had to get up early he slept there so as not to disturb the others. There was, then, no strong need to claim a particular space as one's own. At least in the early years of single-family living, the concept of private *personal* rather than *family* space seems to have been an alien concept.

New furniture and appliances for the new apartment

For many of my respondents, one of the pleasures of moving to a single-family apartment was the opportunity to buy new furniture. 'Before this we lived out of suitcases', Vladimir Borisovich recalled. They remembered most of the furniture for the new apartments coming from neighbouring Eastern bloc countries; Lyudmila Ivanovna recalled buying East German products, while Elena Mikhailovna's new furniture came from Czechoslovakia. Politically, the relationship between the Soviet Union and its post-war buffer zone was not that different from that of other imperial powers and their colonies, but economically it had been turned on its head, with the Eastern European 'colonies' producing manufactured goods for the Soviet market. These goods were of good quality but expensive, and since, as Emma Aleksandrovna pointed out, so many people were moving into their own apartments at the same time, there was not enough to go round. Accordingly, my respondents remembered buying their furniture in an ad hoc manner rather than in accordance with a plan, and much of it did not match. In some families decisions were taken collectively, and there were no quarrels about what to get. Galina Mikhailovna, however, insisted that, as the woman, she made these decisions; 'I was the matriarch!' she declared with pride. Anatolii Aleksandrovich and Lyudmila Petrovna had as unconventional an attitude towards furniture as they had towards the home: for a long time the main piece of furniture in their new single-family apartment was a ping-pong table.

Domestic appliances were also acquired as and when they could be procured and paid for. When Vladimir Borisovich's father won the Stalin Prize in 1953, they used the money to buy a washing machine and a vacuum cleaner, two appliances which were just beginning to become available. These were really for his mother, he added, since she was the only one who did any domestic work:

> Back then there was no conception of men doing housework. Women did everything, even before they had any domestic appliances. The shopping, which was itself a tough job which involved standing in lines; the cooking, the washing, and all by hand before they got washing machines.

Yet some of the female respondents wondered if the appliances had really been that useful. Before Lyudmila Ivanovna's family got their first washing machine in the mid-1960s they would use the local laundry, where they would pay a few kopecks to have the washing and ironing done. It took half an hour to take the laundry there, and half an hour to go and collect it. The same amount of washing and ironing took around four hours to do at home, even with the help of the washing machine and electric iron. As both Elena Mikhailovna and Emma Aleksandrovna pointed out, domestic washing machines were initially of poor quality and had a tendency to ruin clothes, so they both used them only to wash sheets and continued to take their clothes to the laundry.

Many of my respondents could only afford the cheapest appliances, and these were not much help. The first iron Mariya Efimovna had in her single-family apartment had to be heated up on the stove, while the washing machine, a gift from her parents, had separate tubs for washing and drying, and the wet washing had to be dragged from one to the other. She too found it faster and easier to go to the laundry.

Children and child care

The demographic situation was always a concern in the Soviet Union, and young people were encouraged to marry and start their families early. Many did so, often while they were still in higher education. With the majority of women going on to work full time, this made child care a big issue.

As we have seen in previous chapters, socialised child care was strongly promoted in the early years of the Revolution, with some commentators calling for entirely separate accommodation for children. This would ensure that neighbours – and, indeed, mothers themselves – would not have their peace disturbed by the 'continual racket' of children.[7] By the 1930s, however, the official attitude towards child care had become more contradictory. This is reflected in my respondents' stories.

According to Elena Mikhailovna, having a nanny was not at all uncommon even amongst people committed to socialist ideals. Her own father was a Communist Party official, and they always had a nanny:

> These nannies were usually young girls who had come directly from the countryside. Our nanny was even registered with the trade union as a hired worker [*naemnaya trud'nitsa*], which meant she had the right to a pension ... She did everything; I remember her washing sheets in a huge tub, using her feet!

Emma Aleksandrovna and her family, as noted earlier, were in the unusual position of having their own kitchen in the pre-war years. Accordingly they were able to take on a nanny and accommodate her in the kitchen. She became a friend of the family, and Emma Aleksandrovna's father encouraged her to try to do better for herself; so she got a factory job which came with barracks accommodation. Later she had a child of her own, which, in an ironic reversal of roles, Emma Aleksandrovna would sometimes look after for her.

Not having any obvious space in which to accommodate a nanny did not put people off. Elena Mikhailovna started life in a communal apartment in the Arbat, where the four of them – the parents and two children – had just one room, but they still squeezed a nanny into these cramped quarters. When Elena Mikhailovna became a mother herself, in 1963, she and her husband also had only one room, but somehow found the space to accommodate a nanny.

Some of the apartments built in the Stalin era included a small 'housekeeper room', on the understanding that it would eventually become the norm for families, or at any rate those of the intelligentsia or the worker elite, to have their own domestic worker. In some cases they already did. According to Lyudmila Ivanovna, 'these [housekeeper rooms] were very common in apartments built in Stalin's time. Sometimes the state even paid for privileged workers to have a housekeeper.'

Yet just as it was virtually impossible for an 'ordinary' family to have a single-family apartment to itself, so too was it unimaginable that they could set aside even such a minute room for a nanny. The housekeeper room usually had to accommodate family members, and sometimes much else besides. As a teenager in the hungry post-war years, Lyudmila Ivanovna shared her housekeeper room with cages full of rabbits, which her family and neighbours had bred for food.

Despite what Elena Mikhailovna described as 'the Stalinist process of embourgeoisement', socialist ideas about child care had not died out completely, but sat awkwardly alongside the rehabilitation of the family and the single-family apartment. Between the ages of two and eight, Lyudmila Ivanovna spent the weekdays at a residential kindergarten in Moscow, returning to her family in Zhukovskii only at weekends. Her parents were both high-ranking engineers and had been given a package of benefits which included this full-time child care. They did not question whether or not it was a good thing: 'It fit in with the ideology, to raise children communally', she explained.

Because she only lived in the communal apartment at weekends, Lyudmila Ivanovna was not that aware of its day-to-day problems and frustrations. In general, however, children seem to have had a much more positive experience of communal living. We have noted already Sasha Sergeevich's close relationship with his 'Uncle Misha', and the pleasure he got from their regular outings to the park. The presence of other children could also be a boon. It was mainly for this reason that Emma Aleksandrovna remembered her cramped childhood home in Fili with fondness. Her parents had little in common with their neighbours, who were factory workers while they were members of the *intelligentsia*, but the children were less concerned about such distinctions and would happily play together. Lyudmila Ivanovna recalled her childhood home as a magical playground.

The move to the single-family apartment made child care a more pressing issue. There were no longer neighbours who might be willing to keep on eye on the child, or at the very least deal with an emergency. In the new micro-district things were particularly difficult, since the promised network of child care facilities usually lagged behind the construction of housing. Accordingly, unless the family had a resident *babushka* who would look after the children, the nanny was likely to remain a crucial feature of their lives.

Mariya Efimovna had to take on a nanny when she and her family were assigned an apartment in a new micro-district which for the first three years had no crèche or kindergarten. The nanny lived in a tiny windowless room which had been intended as a cloak room. They fired her after her attention wandered and she let her young charge fall down an open manhole; but despite the miserable accommodation on offer there was no shortage of new applicants for the post, and the family was able to replace her immediately. The next nanny left some two years later when she had a better offer, but by then there was a local crèche.

From the time of the birth of her first child, Elena Mikhailovna was never without a nanny. She had a succession of them until 1972, when she took on Zina, who has been with her ever since. At the time of the interview Elena Mikhailovna and Zina were the only residents of Elena Mikhailovna's two-room apartment. With the children now grown and gone, the elderly Zina was housekeeper and companion rather than nanny. The two women had become so close over the years that Elena Mikhailovna joked that they would be buried in a single grave.

The post-Soviet situation: privatisation and its problems

This study has been concerned with housing in the Soviet era. The interviews were all conducted after the collapse of the Soviet Union, however, and a number of my respondents were keen to talk about the latest developments in housing provision, most notably the problems stemming from the privatisation of the housing stock.

In the early post-Soviet era, the so-called 'New Russians' were investing heavily in housing, in some cases buying up communal apartments and converting them into single-family homes. At this time Sasha

Sergeevich was newly married, and keen to set up home with his wife. They started out living with her parents, but then moved into a privately rented room in a communal apartment. At first they felt very fortunate:

> This was a four-room apartment: we had one room. But no one else actually lived in the apartment. Sometimes a neighbour would appear, then disappear again. But then someone or other bought this apartment and began to take possession. And the militia came and said we had to leave.

Those who were registered in accommodation which they rented from the state or from their workplace were in a stronger position. As noted previously, a decree 'On the Privatisation of the Housing Stock in the RSFSR' was introduced in 1988, which gave them the right to buy their existing living space at very low cost, and in July 1991 this was amended so that they could privatise their accommodation free of charge. Yet these free apartments turned out to have hidden costs. Indeed, privatisation is viewed by some as the state's attempt to shed its responsibilities in relation to housing and pass them on to residents. As Vladimir Nikolaevich explained:

> Under socialism there was no private ownership and the state paid for everything. Repairs were all done by the government, and people didn't think about it. Now we have to pay for a lot of things ourselves, like the cleaning of the courtyard and the staircase and the maintenance of the lift.

Everything is listed on the bill they receive every month, he continued. Around eighteen months ago an additional charge began to appear on this bill to cover future capital repairs, but the horrified residents wrote letters of protest and the charge was dropped. However, he feels that it is only a matter of time before it is reinstated. His own apartment block was well built and is unlikely to need extensive repairs in the near future, but those dating from the Khrushchev era are now falling apart, and if the residents have to pay for the repairs themselves this will place an impossible financial burden on them.

Privatisation is no longer restricted to those living in single-family apartments. The residents of communal apartments are now entitled to buy their living space and Svetlana Ivanovna privatised her room as soon as this was possible, believing that owning any property, even just a room in a communal apartment, was better than nothing. However, she subsequently came to realise that this did not give her increased security. All privatised properties in Russia are leasehold, so the state continues to own the ground beneath the building, and Svetlana Ivanovna has heard of people being forced out of apartments they have privatised because the state wants to sell the land to property developers. Even if they now own the property, she concludes, people are in a more uncertain situation than they were in Soviet days when they were tenants of the state or their workplace. The development of post-Soviet Russia's cut-throat version of capitalism had made Svetlana more sympathetic towards the Soviet authorities. She now felt that many of the negative aspects of life in the Soviet Union resulted from the country's financial difficulties, and that the authorities had probably done the best they could.

Paulina Aleksandrovna was in the unusual position, at the time of the interview, of having a share in an apartment that she did not actually want. Her mother had privatised her three-room apartment in a provincial city in both of their names, wanting to ensure that Paulina would always have somewhere to live. Paulina now wanted to privatise her room in Moscow, but was unable to do so since people were only entitled to privatise one property. If Paulina were to buy her Moscow room from the state rather than privatising it, she would have to pay around $5,000 per square metre, which would amount to an impossible total figure of $200,000. Accordingly, she told me that she had bribed a local administrator in the provincial city to destroy the document she had signed in relation to the privatisation of her mother's apartment, and that she was now planning on trying to relinquish her share of this property through the courts on the grounds that had never agreed to the privatisation.

I asked how young people were able to afford to buy apartments, given the rapid growth in the cost of housing in the major cities, particularly Moscow. My respondents explained that low-interest mortgages were now available, and that while older people were still dubious about taking out long-term loans because of the instability of the banking system in the past, this was not the case with younger people. Paulina also referred to a government pledge that young parents would be entitled to state assistance with the purchase of housing. This, she said, followed President Putin's State of the Nation address in May 2006, in which he expressed grave concern about the low birth rate and announced that measures would be introduced to encourage young people to have children. These included a pledge to give young families an allowance of 250,000 rubles on the birth of their second or third child, which they could put towards the cost of housing, education or child care. As in the past, then, housing was to be used as an incentive, this time in relation to reproduction rather than production.

'The love boat has crashed against *byt*'

While overcrowded accommodation is not unknown in capitalist countries, it is largely a working-class phenomenon. This was not the case in the Soviet Union. All of my respondents were white-collar professionals, but they had all experienced housing conditions which would have been unimaginable for the middle class in the West.

Anatolii Aleksandrovich and Lyudmila Petrovna had unusually sanguine memories of their experience of communal housing. It must have helped, however, that they lived with people who had the same educational level, worked in the same field, and had similar values and views. Despite their insistence that they did not see their hostel as a home, and did not aspire to have a home in the conventional sense, their recollections of hostel life are peppered with references to congenial, supportive relations between themselves and their neighbours. Meals and domestic duties were shared, as well as their enthusiasm for their work. Friendships developed which in some cases have survived to the present day. In their case, their neighbours seemed to have functioned as a surrogate family.

My other respondents were less happy with their accommodation and, even if work was their priority, the struggle to improve their housing conditions was a constant backdrop to their lives. However long they lived in an apartment, it often seemed to them like a temporary arrangement. Mariya Efimovna talked of her family's unsuccessful attempts to get a cooperative apartment by means of *blat* (the use of connections); they did not succeed, and had to live for seventeen years in an apartment they had always felt was too small for them and had seen as a stopgap arrangement. Vladimir Borisovich talked of his family living out of suitcases because the room they shared was too small to accommodate cupboards and wardrobes.

There is some contradiction over the understanding of privacy and personal space in the communal apartment. Most of my respondents said that there was no real chance of achieving privacy in a communal apartment and, as we noted, Sasha Sergeevich, as a young boy, was unaware of any meaningful division between the individual rooms and the communal corridor in his apartment. Yet it could be said that Paulina Aleksandrovna and her neighbours showed an inviolable respect for what little privacy the individual room could offer when they felt unable to come to the aid of a female neighbour being beaten by her husband behind the closed door of their room. This room was the husband's 'sphere of control', she explained, and the neighbours only felt they could intervene if the woman made her escape to the apartment's communal spaces. As we saw in previous chapters, neighbours had no such qualms in the earlier decades of Soviet rule. Perhaps, over the years, the desire for privacy had grown, to the extent that it overrode all other considerations. Most surprisingly, we have seen how the desire for privacy could result in some residents ignoring their neighbours to such an extent that, as in the case of Arkadii Abramovich, they could be unaware of the existence of one of them.

The desire to improve their housing resulted in some Soviet citizens becoming adept at 'working the system'. As we have noted, Vladimir Nikolaevich talked of elderly people registering theiir children in their new apartments and then putting themselves back on the housing list in the hope of eventually obtaining another apartment. It was also common for more people to be registered in an apartment than actually lived there, at least partly to ensure that nobody else could be moved in by the authorities. At one time six people were registered to live in Vladimir Nikolaevich and Lyudmila Armenakovna's apartment, but they were the only two who actually did; all of the others lived in the family *dacha*. Paulina Aleksandrovna went so far as to enter a marriage of convenience in order to get residence rights in Moscow and an entitlement to living space in the capital.

This, perhaps more than anything, illustates the importance of housing, and the ways in which the housing shortage distorted people's intimate lives. More than once in the course of his interview, Vladimir Nikolaevich recited the Mayakovskii line we have referred to before: 'the love boat has crashed against *byt*'. Asked what he understood this to mean, he explained: 'the dream of socialism collapsed under the weight of everyday trifles [*melochi*]'. That could be the epitaph for this book.

Notes

1 C. Merridale, *Night of Stone: Death and Memory in Russia* (London: Granta, 2000), p. 17.
2 A particularly enthusiastic discussion of the development of Fili in the 1930s is found in an article by E. Kriger in *Ogonek*. After gushing about the new asphalted roads, public transport, shops, clubs, etc., he insisted that Muscovites were clamouring to move out to Fili: 'The torrent has flowed back! "To Fili, to Fili!", the heroes of a new Chekhov might now exclaim', he concluded, referring to the eponymous heroines of Chekhov's play *The Three Sisters* who were longing to return to Moscow from their 'exile' in the countryside. E. Kriger, 'V Fili, V Fili!', *Ogonek* no. 22 (1933), pp. 10–11.
3 S. Boym, *Common Places: Mythologies of Everyday Life in Russia* (Cambridge, Mass.: Harvard University Press, 1994), p. 121.
4 S.E. Harris, 'In Search of "Ordinary" Russia: Everyday Life in the NEP, the Thaw, and the Communal Apartment', *Kritka: Explorations in Russian and Eurasian History* 6:3 (2005), p. 612.

5 Since these were state-owned apartments, I asked Sasha if people had to get permission to make such major changes. He laughed at my naivety; they just did it, he said.
6 As a researcher in the Soviet Union in the late 1970s, I spent much of my time crammed into diminutive kitchens in cramped apartments with vast numbers of people. One would invariably come out with the distinctly Russian saying, '*V tesnote, da ne v obide!*' My Russian–English dictionary translates this as 'The more the merrier', but a more literal translation would be 'Cramped, but not actually irritating each other'.
7 M. Ilyushina, 'Ya golosuyu za dom-kommunu', *Rabotnitsa* no. 19 (1931), pp. 4–5.

Conclusion

This study has explored Soviet housing throughout the entire span of Soviet history. It has also demonstrated the ways in which housing has been bound up with a range of social issues such as the changing understanding of new *byt,* attitudes towards gender, and the distinction between 'public' and 'private'. In this way, housing has served as the starting point for a broader study of Soviet social history. We will now draw out the study's major conclusions.

Post-revolutionary housing policy was, we have argued, developed in accordance with ideological principles. These included a commitment to new *byt*, equality between men and women, and the creation of a new and more communally oriented person. However, in the appalling conditions of those times, ideology had to play second fiddle to practical considerations. Accordingly, housing policy in reality amounted to simply trying to deal with the housing crisis in the cheapest way possible: in other words, trying to house the most people at the least cost.

In the early years, ideology and practical considerations were largely compatible. While most commentators espoused communal housing as a means of encouraging collective behaviour, freeing women from private housekeeping and enabling them to enter the workforce, it also made economic sense. Even if individual family homes had been seen as desirable, at that time building enough of them to house the swelling urban population was simply unfeasible.

In the 1920s the house commune was hailed as the ideal form of housing for a socialist society, and competitions were held to design the most appropriate models. None of these was actually built, however. Although they predated the official onset of Socialist Realism, the competitions bear its chief hallmark: they presented an idealised image of life as it should be, rather than as it actually was. There was insufficient money – and, it would seem, political will – to turn these designs into reality. The competitions did, however, provide an image of the glorious socialist future, and helped to keep alive the notion that Soviet society was on its way there.

While some idealistic communes were set up by groups of students or young workers, most urban workers in the 1920s lived in multi-occupancy apartments, hostels or barracks. The cornerstone of housing policy in the immediate aftermath of the Revolution had been to move workers and their families into rooms in requisitioned apartments or town houses. While this was justified by Engels' writings on solving the housing shortage, the articles we have looked at suggest that it was an unsatisfactory arrangement all round. The workers had to make long journeys from their new homes in the city centre to their factories in the outskirts, which was no mean feat given the state of public transport. The former owners sometimes continued to live in one or two rooms of their old homes, and inevitably resented the intruders. Furthermore, these apartments were rarely appropriate for multi-occupancy. New partitions created rooms without windows or stoves; 'walk-through' rooms provided their inhabitants with no privacy. These were not homes, but, as they were aptly termed in Russian, *zhilishchnoe ploshchad'*: 'living space'.

Most other forms of urban housing were even worse. Many families were forced to live in hostels and barracks provided by their place of work, sharing dormitories with strangers. These were overcrowded, dirty, smelly, full of untended children, drunken men and overworked women. Housing rented by groups of people who formed themselves into cooperatives was generally little better. Housing which was actually built by the cooperatives gave members more say in how they organised their domestic lives, at least in theory, but the costs involved made this unfeasible for most people, and the system was so beset with bureaucratic problems and corruption that people often did not get the accommodation they were entitled to and had paid for.

During the NEP period, much requisitioned housing returned to private hands. The state retained some control, particularly with regard to determining what rent should be paid and what rules adhered to. However, the queries sent to magazines and the cases brought before the courts reveal enormous confusion over housing rights and responsibilities. Many people turned to the authorities for help in resolving problems in what would once have been considered their 'private' lives. This involved attempts to rid themselves of unpleasant neighbours, violent partners, or simply people who were taking up living space they wanted for themselves.

It was repeatedly claimed that women had the most to gain from communal living. In fact, its effects were ambiguous. On the one hand, women were vulnerable to unwelcome advances from male neighours. On the other, those with violent partners derived some protection from the presence of other people. In theory, communal living would free women from domestic servitude; in reality they were still held responsible for domestic tasks, and it was envisaged that this would continue even when those tasks were socialised. This might explain, at least in part, why women were generally rather unenthusiastic about living communally, despite the efforts of magazines like *Rabotnitsa* to convince them of its benefits.

An awkward combination of ideology and practical considerations was a feature not only of housing, but also of new *byt*. We discussed the fact that new *byt* was both a utopian vision of the new society and a set of mundane domestic matters such as improved hygiene, better ventilation and more temperant alcohol use. This combination was bound to lead to disappointment and disillusionment, especially amongst the more committed and idealistic revolutionaries. To paraphrase Mayakovskii's lines once more, the love boat would inevitably crash against *byt* – that is, the dream of a new life was bound to be destroyed by daily domestic trivia.

The first Five Year Plan brought about renewed enthusiasm for the socialist project. A few custom-built house communes finally appeared, and there were plans to build entire Socialist Cities in accordance with the principles of communal life. However, priority was given to the new industrial developments which these cities were to serve, and there was little money left over for housing or domestic services.

By the end of the first Five Year Plan there was a distinct change in the approach to new *byt*. The commune was no longer the official ideal. The individual family was back in favour, ideally living in its own self-contained family apartment. Yet there was now a yawning gap between ideology and practice. New housing construction focused on individual apartments, but only the new elite which had emerged during the course of the first Five Year Plan had any chance of living in their own family apartment. The housing shortage, made worse by the rapid urbanisation which accompanied Stalin's industrialisation drive, meant that in the case of 'ordinary' people several families had to be crammed into each of them. Housing in this era seems, again, to reflect the tenets of Socialist Realism. Building individual family apartments in the knowledge that in most cases it would not be possible for individual families to actually live in them was, once more, presenting life as it should be, not as it was.

For the majority of people, housing in the Stalin era bore little resemblance to 'home', as defined at the start of this study. There was no privacy, no sense of self-control over their living space, and little chance of being alone. Indeed, shared housing was seen by the authorities as public space, subject to the same rules of conduct as other public places.

In the wake of the first Five Year Plan there was also a notable shift in approach to domestic services such as laundries and communal child care. While the authorities still supported them in principle, they would no longer accept responsibility for them. Despite the continuing rhetoric about gender equality, a traditional understanding of gender roles was invoked. Women were largely responsible for domestic matters; ergo, it was women who would benefit most from these domestic institutions, so they should set them up and find ways of funding them.

The Stalin era witnessed a further erosion of what was already a weak distinction between work and home, public and private. On the one hand, there was a vast increase in the proportion of housing owned by factories and enterprises. This was distributed to its workers both as an incentive and reward for hard work and loyalty. However, in some respects this backfired, since the hunt for better accommodation encouraged some workers to move from job to job in the hope of finding one which offered better accommodation.[1]

While the home and the workplace were increasingly tightly bound, the public space was portrayed as a alternative form of home. In its enthusiastic reports on the reconstruction of Moscow, *Ogonek* portrayed the city as home to its citizens, with its great squares, beautiful parks and huge open spaces offering respite from the cramped quarters in which they only had to sleep.

The 'Great Patriotic War' resulted in enormous damage to the housing stock. It also led to the drastic depletion of the population. Both resulted in a need for more and better housing. Increased procreation was essential and, as *Rabotnitsa* pointed out, a married couple living in separate hostels would be less likely to have children than a couple set up in its own apartment. Post-war reconstruction did include residential buildings, with the emphasis on single-family accommodation, and this in turn led to a new interest in domestic life. The magazines we have looked at were now illustrated with photographs of apartment interiors, and families were pictured enjoying leisure time at home instead of strolling in their city's public squares and gardens. In reality, however, housing construction in the late Stalin era did little more than scratch the surface of housing need.

When Khrushchev came to power, a determined attempt was finally made to provide families en masse with their own apartments. Furthermore, there was a pledge to fill them with a range of new domestic appliances. This fed the interest in domestic life which began in the late Stalin era. It focused, inevitably, on women. Despite its name, *Rabotnitsa* - 'The Woman Worker' - became an enthusiastic proponent of homemaking, and the *domozhozyaika* or housewife figured prominently in its pages, though in the Soviet context this was not a full-time position but had to be combined with work outside the home.

The move to single-family apartments was accompanied by much rhetoric about new forms of socialist community, based on the apartment block and the 'micro-district'. This reflected a concern that families might be tempted to close the doors of their new apartments and disappear into private space, which would not be appropriate in a socialist society. Yet despite the Party's attempts to incorporate the single-family apartment into a new socialist community, in reality it did lead to a privatisation of family life. This does not mean that there had been a genuine sense of community in communal apartments, however. In fact, most residents had attempted to create as much privacy as was possible within that environment. The move to single-family accommodation indulged an already existing desire for private family life.

In the Brezhnev era, the housing programme and the development of more home comforts continued to feature prominently in the press. Some of the unpopular features of the Khrushchev apartments, such as the walk-through rooms and tiny kitchens, were rectified in the new designs. However, people who had been assigned single-family apartments in the Khrushchev era were stuck with what they had got. Their housing problem had officially been solved; they were unlikely to be rehoused even if their families had gone through changes which rendered their old apartments inappropriate. The supposedly 'average' family which was the focus of the Khrushchev housing programme had consisted of two adults and two dependent children. Over time these had grown into two generations of adults whose needs were unlikely to be compatible. When an adult child added a spouse and then a child to the mélange, conflict was almost inevitable.

Relations between women in a multi-generational single family apartment could be particularly tense, with conflicts breaking out over such matters as shared use of the kitchen and different approaches to child rearing. These could be even more bitter in single-family homes than in communal apartments, since blood relatives felt more entitled to intervene and interfere. Apartment exchanges were the most common means of escape, and their frequently tortuous complexity ensured that they became a comic theme in many articles and short stories of the era.

Communal housing continued to exist alongside the single-family apartment. In some articles *Rabotnitsa* tried to present hostel life in a positive light, explaining that young single people enjoyed the camaraderie which was an inevitable result of living with others of the same age and interests, and also developed valuable skills such as cooperation and compromise, which would stand them in good stead in their future family lives. Other articles, however, painted a rather different picture, of soulless institutions ruled over by dictatorial and intrusive administrators. Furthermore, for many women this was not a short-term housing solution for when they were young and single, but turned out to be a life sentence.

When Gorbachev came to power there was a complete change in approach to housing. It was now openly acknowledged that overcrowding was a problem even in single family apartments, and that state resources were not sufficient to deal with it.² Privatisation was the only way forward; private capital had to be harnessed to the house-building programme. As we have seen, this was also the principal aim of the cooperative house-building movement which began in the 1920s and was revived in the 1960s. However, that had been a much more modest programme, aimed at taking pressure off the state by getting future residents to contribute to the building costs of a small portion of the housing stock. Now, the aim was to pass the ownership of virtually all state housing to its residents. People were also encouraged to build their own houses, a practice which had been applauded in the late Stalin and early Khruschchev eras but outlawed in urban areas from 1961.³ The state would continue to provide housing only for a few categories of people, such as servicemen and their families, people who had been disabled at work and those on very low incomes.⁴

Even though the Soviet Union officially remained a socialist country, there were few expressions of support for communal living in the Gorbachev era. Communal apartments were portrayed as a relic of the past, to be 'resettled' or reconstructed into self-contained apartments as quickly as possible. Hostels were no longer presented as useful conductors of socialist values, but a cause of psychological damage. Instead of resulting in the fair distribution of accommodation, past housing policies were said to have led to corruption, speculation and criminality.

The Soviet Union may not have succeeded in bringing about genuine communal living, but it did bring together people from very different professions and educational backgrounds, placing them in the same districts, streets and apartments. By the late Gorbachev era this was also rejected. The economist Larisa Piyasheva called for the development of separate districts for different social classes, so that the middle class would not have to suffer the anti-social behaviour of the poor.⁵ At the same time, the English expression 'my home is my castle' was adopted by Soviet commentators, creating an image of the middle-class Soviet home as a fortress protecting its inhabitants from the perils of the outside world. For those with the means to afford it, the home in the final years of the Soviet era had become the ultimate private space.

Yet there were some expressions of nostalgia for the communal housing of the past. It is unlikely that those reminiscing about communal apartments would have actually wanted to live in them, but this distinctly Soviet phenomenon was now hailed as an important feature of Soviet history and perhaps, even, a part of national identity.

In short, this study has demonstrated that the original ideas about what housing was most appropriate in a socialist society were altered and distorted over the decades in accordance with changes in leadership, ideology and practical concerns. Although radical ideas about the future of the home, the family and gender relations were expressed in the early years of the Soviet regime, putting them into practice was not so easy. Traditional ideas about male and female roles proved particularly resilient, and remained at the heart of the supposedly 'new' gender relations. Throughout Soviet history, though the vast majority of women worked outside the home, they were still seen as the primary homemakers and held responsible for dealing with their families' domestic needs. Behind the door of the Soviet apartment, the 'new woman' was not so different from her Western counterpart. Perhaps the main difference was that the Soviet woman was more likely to employ a live-in maid or nanny. The large number of peasants fleeing the rural chaos and hardship resulting from collectivisation of agriculture ensured a steady supply of domestic servants at a cost which was not beyond the reach of many 'ordinary' Soviet citizens.

Housing remains a problematic issue in post-Soviet Russia, but in a different way; instead of the 'equality in poverty' of the Soviet period, there is now a sharp differentiation between the housing of different socioeconomic groups. The situation is particularly difficult for those who did not have apartments they could privatise; finding affordable accommodation in the private housing market, particularly in Moscow and St Petersburg, has become extremely difficult. The new elite, on the other hand, has ensconced itself in renovated 'Western-style' city apartments and large country houses, the ironically termed 'cottages'.

While women are still held largely responsible for domestic chores, there are indications of what could be termed a patriarchal appropriation of domestic space. This is particularly the case with men of the new Russian elite, who appear to have a greater interest in housing and the home than Soviet men. This is indicated by the plethora of glossy magazines on home design and furnishings,[6] which seem to be aimed primarily at them. Like automobile advertisements in the West which habitually use women's bodies to seduce male buyers, images of domestic interiors in these magazines have women draped over sofas and beds instead of cars.

It could be argued that in some respects renovating city apartments and rural 'cottages' is an extension of the male interest in the *dacha* in Soviet times, when those fortunate enough to have access to a weekend cottage would spend much of the weekend working on it. However, the luxury home in post-Soviet Russia provides men of the new elite with more than just the excuse to chop wood and build extensions; it also gives them the opportunity to display their wealth, taste and power.[7] This, however, is the subject of another study.

Notes

1. See S.E. Harris, 'Moving to the Separate Apartment: Building: Distributing, Furnishing, and Living in Urban Housing in Soviet Russia, 1950s-1960s', Ph.D. dissertation, University of Chicago, 2003, pp. 6, 40.
2. B. Kosareva, A.S. Puzanov and M.V. Tikhomirova, 'Russia: Fast Starter – Housing Sector Reform 1991–1995', in R.J. Struyk (ed.), *Economic Restructuring of the Former Soviet Bloc: The Case of Housing* (Avebury: Urban Institute Press, 1996), p. 263.
3. Ibid., p. 264.
4. Ibid., p. 258.
5. Interview with economist L. Piyasheva, conducted by N. Fedorova, 'Kuplyu kvartiru!', *Rabotnitsa* no. 10 (1990), p. 20.
6. For example, *Chetyre komnati*, *Idei Vashego Doma* and *Salon*.
7. In some cases this display of power involves control of and violence over wives and partners See L. Attwood, '"She was Asking for it": Rape and Domestic Violence against Women', in M. Buckley (ed.), *Post-Soviet Women: From the Baltic to Central Asia* (Cambridge: Cambridge University Press, 1997), pp. 99–118.

Bibliography

The following magazines, journals and newspapers were used systematically for all or part of the period under study:

Ogonek, from 1923 to 1991.
Rabotnitsa, from 1923 to 1991.
Sovetskaya zhenshchina, from 1945 to 1964.
Trud, from 1956 to 1964.
Zhilishchnoe delo, from 1924 to 1930.
Zhilishchnoe khozyaistvo, from 1935 to 1941.

Other material in Russian

Artyukhina, A. (1927), *Ocherednye zadachi partii v rabote sredi zhenshchin* (Moscow: Gosudarstvennoe izdatel'stvo).
Barkhin, M.G. (1974), *Gorod 1945-1970: Praktika, proekty, teoriya* (Moscow: Stroizdat).
Borovoi, V., and L. Balanovskii (1963), 'Eksperimental'nyi krupnopanel'nyi zhiloi dom novogo tipa', *Arkhitektura SSSR* no. 5, pp. 3-7.
Bumazhnyi, L. and A. Zal'tsman (1959), 'Perspektivnye tipy zhilykh domov i kvartir', *Arkhitektura SSSR* no. 1, pp. 2-3, 6, 9.
Davydov (1935), 'Zapushchennye obshchezhitiya', *Zhilishchnoe khozyaistvo* no. 3, pp. 10-11.
Delle, V. (1956), 'Za prostotu i udobstvo sovremmennoi mebeli', in *Arkhitektura SSSR*, no. 1, pp. 33-6.
Druzhinin, V. (1942), 'Oboima', *Leningrad* no. 4-5, p. 27.
Dyushen, V. (1921) 'Problemy zhenskogo kommunisticheskogo dvizheniya: problemy sotsial'nogo vospitaniya', *Kommunistka* no. 12-13, pp. 25-8.
Gerasimova, E. (2000) *Sovetskaya kommunal'naya kvartira kak sotsial'nyi institut: istoriko-sotsiologicheskii analiz (na materialakh petrograda-Leningrad, 1917-1991)*. Synopsis of Candidate of Science Dissertation, December 2000, St Petersburg.
Gradov, G.A. (1955), 'Sovetskuyu arkhitekturu na uroven' novykh zadach', *Arkhitektura SSSR*, no. 2, pp. 4-8.
Gradov, G.A. (1968), *Gorod i byt* (Moscow: Izdatel'stvo literatury po stroitel'stvu).
Isaev, V.I. (1996), *Kommuna ili kommunalka? - izmeneniya byta rabochykh sibiri v gody industrializatsii* (Novosibirsk: Nauka: Sibirskaya izdatel'skaya firma RAN).
Kaganovich. L.M. (1931), *Za sotsialisticheskuyu rekonstruktsiyu Moskvy u gorodov SSSR* (Moscow and Leningrad: Moskovskii rabochii).
Kollontai, A. (1919), *Sem'ya i Kommunisticheskoe Gosudarstvo*, Kiev: Ukrainskoe tsentral'noe agenstvo.

BIBLIOGRAPHY

Kollontai, A. (1921), 'Tezisy o kommunisticheskoi morali v oblasti brachnykh otnoshenii', *Kommunistka* no. 12-13, pp. 28-34.

Kollontai. A. (1923), *Revolyutsiya byta*, Moscow: Gosudarstvenno izdatel'stvo.

Kollontai, A. (1974) *Iz moei zhizni i raboty* (Moscow: Proveshchenie).

Kostandi, M., and E. Kapustyan (1961), 'Tipy zhilykh domov dlya eksperimental'nogo zhilogo raiona Moskvy', *Arkhitektura SSSR* no. 4, pp. 17-28.

Krupskaya, N. (1921), 'Problemy zhenskogo kommunisticheskogo dvizheniya v Rossii: Problema kommunisticheskogo vospitaniya', *Kommunistka* no. 8-9, pp. 22-6.

Krupskaya, N. (1984), *Deti - nashe budushchee* (Moscow: Proveshchenie).

Krylenko, N. (1936), Sotsializm i sem'ya, *Bol'shevik* no. 18 (15 September 1936), pp. 65-78.

Lebina, N.B. (1999), *Povsednevnaya zhizn' Sovetskogo goroda: normy I anomalii. 1920-1930 gody* (St Petersburg: Zhurnal 'Neva' - izdatel'stvotorgovyi dom 'Letnii Sad').

Luppov, N. (1959), 'Mebel' dlya kvartir novogo tipa', in *Arkhitektura SSSR* no. 5, pp. 11-15.

Manuilov,V. (1942), 'Novye knigi', review of Inber's 'Dusha Leningrad', *Leningrad* no. 1, p. 24.

Mesheryakov, N. (1921) 'Chto delaet sovetskaya vlast' dlya uluchsheniya zhilkishch rabochikh', *Kommunistka* no. 8-9, pp. 30-2.

Meshcheryakov, N. (1926), *Zhilishchnaya kooperatsiya v kapitalisticheskom i sovetskom stroe* (Moscow and Leningrad: Knigosoyuz).

Mikulina, E. (1958), 'My stroim dom - svoimi silami', *Novyi Mir* no. 4, 1, pp. 1-4.

Nemtsov, N.M. (ed.) (1932), *Zhilishchnye dela* (Moscow: Sovetskoe zakonodatel'stvo).

Olesin, M. (1990) *Pervaya v mire: biograficheskii ocherk ob A.M. Kollontai* (Moscow: Izdatel'stvo).

Perchak, L. (1932) 'O "zhilishchnom voprose" F. Engel'sa', *Bol'shevik* no. 10, pp. 47-58.

'Pravil'no, nauchno reshat' problemy tipizatsii zhilykh domov' (1956), editorial in *Arkhitektura SSSR* no. 5, pp. 1-4.

Rumyantseva, M.S. and A.I. Pergament (1975), *Spravochnik zhenshchiny-rabotnitsy* (Moscow: Izdatel'stvo politicheskoi literatury).

Sokolov, A. K., and V. M. Koz'menko (eds) (2002), *Rosiiya v XX veke: lyudi, idei, vlast'* (Moscow: Rossiiskaya Politicheskaya Entsiklopediya).

Svetlichnyi, B. (1958), 'Zaboty gradostroitelei', *Novyi Mir* no. 10, pp. 211-16.

Tyazhel'nikova (2002), 'Povsednevnaya zhizn' Moskovskikh rabochikh v nachale 1920-kh godov', in A.K. Sokolov and V.M. Koz'menko (eds), *Rosiiya v XX veke: lyudi, idei, vlast'* (Moscow: Izdatel'stvo Rosspen).

Utekhin, I. (2001), *Ocherki kommunal'nogo byta* (Moscow: OGI).

Vasil'eva, L. (1993), *Kremlevskie zheny* (Moscow: Kantor).

'Zabota o cheloveke - osnova sovetskogo gradostroitel'stva' (1960), editorial article in *Arkhitektura SSSR* no. 6, pp. 1-3.

Zhilishchnyi vopros i zadachi zhilishchnoi kooperatsii (Materialy dlya dokladchikov) (1927), Leningrad: Izdachi Zhilishchsoyuza.

Zhukhov, K. (1963) 'Bol'shoe novosel'e i bol'shie zadachi', *Novyi mir* no. 2, pp. 230–8.

Material in English

Adamovich, A. and D. Granin (1983), *A Book of the Blockade* (Moscow: Raduga).

Alexopoulos, G. (2003), *Stalin's Outcasts: Aliens, Citizens and the Soviet State, 1926–1936* (Ithaca, N.Y.: Cornell University Press).

Alpern Engel, B. (1994), *Between the Fields and the City: Women, Work and Family in Russia, 1861–1914* (Cambridge: Cambridge University Press).

Andrusz, G. (1984), *Housing and Urban Development in the USSR* (Basingstoke: Macmillan).

Andrusz, G., M. Harloe and I. Szelenyi (eds) (1996), *Cities after Socialism: Urban and Regional Change and Conflict in Post-Socialist Cities* (Oxford: Blackwell).

Atkinson, D., A. Dallin and G.W. Lapidus (eds) (1978), *Women in Russia* (Hassocks, Sussex: Harvester).

Attwood, L. (1997), '"She was Asking for it": Rape and Domestic Violence against Women', in M. Buckley (ed.), *Post-Soviet Women: From the Baltic to Central Asia* (Cambridge: Cambridge University Press), pp. 99–118.

Attwood, L. (1999), *Creating the New Soviet Woman: Women's Magazines as Engineers of Female Identity, 1922–53* (Basingstoke and London: Palgrave).

Attwood. L. (2000), 'Celebrating the "Frail-Figured Welder": Gender Confusion in Women's Magazines of the Khrushchev Era', *Slavonica* 8:2, pp. 158–76.

Baker, J.H. (1980), *The Soviet City: Ideal and Reality* (Beverly Hills, Sage).

Barber, J. and M. Harrison (1991), *The Soviet Home Front* (London: Longman).

Bebel, A. (1917), *Woman under Socialism* (New York: New York Labor News Company).

Bertaux, D., P. Thompson and A. Rotkirch (eds) (2004), *On Living through Soviet Russia* (London: Routledge).

Bessanova. O. (1992), 'The Reform of the Soviet Housing Model in Search of a Concept', in B. Turner, J. Hegedus and I. Tosics, *The Reform of Housing in Eastern Europe and the Soviet Union* (London and New York: Routledge), pp. 276–89.

Bliznakov, M. (1976), 'Urban Planning in the USSR: Integrative Theories', in Michael F. Hamm (ed.), *The City in Russian History* (Lexington: University Press of Kentucky), pp. 243–56.

Bliznakov, M. (1990), 'The Realization of Utopia: Western Technology and Soviet Avant-garde Architecture', in W.C. Blumfield (ed.), *Reshaping Russian Architecture: Western Technology, Utopian Dreams* (Cambridge: Woodrow Wilson Centre and Cambridge University Press), pp. 145–75.

Bliznakov, M. (1993), 'Soviet Housing during the Experimental Years, 1918–1933',

BIBLIOGRAPHY

in Brumfield and Ruble (eds), *Russian Housing in the Modern Age: Design and Social History* (Cambridge: Cambridge University Press), pp. 85-148.

Boym, S. (1994), *Common Places: Mythologies of Everyday Life in Russia* (Cambridge, Mass.: Harvard University Press).

Brumfield, W.C. (1993), 'Building for Comfort and Profit', in W.C. Brumfield and B. Ruble (eds), *Russian Housing in the Modern Age: Design and Social History*, pp. 55-84.

Brumfield, W.C. and B.A. Ruble (eds) (1993), *Russian Housing in the Modern Age: Design and Social History* (Cambridge: Cambridge University Press).

Buchli, V. (1997), 'Khrushchev, Modernism, and the fight against *Petit-bourgeois* Consciousness in the Soviet Home', *Journal of Design History* 10:2, pp. 161-75.

Buchli, V. (1999), *An Archaeology of Socialism* (Oxford and New York: Berg).

Buckley, M. (1993), *Redefining Russian Society and Polity* (Boulder, Col. and Oxford: Westview Press).

Buckley, M. (ed.) (1997), *Post-Soviet Women: From the Baltic to Central Asia* (Cambridge: Cambridge University Press).

Bulgakov, M. (1983), *Master and Margarita*, translated by Michael Glenny (London: Fontana).

Castillo, G. (2003), 'Stalinist Modern: Constructivism and the Soviet Company Town', in J. Cracraft and D. Rowland (eds), *Architectures of Russian Identity, 1500 to the Present* (Ithaca and New York: Cornell University Press), pp. 135-49.

Chernyshevsky, N.G. (1982), *What is to be Done?: Tales about New People*, translated by B.R. Tucker (London: Virago Russian Classics).

Chukovskaya, L. (1989), *Sofia Petrovna*, translated by David Floyd (London: Collins Harvill).

Cracraft, J. and D. Rowland (eds) (2003), *Architectures of Russian Identity, 1500 to the Present* (Ithaca and New York: Cornell University Press).

Crowley, D. and S. Reid (eds) (2002), *Socialist Spaces: Sites of Everyday Life in the Eastern Bloc* (New York: Berg).

Dant, T. (1999), *Material Culture in the Social World: Values, Activities, Lifestyles* (Buckingham: Open University Press).

DiMaio, Jr., A.J. (1974), *Soviet Urban Housing: Problems and Policies* (New York and London: Duke University Press).

Dunham, V.S. (1991), *In Stalin's Time: Middleclass Values in Soviet Fiction* (Durham and London: Duke University Press).

Figes, O. (1996), *A People's Tragedy: The Russian Revolution 1891-1924* (London: Jonathan Cape).

Figes, O. (2007), *The Whisperers: Private Life in Stalin's Russia* (London: Allen Lane).

Filtzer, D. (2006), 'Standard of Living versus Quality of Life: Struggling with the Urban Environment in Russia during the Early Years of Post-War Reconstruction', in P. Jones (ed.), *The Dilemmas of De-Stalinization: Negotiating Cultural and Social Change in the Khrushchev Era* (London and New York: Routledge, 2006), pp. 81-102.

Fitzpatrick, S. (1999), *Everyday Stalinism* (Oxford and New York: Oxford University Press).
Fitzpatrick, S. (ed.) (2000), *Stalinism: New Directions* (London: Routledge).
Fitzpatrick, S. and Y. Slezkine (2000), *In the Shadow of Revolution: Life Stories of Russian Women* (Princeton, N.J.: Princeton University Press)
Fitzpatrick, S. (2003), 'The Good Old Days', *London Review of Books*, 25(19), www.lrb/co.uk., accessed 17 February 2006.
Fitzpatrick, S. (2005), *Tear off the Masks! Identity and Imposture in Twentieth-Century Russia* (Princeton and Oxford: Princeton University Press).
French, R.A. and I. Hamilton (1979), *The Socialist City; Spatial and Urban Policy* (Chichester: Wiley).
Fuerst, J. (2008), 'Between Salvation and Liquidation: Homeless and Vagrant Children and the Reconstruction of Soviet Society', *Slavonic and East European Review*, 86:2, pp. 231–58.
Garros, V., N. Korenevskaya and T. Lahusen (eds) (1995), *Intimacy and Terror: Soviet Diaries of the 1930s* (New York: The New Press).
Geiger, H.K. (1968), *The Family in Soviet Russia* (Cambridge, Mass.: Harvard University Press).
Gerasimova, K. (1999), 'The Soviet Communal Apartment', in J. Smith (ed.), *Beyond the Limits: The Concept of Space in Russian History and Culture* (Helsinki: SHS).
Gerasimova, K. (2002), 'Public Privacy in the Soviet Communal Apartment' , in D. Crowley and S.E. Reid (eds), *Socialist Spaces: Sites of Everyday Life in the Eastern Bloc* (New York: Berg), pp. 207–30.
Goldman, W.Z. (1993), *Women, the State and Revolution* (Cambridge: Cambridge University Press).
Gronow, J. (2003), *Caviar with Champagne: Common Luxury and the Ideals of the Good Life in Stalin's Russia* (Oxford and New York: Berg).
Habermas, J. (1999), *The Structural Transformation of the Public Sphere: An Inquiry into a Category of Bourgeois Society*, translated by T. Burger with the assistance of F. Lawrence (Oxford: Polity Press).
Hamm, M. (1976), *The City in Russian History* (Lexington: University Press of Kentucky).
Harris, S.E. (2003), 'Moving to the Separate Apartment: Building, Distributing, Furnishing, and Living in Urban Housing in Soviet Russia, 1950s–1960s', Ph.D. dissertation, University of Chicago.
Harris, S.E. (2005), 'In Search of "Ordinary" Russia: Everyday Life in the NEP, the Thaw, and the Communal Apartment', *Kritika: Explorations in Russian and Eurasian History* 6:3, pp. 591–2.
Hodgson, K. (1996), *Written with the Bayonet: Soviet Russian Poetry of World War Two* (Liverpool: Liverpool University Press).
Holmgren, B. (1993), *Women's Works in Stalin's Time: On Lidiia Chukovskaia and Nadezhda Mandelstam* (Bloomington, Ind.: Indiana University Press).
Hooper, C. (2006), 'Terror of Intimacy: Family Politics in the 1930s Soviet Union', in C. Kiaer and E. Naiman (eds), *Everyday Life in Early Soviet Russia: Taking*

the Revolution Inside (Bloomington, Ind.: Indiana University Press), pp. 61–91.
Horsbrugh Porter, A. (ed.) (1993), *Memories of Revolution* (London and New York: Routledge).
Hosking, G. (1985), *The First Socialist Society: A History of the Soviet Union from Within* (Cambridge, Mass.: Harvard University Press).
Kelly, C. (2001), *Refining Russia: Advice Literature, Polite Culture, and Gender from Catherine to Yeltsin* (Oxford: Oxford University Press).
Kelly, C. (2002), 'Ordinary Life in Extraordinary Times: Chronicles of the Quotidian in Russia and the Soviet Union', *Kritika: Explorations in Russian and Eurasian History* 3:4, 631–51.
Kettering, K. (1997), '"Ever More Cosy and Comfortable": Stalinism and the Soviet Domestic Interior, 1928–1938', *Journal of Design History* 10:2, pp. 120–32.
Kharkhordin, O. (1999), *The Collective and the Individual in Russia* (Berkeley and London: University of California Press).
Khrushchev, N.S. (1974), *Khrushchev Remembers*, translated by Strobe Talbott (London: André Deutsch).
Kiaer, C. and E. Naiman (eds) (2006), *Everyday Life in Early Soviet Russia: Taking the Revolution Inside* (Bloomington, Ind.: Indiana University Press).
Kollontai, A. (1977), *Love of Worker Bees* (London: Virago).
Kollontai, A. (1977), *Selected Writings*, translated, and with commentary, by A. Holt (London: Allison and Busby).
Kollontai, A. (1984), *Selected Articles and Speeches* (Moscow: Progress Publishers).
Kopp, A. (1993), 'Foreign Architects in the Soviet Union During the First Two Five-Year Plans', in W.C. Brumfield (ed.), *Reshaping Russian Architecture: Western Technology, Utopian Dreams* (Cambridge: Woodrow Wilson Centre and Cambridge University Press), pp. 176–214.
Kosareva, N.B., A.S. Puzanov and M.V. Tikhomirova (1996), 'Russia: Fast Starter – Housing Sector Reform 1991–1995', in R.J. Struyk (ed.), *Economic Restructuring of the Former Soviet Bloc: The Case of Housing* (Avebury: Urban Institute Press), pp. 255–305.
Kotkin, S. (1993), 'Shelter and Subjectivity in the Stalin Period: A Case Study of Magnitogorsk', in W.C. Brumfield and B. Ruble (eds), *Russian Housing in the Modern Age: Design and Social History* (Cambridge: Cambridge University Press), pp. 171–210.
Kotkin, S. (1995), *Magnetic Mountain: Stalinism as a Civilisation* (Berkeley and London: University of California Press).
Lapidus, G.W. (1978), 'Sexual Equality in Soviet Policy: A Developmental perspective', in D. Atkinson, A. Dallin and G.W. Lapidus (eds), *Women in Russia* (Hassocks, Sussex: Harvester), pp. 119–24.
Lapidus, G.W. (1979), *Women in Soviet Society: Equality, Development and Social Change* (Berkeley: University of California Press).
Larina, A. (1993), *This I Cannot Forget* (London: Pandora).
Leder, M.M. (2001), *My Life in Stalinist Russia: An American Woman Looks Back* (Bloomington, Ind.: Indiana University Press).

Lenin, V.I. (1977), *Selected Works* (Moscow: Progress Publishers).
Lewin, M. (2005), *The Soviet Century* (London and New York: Verso).
Littlejohn, G. (1984), *A Sociology of the Soviet Union* (London and Basingstoke: Macmillan).
Lodder, C. (2006), 'Searching for Utopia', in C. Wilk (ed.), *Modernism 1914-1929: Designing a New World* (London: V&A Publications).
Lovell, S. (1996), '*Ogonek*: The Crisis of a Genre', *Europe-Asia Studies* 48:6, pp. 989-1006.
Lovell, S. (2002), 'Soviet Exurbia: Dachas in Postwar Russia', in D. Crowley and S.E. Reid (eds), *Socialist Spaces: Sites of Everyday Life in the Eastern Bloc* (New York: Berg), pp. 105-21.
Lovell, S. (2003), *Summerfolk 1710-2000: A History of the Dacha* (Ithaca and London: Cornell University Press).
Manley, R. (2006), 'Where Should We Resettle the Comrades Next?', in J. Fuerst (ed.), *Late Stalinist Russia: Society between Reconstruction and Reinvention* (London and New York: Routledge), pp. 233-46.
Marx, K. (1983), *The Portable Karl Marx*, edited and translated by E. Kamenka (Harmondsworth: Viking Penguin).
Mehnert, K. (1933), *Youth in Soviet Russia*, translated by Michael Davidson (London: George Allen and Unwin).
Merridale, C. (2000), *Night of Stone: Death and Memory in Russia* (London: Granta).
Meshcherskaya, E. (1989), *Comrade Princess: Memoirs of an Aristocrat in Modern Russia* (London and New York: Doubleday).
Mills, C.W. (1977), *The Marxists* (Harmondsworth: Penguin).
Mills Todd III, W. (1986), *Fiction and Society in the Age of Pushkin: Ideologies, Institutions and Narratives* (Cambridge, Mass.: Harvard University Press).
Paperny, V. (1993), 'Men, Women and the Living Space', in W.C. Brumfield and B. Ruble (eds), *Russian Housing in the Modern Age: Design and Social History* (Cambridge: Cambridge University Press), pp. 149-69.
Passerini, L. (ed.) (1992), *International Yearbook of Oral History and Life Stories*, vol. 1, *Memory and Totalitarianism* (Oxford: Oxford University Press).
Prost, A. and G. Vincent (eds) (1991), *A History of Private Life*, vol. V, *Riddles of Identity in Modern Times* (Cambridge, Mass. and London: Belknap Press of Harvard University Press).
Reid, S.E. (1997), 'De-Stalinization and Taste, 1953-1963', *Journal of Design History* 10:2, pp. 177-202.
Reid, S.E, (2004), 'Women in the Home', in M. Ilič, S.E. Reid and L. Attwood, *Women in the Khrushcher Era* (Basingstoke: Palgrave Macmillan), pp. 149-76.
Ruble, B. (1990), *Leningrad: Shaping a Soviet City* (Berkeley: University of California Press).
Ruble, B. (1993), 'From Khrushcheby to Korobki', in W.C. Brumfield and B. Ruble (eds), *Russian Housing in the Modern Age: Design and Social History* (Cambridge: Cambridge University Press), pp. 232-69.
Salisbury, H. (1969), *The Siege of Leningrad* (London: Secker and Warburg).

Scott, J. (1989), *Behind the Urals* (Bloomington, Ind.: Indiana University Press).
Semenova, V. (2004), 'Equality in Poverty: The Symbolic Meaning of *kommunalki* in the 1930s–50s', in D. Bertaux, P. Thompson and A. Rotkirch (eds), *On Living through Soviet Russia* (London: Routledge), pp. 54–67.
Shlapentokh, V. (1989), *Public and Private Life of the Soviet People: Changing Values in Post-Stalin Russia* (Oxford and New York: Oxford University Press).
Shvidovsky, O.A. (ed.) (1971), *Building in the USSR 1917–1932* (London: Studio Vista).
Siegelbaum, L.W. (1988), *Stakhanovism and the Politics of Productivity, 1935–1941* (Cambridge: Cambridge University Press).
Siegelbaum, L.W. (2000), '"Dear Comrade, You Ask What We Need": Socialist Paternalism and Soviet Rural "Notables" in the Mid-1930s', in S. Fitzpatrick (ed.), *Stalinism: New Directions* (London: Routledge), pp. 210–30.
Simmons, C., and N. Perlina, (2005), *Writing the Siege of Leningrad* (Pittsburgh: University of Pittsburgh Press).
Smith, A. (1937), *I Was a Soviet Worker* (London: Robert Hale and Co).
Smith, D.M. (1996), 'The Socialist City', in G. Andrusz, M. Harloe and I. Szelenyi (eds), *Cities after Socialism: Urban and Regional Change and Conflict in Post-Socialist Cities* (Oxford: Blackwell), pp. 70–99.
Smith, M.B. (2008), 'Individual Forms of Ownership in the Urban Housing Fund of the USSR, 1944–64', *Slavonic and East European Review* 86:2, pp. 83–305.
Sobel, A. (ed.) (1971), *Russia's Rulers: The Khrushchev Period* (New York: Facts on File).
Stites, R. (1989), *Revolutionary Dreams: Utopian Vision and Experimental Life in the Russian Revolution* (Oxford and New York: Oxford University Press).
Struyk, R.J (ed.) (1996), *Economic Restructuring of the Former Soviet Bloc: The Case of Housing* (Avebury: Urban Institute Press).
Thurston, R.W. (1991), 'The Soviet Family during the Great Terror, 1935–41', *Soviet Studies* 43:3, .pp. 553–74.
Timasheff, N.S. (1946), *The Great Retreat: The Growth and Decline of Communism in Russia* (New York: E.P. Dutton and Co).
Tyler May, E. (1988), *Homeward Bound* (New York: Basic Books).
Varga-Harris, C. (2006), 'Forging Citizenship on the Home Front: Reviving the Socialist Contract and Constructing Soviet Identity during the Thaw', in P. Jones (ed.), *The Dilemmas of De-Stalinization: Negotiating Cultural and Social Change in the Khrushchev Era* (London and New York: Routledge), pp. 101–16.
Volkonskaia, S. (2000), 'The Way of Bitterness', in S. Fitzpatrick and Y. Slezkine, *In the Shadow of Revolution: Life Stories of Russian Women* (Princeton, N.J.: Princeton University Press).
Volkov, V. (2000), 'The Concept of Kul'turnost'', in S. Fitzpatrick (ed.), *Stalinism: New Directions* (London: Routledge), pp. 210–230.
Vysokovskii, A. (1993), 'Will Domesticity Return?', in W.C. Brumfield and B. Ruble (eds), *Russian Housing in the Modern Age,: Design and Social History* (Cambridge: Cambridge University Press), pp. 271–308.

Ward. C. (1999), *Stalin's Russia* (London: Arnold).
Werth, A. (1961), *The Khrushchev Phase: The Soviet Union Enters the 'Decisive' Sixties* (London: Robert Hale).
Westwood, J.N. (1973), *Endurance and Endeavour: Russian History 1812–1971* (London: Oxford University Press).
Wetlin, M. (1994), *Fifty Russian Winters: An American Woman's Life in the Soviet Union* (New York: John Wiley and Sons).
Wilk, C. (ed.) (2006), *Modernism 1914–1939: Designing a New World* (London: V&A Publications).
Zetkin, C. (1965), 'My Recollections of Lenin', Appendix to *Lenin on the Emancipation of Women* (Moscow: Progress Publishers).
Zubkova, E. (1998), *Russia after the War: Hopes, Illusions, and Disappointments, 1945–1957* (London: M.E. Sharpe).

Index

'fn' after a number indicates a footnote on that page

abortion 81, 116
adoption 145, 214
alcohol abuse 25–7, 52–3, 55, 70, 84, 158, 185, 188, 213, 223–4, 226, 243
'apartment denunciation' 4, 90, 136
apartment exchanges, *see* exchanging accommodation
appliances, domestic 26, 91, 167–8, 181, 195, 230, 232–3
aristocratic homes (requisitioned for workers) 24, 32–6, 42–3, 54
Artyukhina, Aleksandra 61, 91, 113

barracks 4, 17, 22, 70, 76, 79, 83–4, 102, 123–5, 134, 148, 150, 191, 221, 233, 241, 242
'*barskie kvartiry*', *see* aristocratic homes
besprizorniki, *see* homeless children
birth rate, concern about 109, 115, 116, 146, 156, 233, 237

child abandonment 31, 40, 116, 130, 194
  see also homeless children
child benefits, *see* state benefits
child care, socialised 29, 30–1, 66, 69, 71, 77, 81, 93, 95, 100, 102, 108–9, 111–13, 163, 168, 234, 243
child neglect and abuse 2, 51, 119
children's experience of communal housing 54, 57–8, 66, 84, 223, 226, 234–5
choice, ability to exercise 2–3, 8, 10–11, 29, 47, 56, 67, 71, 76, 79, 94, 130, 156, 163, 202–3, 208–9, 214
Civil War 12, 22, 27, 31, 35, 43, 46, 62
  see also War Communism
communal apartments 3–6, 9, 16–7, 19 fn 26, 23, 45, 56–7, 117, 119, 123, 125–7, 129, 132, 133–5, 139 fn 45, 142–3, 146, 150–1, 156, 158, 162, 168, 171, 184–5, 187–9, 190–1, 193–5, 200, 207, 210, 212–15, 220–30, 234–6, 238, 245–7
communal dining 28–9, 61, 63–4, 67–8, 77, 81–2, 91, 94, 96, 100–2, 111–12, 115, 162, 167, 168
  see also kitchens, communal
communist youth organisations 78, 83, 89, 97, 98, 103, 118
'compression' (*uplotnenie*) 17, 33, 46, 194
cooperative apartments, *see* housing cooperatives
cooperative movement 13, 61
corruption in housing distribution 1, 4–5, 61, 128, 157, 190–1, 194, 201, 204–5, 209, 211, 239, 242, 246
crèches, *see* preschool child care institutions

dachas (weekend and holiday cottages) 34, 239, 248
demographic crisis, *see* birth rate, concern about
disenfranchisement 32, 63, 89, 90, 136
  see also 'formers'
divorce 28, 96, 116, 130–1, 155, 169, 184, 190, 191, 194, 204–5, 215, 227
dom kommuna, *see* house communes
domestic servants 24, 42, 54, 66, 80, 115, 117, 129, 133, 156, 229, 233–5, 247
domestic violence, *see* physical abuse, sexual harassment
double burden, women's 25, 116

259

INDEX

education 3, 6, 26, 52–3, 66, 82, 89, 94, 96, 100, 109, 126, 134, 144, 219, 233, 237, 238, 246
  see also 'Red Corner'
elderly, the 48, 89, 133, 143–4, 155, 158, 162, 184, 186–8, 190–1, 195, 199 fn 70, 202, 207, 211–14, 226–7, 231, 235, 239
Engels, Friedrich 1, 31, 92
enterprise housing, *see* work-place owned housing
entertaining 25, 54, 56, 67–8, 163, 166–7, 192, 203, 223, 230
equality, gender 24–6, 28–9, 52, 70, 79–82, 108–9, 115–19, 157, 159, 169, 173–4, 241, 244
equality, women's, *see* equality, gender
exchanging accommodation 131–2, 156, 161, 169, 184–7, 194, 204, 213, 245

'family hearth' 3, 77, 116, 203
'formers' 5, 32–3, 42, 44, 47, 63, 72, 89
Fourier, Charles 23, 77

guests, *see* entertaining

Habermas, Jurgen 7–10
'Hero-Mothers', *see* motherhood awards
'home' (meaning of) 1–4, 6–8, 11–12, 16–17, 25, 36, 49, 55, 64, 80, 89, 91, 98–9, 108, 115–16, 119, 131, 134, 139 fn 45, 143–4, 148–50, 159, 161, 172–3, 192, 203, 208, 212–14, 227, 229, 238, 242–3, 244, 246–7
homeless children 40, 66
homelessness 31, 66, 89, 145, 146, 151 215–16
  see also homeless children
'hooliganism' 26, 84, 109, 125, 150, 185
  see also physical abuse
hostels 17, 22, 67, 83–4, 96, 123–5, 134, 144, 150–1, 157, 175 fn 21, 191–3, 215, 221–2, 228, 241–2, 244, 246

house communes 76–82, 91, 96–7, 109–12, 241, 243
housekeepers, *see* domestic servants
housewives 25, 52, 64, 66, 68, 71, 73, 91–2, 98, 111, 114, 119, 135, 143, 155, 162, 164, 165–8, 172–3, 244
housework,
  as female function 26–9, 36, 64, 70, 73, 79, 82, 91, 96, 101, 167, 173, 229, 230, 247
  men's contribution to 80, 117, 173, 232
  socialisation of 17, 53, 67, 73, 79, 82, 91, 96, 167
housing
  as reward and incentive 5, 115, 231, 237, 244
  affect on personal relationships 4, 52, 55–7, 96, 169–70, 202, 229, 239
housing cooperatives 52, 61–75, 78, 112, 129–31, 160–1, 183–4, 187, 211, 238, 246

informers 5–6, 11, 14–15, 33, 58, 126, 133, 136, 195, 223

Jews, special treatment in relation to housing 147–8, 151

Kaganovich, Lazar 110
kindergartens, *see* pre school child care institutions
'kitchen debate' (between Khrushchev and Nixon) 173
kitchens, communal 3, 28, 35, 36, 43–4, 48, 54–5, 63–71, 76–7, 81–3, 93–4, 96, 100–2, 112, 117–19, 124–5, 127, 135, 150, 185, 189, 191, 193, 195, 212, 214, 221, 224–5, 229–30
  see also communal dining
kitchens, separate 6, 77, 100, 103, 110–12, 115, 132, 156, 163, 168, 170–1, 173, 181–2, 186–8, 195, 204, 207, 222, 229–30, 233, 245,

Kollontai, Aleksandra 29, 30
kommunalka, see communal apartments
Komsomol, see communist youth organisations
Krupskaya, Nadezhda 28, 30, 64, 95

labour saving devices, see appliances, domestic
Larin, Yuri 91,108
laundry and laundries 17, 28, 36, 56, 61, 63–6, 69–71, 76–7, 80, 82, 91, 96, 101–2, 110, 113, 120, 124, 127, 163, 167–8, 173, 181, 232–3, 243
leisure 4, 23, 26–7, 67, 101, 131, 134, 149–50, 162–3, 244
see also entertaining
Lenin, V.I. 1, 12, 28–9, 33, 40, 42, 70, 92, 140
Lilina, Zlata 30
limitchiki (people with limited residence rights) 215
'living space' as concept 3, 4, 17, 42–8, 83, 116, 144, 146, 149, 157, 183–4, 190, 193–4, 201, 203–4, 210–11, 228, 236, 239, 242–3

Magnitogorsk 93, 94, 101–3
see also Socialist Cities
maids, see domestic servants
Marx, Karl 1, 92, 98, 114
maternity benefits, see state benefits
May, Ernst 101–3
Mayakovskii, Vladimir 1, 27, 37 fn 28, 98, 99, 239, 243
Medals of Maternity, see motherhood awards
Mehnert, Klaus 79, 80–1, 85 fn 21, 114
micro-districts 162–3, 167, 180, 182, 196, 235, 245
military housing 33, 120, 202, 209
Modernism 88, 98–99
motherhood awards 146, 193
'multi-child' families 155, 157, 193, 202

municipalised housing, see state-owned housing

nannies, see domestic servants
Nepmen 40, 41, 44, 46, 53, 54, 72, 89
new *byt*, meaning of 1, 12, 26–7, 52, 53, 64–6, 69–73, 81–3, 90–2, 103, 107–17, 195–6, 239, 241, 243
NOTists (Nauchnaya Organizatsiya Truda) 80

obshchestvennitsy (female social activists) 114
OZhSKT, see housing cooperatives

passports, internal 136
phalansteries, see Fourier, Charles
physical abuse 26–8, 48, 51, 55–6, 84, 193, 194, 196
see also 'hooliganism'
physical culture 95–6, 99, 134
prefabricated housing 46, 149, 163, 169–70, 181–2, 205
preschool child care institutions, see child care, socialised
prisoners 215–6
privately-owned housing 2–3, 6, 8, 17, 23, 32, 34, 41, 45–6, 51, 61, 128, 149, 158, 159–61, 172–3, 200, 208–12, 220, 236, 242, 246–7
propiska (registration) 202, 215
prostitution 31, 41, 48, 89
protective legislation for female workers 41, 115

rape 9–10, 103
see also sexual harassment and abuse
Red Corner 26, 52, 63–4, 68, 94, 125, 144
Revolution, October 1, 3, 8, 11, 13–14, 16, 22–8, 31, 32, 36, 41, 43, 46, 62, 76, 87, 90–1, 93, 110, 116, 125, 222, 233, 241
RZhSKT, see housing cooperatives

Sabsovich, Leonid 93, 108
'self-build' housing, *see* privately-owned housing
'self-compression' (*samo-uplotnenie*) 17, 47–8
'senior tenant' (*otvetsvennyi kvartiro'semshchik*) 5, 223
separate apartments, *see* single family housing
sexual harassment and abuse 10, 57, 224
   see also rape
sexual relations 10, 29, 52, 81, 85 fn 31, 94, 129, 163, 173
shock workers 5, 107, 120, 135
single-family housing 3, 5–6, 13, 17, 24, 32, 35, 46, 110–11, 131, 134–5, 151, 154–79, 190–1, 201, 207, 212–14, 222, 228–34, 244–6
single parent families 189, 193, 199 fn 70, 204, 213
single people 42, 51, 57, 67, 93, 125, 133, 156–7, 173, 175 fn 21, 189, 190–3, 206, 213, 221–2, 224, 228–9, 245–6
'socialist cities' 4, 17, 92–5, 100–3, 110, 134, 146, 162, 191, 222, 243

'socialist competition' 99, 125
Socialist Realism 108, 131–2, 134, 241, 243
speculation in housing distribution, *see* corruption in housing distribution
Stakhanovites 5, 107, 114–15, 132, 135
state benefits 62, 116, 234, 237
state-owned housing 3, 5, 33–4, 41, 72, 76, 89, 127–9, 149, 158–62, 172, 183–5, 194, 201, 207–12, 220, 236–7, 240 fn 5, 242, 246

violence, *see* physical abuse

'walk through' rooms 35, 42–3, 131, 135, 163–4, 229, 231, 242, 245
War Communism 22, 31–6, 40–1, 46, 88
Women's Department, *see* Zhenotdel
workplace-owned housing 5, 13, 22, 76, 115, 148, 149, 157, 159, 194, 202, 204, 208, 228, 236–7, 244

Zhenotdel 91, 113
ZhAKT, *see* housing cooperatives
ZhSK, *see* housing cooperatives

EU authorised representative for GPSR:
Easy Access System Europe, Mustamäe tee 50,
10621 Tallinn, Estonia
gpsr.requests@easproject.com

www.ingramcontent.com/pod-product-compliance
Lightning Source LLC
Chambersburg PA
CBHW021350300426
44114CB00012B/1165